Monopolizing Knowledge:
A scientist refutes religion-denying, reason-destroying scientism

Ian Hutchinson

Fias Publishing.
20 Horace Road, Belmont, Massachusetts, USA.
http://monopolizingknowledge.net/

ISBN: 978-0-9837023-0-6 (paperback)

SDG

Contents

Preface

In a sense this is a book about science and religion, but that may not be obvious at first glance. In my intellectual journey as a follower of Jesus Christ and as a professional scientist, I came to believe a long time ago that the much-discussed tensions between science and Christianity are part of a wider disagreement between an improper extrapolation of science and — well — everything else. The improper extrapolation of science is approximately the belief that science, modelled on the natural sciences, is the only source of real knowledge. I call that belief scientism. It is an awkward, ugly word and that's fine with me, because I think it's an awkward, ugly, and erroneous world-view. I choose this word because it points directly at the world-view's foundational character and because the traditional alternatives capture only a fraction of the scope to which I think scientism's influence extends.

To call my approach here to science and religion indirect may well seem an absurd understatement. That is because, to explain my way of understanding the relationship between science and religion, I need to show how the "everything else" comes in. The first three quarters of what I have to say will give the impression of wandering through regions that to many scientists and Christians are foreign, and inhospitable. We will spend time to understand science. We will meet some of its most famous practitioners, discover some of its history: both what it is and what people have thought and said it is. We'll identify its most important characteristics, which is as much philosophy as science. We'll talk about what those characteristics imply about its scope of competence. We'll spend a couple of nights with the History and Philosophy of science crowd to get a feel for their concerns and how they bear on our issues. We'll talk about the arguments for and against scientism. We'll be hosted by some hard-core postmodern philosophers and spar with some hard-core atheists. And on the way we'll dip liberally into ideas concerning music, art, language, sociology, politics, law, and technology as well as science and religion.

As a guide to all the intellectually foreign regions, I cannot claim the qualification of being a resident or expert. But I do claim the qualification of understanding the fundamental commitments and concerns, and speaking the language, of both scientists and Christians. And I hope to offer a tolerably well-informed tour through the unfamiliar territory. On the way, I shall also offer commentary that the residents — those who routinely live and work in the different regions of this intellectual country — might consider impertinent. They might say, Who does this scientist think he is to editorialize about what we do for a living? That's the sort of question it is best to acknowledge, but not to answer. The content of the commentary is the only real justification it can have. But I do want to indicate my intention, which is to discuss those features of the intellectual landscape that are relevant to my topic at the level of a tourist. In other words, I am trying to write in a way that is tolerably accessible to an intelligent non-expert — to act in the way a tour guide should: as an interpreter. This intention requires simplification, summarization, and glossing over nuances in a way that might scandalize the local residents. I hope that any residents who choose to tag along with the tour will, nevertheless, be able to recognize some truth in what I say, and perhaps on occasions will gain new insights from the different perspective that I offer, even of their own localities.

Why do I take my readers on this round-about route? In the first place it is because scientism is busily, but largely surreptitiously, at work throughout practically the entire intellectual and cultural landscape. Making sense of its influence in the regions that most interest me is very hard unless one has a feel for the wider picture. Secondly, it is because if one just jumps straight into talking about science and religion, it is easy to give the impression that there are just those two disjoint areas of human knowledge. That impression can lead into unsatisfying and unsatisfactory attempts to reconcile just those areas without realizing that all disciplines are struggling with the question of scientism. Third, it is because both scientists and Christians are frequently misled, in ways that I will explain, into adopting scientistic positions. If one pays attention to the bigger picture, it helps to avoid that mistake. Finally, it is because the case that scientism *is* a mistake depends upon a fairly deep understanding — an understanding which is subject to controversy — of what science is and how it relates to the rest of knowledge. Obviously, I'm trying to make all this interesting, but I'm also trying to make the reader think; so don't be surprised if there are parts that have you puzzled, and maybe feeling a bit lost at first.

Acknowledgements. This book has been half a lifetime in gestation. I owe an enormous debt for what I have learned from authors, friends, colleagues, teachers, and acquaintances, all too numerous for me to be able to recall. Most of the ideas here, even those that I can't remember learning from someone else, I probably owe in part to others. I have always thought it is the greatest triumph for an educator when the ideas they are seeking to inculcate become such an integral part of the student's thinking that the student doesn't remember where they came from. If so, then my own teachers, formal and informal, are triumphant. I am especially grateful, though, to friends and colleagues who have read parts of this work in draft and given me helpful criticisms, soundings, and encouragement on the way: Jesse Rainbow, Roger White, Garry Haake, John Durant. And as ever, my wife Fran has been a constant enabler and encourager beyond my deserving.

Chapter 1

Science and scientism

1.1 Introduction

Science is the most remarkable and powerful cultural artifact humankind has ever created. What is more, most people in our society regard science as providing us with knowledge about the natural world that has an unsurpassed claim to reality and truth. That is one reason why I am proud to be a physicist, a part of the scientific enterprise. But increasingly I am dismayed that science is being twisted into something other than what it truly is. It is portrayed as identical to a philosophical doctrine that I call 'scientism'. Scientism is the belief that all valid knowledge is science. Scientism says, or at least implicitly assumes, that rational knowledge is scientific, and everything else that claims the status of knowledge is just superstition, irrationality, emotion, or nonsense.

The purpose of this book is to show the pervasiveness of the doctrine of scientism; to explore its coherence, and consequences; and to show that it must be repudiated, both to make sense of a vast range of non-scientific human endeavor, and also for science itself. One of the conflicts that is most visible in current culture is between scientism and religion. But the overall confrontation is not just with religious faith, prominent though that part of the debate may be. Religious belief is not at all unique in being an unscientific knowledge. On the contrary, I shall argue that there are many important beliefs, secular as well as religious, which are justified and rational, but not scientific. And if that is so, then scientism is a ghastly intellectual mistake.

But how could it have come about that this mistake is so widespread, if it is a mistake? The underlying reason is that scientism is confused with science. This confusion is commonplace in many, many popularizations of science. Scientists of considerable reputation speak with authority and understanding (but rarely modesty) about the knowledge and technology that science has brought;

1

and frequently they introduce into their explanations, without ac-knowledging it, non-scientific assumptions, unjustified extrapola-tions, philosophy and metaphysics either based on or promoting scientism. It is natural then, for readers, particularly those without inside knowledge of science, to assume that science and scientism are one and the same. After all, many leading scientists, and science popularizers, speak and act as if they are. A major strand within the community of science thus directly promotes this confusion.

What is more, several major strands within the community of religious faith also promote this confusion. On the conservative theological wing, which feels itself in an intellectual battle with a secular academy, there is a deep suspicion of science because it is seen as a countervailing authority against religious orthodoxy. Most of the theologically liberal wing, in contrast, long ago adopted scientism, because they confused it with science. But both sides, whether rejecting or assimilating, have confused science and sci-entism; and that confusion is a major factor in the stance they each take.

Broader non-science academic disciplines — and here I am thinking of subjects such as history, literature, social studies, phi-losophy, and the arts — have related problems. I shall argue that one can understand many of the trends of academic thought in the past century or so as being motivated in part by either embracing or rejecting scientism. Those trends that embrace scientism, do so because they feel compelled by the intellectual stature of science: they confuse the two. Those that (more recently) reject scientism, seeing its sterility, seem often to reject science as well, because they have confused the two.

Scientism is many-faceted. It is, first of all, a philosophy of knowledge. It is an opinion about the way that knowledge can be obtained and justified. My single sentence definition of scientism focuses on this underlying and foundational aspect: " Scientism is the belief that all valid knowledge is science." However, the repercussions of this viewpoint are so great that scientism rapidly becomes much more. It becomes an all-encompassing world-view; a perspective from which all of the questions of life are exam-ined; a grounding presupposition or set of presuppositions which provides the framework by which the world is to be understood. Therefore, from scientism spring many other influences on thought and behavior, notably the principles that guide our understanding of meaning and truth; the ethical and social understanding of who we are and how we should live; and ultimately our answers to the 'big questions': our religious beliefs.

In so far as scientism is an overarching world-view, it is fair to regard it as essentially a religious position. Its advocates are unhappy with such an assertion, and argue that because scientism does not entail the belief in the supernatural, and does not entail ceremonials and rituals, it cannot be regarded as religion. But that is hair-splitting. There are religions that don't involve a belief in God, and religions that don't require participation in ceremonies. What's more, as we will see, several of the historic forms that scientism has taken actually *do* involve ceremonials and rituals of religious intent. In any case, the key aspect of religious conviction that scientism shares with most organized religions is that it offers a comprehensive principle or belief, which itself cannot be proved (certainly not scientifically proved) but which serves to organize our understanding and guide our actions.

Higher education in the West, in its beginnings, was almost exclusively a Christian undertaking. Its rationale and content were dominated by the propagation of Christian truths and the education of people to undertake that mission. As it grew, of course, much broader perspectives were encompassed, but even well into the nineteenth century, religious observance and education were dominant aspects of most colleges and universities. In the second half of that century, though, a transformation occurred, away from religious to more secular motivations and content.[1] To a great extent, that transformation can be viewed as a conversion to scientism. Not that all twentieth century academics subscribed overtly to scientism. But just as Christian presuppositions were a kind of academic mental habitat in earlier centuries, so, scientism became the de facto world-view of the academy. Scientistic viewpoints had been advocated by a vocal minority of intellectuals since the beginning of the Enlightenment, and had gained increasing dominance prior to this transformation. But after it, scientism became practically the orthodoxy of the academy.

In the later parts of this study, I will explore briefly some of the more practical consequences of scientism in modern attitudes to political and social decision making. One can consider the emphasis on technological solutions for the challenges we face as a facet of scientism. The modern reliance on technology to solve all manner of social challenges was increasingly subject to critiques from human and religious perspectives as the twentieth century wore on. The belief in human 'progress', based on technique, failed in the face of the stark realities of world wars and gulags. But because the underlying scientism was not displaced from its intellectual dominance, the technological imperative and the reliance on the technological fix seem as strong as ever.

Repudiation of scientism is the only way that we can break free from some of the more debilitating habits of thought that have dominated modern intellectual life. But this repudiation is unsustainable, even by the most heroic effort, without a distinction between science and scientism. If denying scientism's sway requires us to deny the truthfulness, value, or reality of scientific knowledge — as seems to be implied by some of today's critiques — then in my opinion the move will fail. And it should fail, because in fact science does give real, reliable, knowledge. It is just that science and scientism are not the same thing. Science is not all the knowledge there is.

1.2   Science, what do we mean by it?

Perhaps, gentle reader, you are yourself already highly dubious about the distinction that I am trying to draw. Quite possibly, you take the view that science really is the only reliable route to knowledge: that science is simply the systematic critical study of any field of activity: that the word science simply describes knowledge, which after all is its Latin etymology. If so, then I need to convince you, first, that there is something distinctive about the disciplines that we traditionally call science, something that is different from other disciplines; and second, that that distinctiveness calls for definite characteristics of the things we study using the methods of science, which not all questions possess. In other words, I must show both that there are in fact functional definitions of science, and that not all interesting knowledge falls within the scope of the definitions.

A major cause of confusion is that the word science is used with at least two meanings. Those meanings are completely different; confusing the two has a natural tendency to lead to scientism. One meaning, which I just alluded to, looks to the derivation of the word. It comes from the Latin *scientia* which means simply knowledge. Based on this foundation, the word science is sometimes used to describe *any* systematic orderly study of a field of knowledge; or by extension the knowledge that such study produces. The other meaning of the word science is today a far more common usage. It is that "science" refers to the study of the natural world.

The Encyclopédie and Samuel Johnson

Figure 1.1: Frontispiece of Diderot's *Encyclopédie*[2]. Reason and philosophy revealing truth. Drawn by Charles-Nicolas Cochin, 1764.

Prior to the nineteenth century, the word science was used, especially in continental Europe, to mean simply knowledge. The *Encyclopédie ou Dictionnaire Raisonné des Sciences, des Arts et des Métiers*[3] was edited by Denis Diderot and published in 21 volumes of text and 11 of illustrative plates during the years 1751 to 1777. It was in many ways the embodiment of Enlightenment thinking. Its definition of the word science is this:

> SCIENCE, as a philosophical concept, means the clear and certain knowledge of something, whether founded on self-evident principles, or via systematic demonstration. The word science is, in this sense, the opposite of doubt; opinion stands midway between science and doubt.

(The original was in French.) Clearly, by this definition, science is no different from what we commonly simply call knowledge. If this were all that the word science connoted, there would be no problem. We would use "science" interchangeably with "knowledge" and little else would be implied. But, of course, this is *not* the only connotation in modern usage. Most of the time, today, when people refer to science they are referring to *natural science*, our knowledge of nature, discovered by experiment and (most convincingly mathematical) theory. This is the meaning I use.

The Encyclopédie itself reflects an ambiguity about the usage of the word science, which may have been deliberate. The formal definition it gives, is equivalent to "knowledge". But the Encyclopédie's usage strongly implies the natural and technological knowledge that is captured by the modern meaning, natural science.

Consider the title of the work itself, which might be translated, "Encyclopedia or Reasoned Dictionary of Sciences, Arts, and Trades". Lest the modern reader be misled by this literalistic translation, we should recognize that the word Arts here means predominantly what we would call technology. Here is part of the Encyclopédie's own article on ART, which was evidently Diderot's manifesto for the work.

> Origin of the arts and sciences. In pursuit of his needs, luxury, amusement, satisfaction of curiosity, or other objectives, man applied his industriousness to the products of nature and thus created the arts and sciences. The focal points of our different reflections have been called "science" or "art" according to the nature of their "formal" objects, to use the language of logic. If the

> object leads to action, we give the name of "art" to the compendium of the rules governing its use and to their technical order. If the object is merely contemplated under different aspects, the compendium and technical order of the observations concerning this object are called "science."

Thus, for example, according to Diderot, metaphysics is a science and ethics is an art. Theology is a science and pyrotechnics an art! So arts are the products of applying industriousness to nature, and differ from "science" in that arts are practical, whereas science is contemplative. Moreover, for Diderot, there are subdivisions of arts:

> Division of the arts into liberal and mechanical arts. When men examined the products of the arts, they realized that some were primarily created by the mind, others by the hands. This is part of the cause for the pre-eminence that some arts have been accorded over others, and of the distinction between liberal and mechanical arts.

Then after promoting the value of the mechanical arts and criticizing those who disdain them, who by their prejudice "fill the cities with useless spectators and with proud men engaged in idle speculation", Diderot extols Bacon and Colbert as champions of the mechanical arts and says, "I shall devote most of my attention to the mechanical arts, particularly because other authors have written little about them."

The modern reader may be forgiven for feeling that Diderot has multiplied distinctions in ways that are more confusing than enlightening. Nevertheless, the main point is clear. The Encyclopédie is a work predominantly about natural science and technology. It defines the word science to mean knowledge in general; but then it focuses on natural science and technology. Here we see scientism in its youth. And even in its youth, it seems to be based on deliberate confusion of language. The French philosophes (whose champion Diderot was) and those who followed them were quite deliberate in their attempt to undermine confessional religious faith and any authority based on it. Their avowed aim was to undermine the authority of the clergy and the church; and hence the political system, the Ancien Régime of which clerical power was one foundation stone. Those opposed to the monarchy and aristocracy used every technique at their disposal from the satire of Voltaire to the social activism of the revolutionaries. But one of the most powerful of their techniques, and arguably the most lasting legacy, was to insinuate scientism as an unacknowledged presupposition into much of the intellectual climate of the succeeding two centuries.

Samuel Johnson's dictionary[4], or to give it its full title, *A DICTIONARY of the English Language: in which The WORDS are deduced from their ORIGINALS, and ILLUSTRATED in their DIFFERENT SIGNIFICATIONS by EXAMPLES from the best WRITERS*[5] was perhaps the most definitive work of English usage up to 1755, when it was first published. It had far less of a deliberate agenda than the *Encyclopédie*, and was a remarkable, nine-year, practically solo effort, unlike the French dictionary of the day which took forty scholars forty years. Johnson's boast, based on his initial optimistic estimate of only a three-year schedule, was that this showed "As three to sixteen hundred, so is the proportion of an Englishman to a Frenchman"[6].

The 11th edition, abstracted like some earlier editions by Johnson to produce additional profit through a more accessible, less bulky work, retains only the authors, not the texts by which the meanings are illustrated and its definition of science reads

> Science. 1. Knowledge. *Hammond*. 2. Certainty grounded on demonstration. *Berkley*. 3. Art attained by precepts, or built upon principles. *Dryden*. 4. Any art or species of knowledge. *Hooker, Glanville*. 5. One of the seven liberal arts, grammar, rhetorick, logick, arithmetick, musick, geometry, astronomy. *Pope*.

Evidently this definition conforms to the more general concept as addressing *any* systematic body of knowledge. Several of the original quotations from which these definitions are derived do show signs of preference towards natural science. Nevertheless, the last definition, as liberal art, emphatically retains the breadth of meaning that a classical derivation might imply.

Two Nineteenth Century Historians

Insight into the usage of the word science in the nineteenth century can be gleaned from the writing of Thomas Babington Macaulay (1800-1859), a lawyer, politician, colonial administrator, poet, essayist and historian Macaulay's *The History of England from the ac-*

Figure 1.2: Thomas Babington Macaulay at age 49. After a drawing by George Richmond.[7]

cession of James the second was an immediate bestseller when it was published in mid century (volumes 1 and 2 in 1848), and remains a classic of English literary style and popular history, still in print. Macaulay's writing is considered also a characteristic example of 'Whig History', which means an interpretation of history in terms of the progressive growth of liberty and enlightenment, accompanying the increase of democratic and parliamentary power, as opposed to monarchy and aristocracy. Macaulay, while unromantic in his perspicacious analysis of the motivations of individuals and the sentiments of the populace, is fond of sweeping assessments such as "From the time when the barbarians overran the Western Empire to the time of the revival of letters, the influence of the Church of Rome had been generally favorable to science, to civilization, and to good government. But during the last three centuries, to stunt the growth of the human mind has been her chief object."[8] We see in this quotation that Macaulay refers to science as the intellectual component of the growth of the human mind, which, along with civilization and government, constitutes the progress that he is interested to document. Macaulay's usage of 'science' here is very broad, encompassing all of liberal studies, not just natural science. Yet later in his overview of England in 1685, speaking about historical assessments of the size of the English population (about five million), he writes "Lastly, in our own days Mr. Finlaison, an actuary of eminent skill, subjected the ancient parochial registers of baptisms, marriages, and burials to all the tests which the modern improvements in statistical science enabled him to apply."[9] So 'science' is a natural description of mathematical analysis. But in discussing the low relative degree of militarization of England he says "... the defence of nations had become a science and a calling" meaning that the army was becoming professionalized, and associated with systematic learning, though not necessarily that of natural philosophy.[10]

Macaulay speaks of the far more effective naval officers of that day who had risen through the ranks rather than acquiring their appointment, as did the 'gentlemen captains', by political preferment. "But to a landsman these tarpaulins, as they were called, seemed a strange and half-savage race. All their knowledge was professional; and their professional knowledge was practical rather than scientific."[11] So here he is reflecting the *Encyclopédie*'s distinction between art: the practical; and science: the contemplative, or perhaps in modern terminology theoretical. Macaulay sees science as preeminently the result of formal education, but later refers to the distinguishing of right from wrong as part of "ethical science" (i.e. the science of ethics).

Thus the usage of Macaulay reflects an understanding of science as knowledge that is contemplative and formally-learnt, encompassing the broad scope of human endeavor, yet only somewhat ambiguously focused on situations and methods that are predominantly the province of natural and mathematical studies. That ambiguity, though, is in practice dispelled by his summary under the heading "State of science in England" in 1685. Noting the foundation, just twenty five years before, of the Royal Society (whose concerns surely serve as an indisputable definition of science as natural philosophy), he lists the subjects of his state of science as including agricultural reform, medicine, sanitation, " ... the chemical discoveries of Boyle, and the earliest botanical researches of

Sloane. It was then that Ray made a new classification of birds and fishes, and that the attention of Woodward was first drawn toward fossils and shells. ... John Wallis placed the whole system of statics on a new foundation. Edmund Halley investigated the properties of the atmosphere, the ebb and flow of the sea, the laws of magnetism, and the course of the comets; ... mapped the constellations of the southern hemisphere" [12]. With the sole possible exception of Petty's "Political Arithmetic", an early treatise in economic statistics, what Macaulay refers to are topics in *natural* science.

Figure 1.3: St Paul's cathedral, in London, designed by Christopher Wren, a founder of the Royal Society, and Professor of Astronomy at Oxford, illustrates the harmony of natural science, technology, art, and Christianity in 17th century England.

In the 1898 edition of Macaulay's *History*, however, a particularly telling passage appears in the introduction written by Edward P. Cheyney, then Professor of European History at the University of Pennsylvania, and himself the author of an important *Short History of England* (1904). Cheyney writes

> There are two quite different views of historical writing. The one looks upon it as a form of literature, an artistic product, the materials for which are to be found in the events of the past; the other considers it as a science, the solution of the problems involved in the

same events of the past. Macaulay represents the former rather than the latter. If strict canons of criticism were applied to his methods of investigation and writing, much of his work would fail to stand the test. ... Abundance of illustration and analogy frequently takes the place of a really exhaustive study of the sources.[13]

It is remarkable that a historian would refer to history, or at least history written in the way he approves, as a science. The differences between the subjects and methods of history and those of natural sciences are, as we shall later explore, about as stark as they can be. But for our present purposes the key question is, what Cheyney is getting at when he refers to historians that "treat history as a science" and use "more rigorous methods" while, in contrast to Macaulay they show "almost entire lack of literary ability"? In the first place, it seems Cheyney's complaint is that Macaulay is not rigorous, or critical enough. When he says "There are few things in history quite so certain as he [Macaulay] seems to make them" his advocacy appears to be for greater tentativeness. And when he says "... a spirit of candor and a habit of judicial fairness, was not by any means a characteristic of Macaulay's mind" his criticism appears to be aimed at historical writing that contains specific perspectives and judgements of the merits of actions or events. But when Cheyney portrays Macaulay's writings as if they were some sort of historical artistic literature or almost historical fiction, he goes far beyond what is justified. Whatever may be the shortcomings of Macaulay's work, there can be no doubt that his was a mind of great erudition, not just imagination. His historical facts concerning the era he addresses are carefully documented from original sources. Perhaps he allowed himself greater latitude in speculative interpretation than the academic historian of 1900 (or for that matter 2000) would endorse. But it is remarkable and revealing that in the mind of Cheyney, this makes Macaulay not so much unprofessional, or a populist, or merely biased, but rather: unscientific. This attitude is a consequence of scientism — an effort to distinguish between 'true' scientific historical knowledge on the one hand, and on the other, literature that fails to qualify as science and hence as true knowledge. In effect Cheyney is claiming the credentials of science in support of his view that some of Macaulay's interpretations are erroneous.[14]

Perhaps we can understand Cheyney's position better in the light of his Presidential address to the American Historical Society, some 26 years later[15]. In this oration entitled *Law in History*, although he no longer uses the word scientific to describe it, he still sees history as on a path to discovery of practically deterministic cause and effect.

> So arises the conception of law in history. History, the great course of human affairs, has been the result not of voluntary action on the part of individuals or groups of individuals, much less of chance; but has been subject to law. ...
>
> Such are the six general laws I have ventured to state as discoverable by a search among historical phenomena: first, a law of continuity; second, a law of impermanence of nations; third, a law of unity of the race, of interdependence among all its members; fourth, a law of democracy; fifth, a law of freedom; sixth, a law of moral progress.
>
> May I repeat that I do not conceive of these generalizations as principles which it would be well for us to accept, or as ideals which we may hope to attain; but as natural laws, which we must accept whether we want to or not, whose workings we cannot obviate, however much we may thwart them to our own failure and disadvantage; laws to be accepted and reckoned with as much as the laws of gravitation, or of chemical affinity, or of organic evolution, or of human psychology.

Cheyney's claims and terminology seem aimed to promote professionalism in history: implying that there are certain scientific norms of historiography practiced by the academic historian, but not by writers of much broader experience such as Macaulay.

The effort is not convincing. The distinction between academic and popular history might be significant, but to portray this as a distinction between scientific and unscientific is mostly a power play. The distinction bears no discernible relationship to methods

of the natural sciences. It is mostly a substitution of the judgement 'correct' by 'scientific' for rhetorical effect. Given the present
common usage of 'science', any merit that might once have resided
in references to scientific history is today replaced by confusion.
And the hope that some historical law of (say) "moral progress"
would be accepted "as much as the laws of gravitation", seems to
a scientist just silly.

Metaphysics a Science?

The confusion of usages of the word science throughout the twentieth century may be illustrated by reference to the insightful *An
Essay on Metaphysics* by R.G.Collingwood (1940)[16]. I think it is fair
to say that today metaphysics would be regarded as a subject that
stands in contrast to science. Common sense usage would say
something along the lines that science is about the experimentally
verifiable facts of nature, whereas metaphysics is about the speculative, unverifiable, logical, and philosophical questions that include
religion and the big questions of human life[17]. For Collingwood,
though, classical usages of the words are primary. He explains that
literally metaphysics is simply the expression used by the editors
of Aristotle to describe the writings that are placed *after physics*.
Collingwood defines science (in contrast to common usage even of
1940) as any "body of systematic or orderly thinking". And he calls
metaphysics "an historical science" which attempts to find out, for
the thinkers and arguments it analyzes, their absolute presuppositions.

Ironically Collingwood is himself aware of and concerned to
critique scientism. He addresses a nineteenth century philosophy whose prime tenet is that the "only valid method of attaining
knowledge is the method used in the natural sciences" as *Positivism*.
Undoubtedly the use of 'Positivism' is historically correct and precise terminology to describe the school of philosophy to which it
refers. One reason I avoid it in talking about the larger issue is that
scientism is far broader and more influential than the explicit formulation by Auguste Comte (1798-1857) and his followers, which
Collingwood analyses. No, scientism is not just philosophical and
sociological positivism; it is much more pervasive than that. Nor
is it just postivism's twentieth century extension *Logical Positivism*,

which holds, in brief, that propositions other than scientific ones are meaningless, and which Collingwood colorfully criticizes under the title of the "Suicide of Positivistic Metaphysics"!

I'll have more to say later about these philosophical formulations. But my present point is that calling metaphysics a science, despite the practice adopted by Diderot in the mid 18th century, is by modern standards just plain confusing, since metaphysics is in large measure defined by the fact that it is *not* natural science.

Nothing leads more quickly to sloppy thinking and misunderstandings than terminological confusion of this type. Indeed, the continued robustness of scientism is surely partly attributable to this terminological confusion. If science means simply knowledge, then scientism is just tautologically true. End of story. But if science means a particular type of knowledge, as it does today, then it is essential to recognize that meaning and stick to it. For this reason and others, as a matter of the use of language, when I refer to science, I will mean *natural* science, not simply systematic knowledge. Moreover I mean modern natural science, the inheritor of the revolution in natural philosophy that started in the sixteenth century. I implore the reader to bear this meaning firmly in mind.

New Sciences

A further source of confusion lies in recent trends in academic disciplines to refer to their subjects as various types of "sciences".

It was not a scientist but a philosopher (John Searle) who remarked that most of the disciplines that have the word science in their name are actually not science. He was overstating the idea, even for the 1970s. But he was making the point that most subjects that are unequivocally sciences have descriptive names that don't require the qualification "science". One can think of physics, chemistry, astronomy, biology, geology, zoology, botany, genetics, physiology, and so on. No one would hesitate to classify these as part of science.

In contrast, think about Social Science, Management Sciences, Pharmaceutical Sciences, Archaeological Sciences, Animal Science, Food Science, Behavioral Sciences, Decision Sciences, Family and Consumer Sciences (I am not making these up!) even Computer Science. Practically none of these are science in the sense of the word that I am using, either because they are not natural (about nature) or because they are really technologies or professional studies.

In recent years, it must be conceded, some of the more traditional sciences have taken to using the word science in the titles of academic departments (e.g. Earth Sciences, Biological Sciences, Atmospheric Sciences, Materials Science, Marine Sciences, Life Sciences) but in most cases this seems to be either because they represent a merging of several historically distinct subjects, or because they want to shed a narrow interpretation.

Whatever may be the individual justification, the outbreak of "sciences" in academic descriptions is in part a reflection of scientism at work. If science is all the real knowledge there is, as scientism says, then a self-respecting academic department better be sure that its discipline is understood to be science. But of course, a discipline does not become a science by simply calling itself one. So not all the new "sciences" are science in any useful sense. But what *does* make a discipline a science?

1.3   The Scientific Revolution

Modern natural science came into being during approximately the century that led up to the publication of Isaac Newton's Principia (1687). It is now popular and appropriate to refer to this intellectual birth as the Scientific Revolution. Science historian Steven Shapin begins his 1996 book *The Scientific Revolution*[18] with the paradoxical declaration "There was no such thing as the scientific revolution, and this is a book about it." Shapin warns us that the actual phrase 'the Scientific Revolution' was probably coined by Alexandre Koyré as recently as 1939; even though the "beginnings of an idea of revolution in science date from the eighteenth century writings of French Enlightenment philosophes" [like Diderot and the other authors of the Encyclopédie] "who liked to portray themselves and their disciplines as radical subverters of Ancien Régime culture". "In just this sense, the first revolution may have been scientific, and the American, French, and Russian Revolutions are its progeny". The key characteristics of the new philosophy, the new science, that Shapin points to are (1) that it was to be arrived at by *dependence on natural evidence* rather than textual authority, (2) that its content was primarily *mechanical* and (3) that its purposes were diverse. Those purposes were intellectual: offering an alternative to scholastic wrangling, cultural: providing luster to the courts that sponsored it, and practical: giving rise to improvement of the human condition.

The idea that science must be founded on observations of nature, on experiments, and on the gathering of facts, is taken for granted today. So much so that we should pause to remind ourselves of how radical an idea that was, at the start of the Scientific Revolution.[19] It is not that no natural philosophy (as science was called until the nineteenth century) existed in medieval times. On the contrary, there was an elaborate medieval system of the world based largely on Greek philosophy. Much of this world view had been inherited with the rest of the writings of antiquity as they had been rediscovered after the dark ages in Europe — preserved and elaborated first, incidentally, by Byzantine and Nestorian Christians and subsequently reintroduced into a Europe ignorant of the Greek language by translations initiated from Baghdad under Islam.

An important thread of medieval philosophy that it inherited from its Greek forebears was an emphasis on the contemplative, and a disdain for manual activity. These attitudes were debilitating for truly experimental science. In the Platonic and scholastic medieval intellectual world, the roost was ruled by what would today be considered armchair philosophizing, combined with a deference to the authority of the Greek texts and an emphasis on *deduction* from authority, rather than *discovery* in nature. To make experimental evidence the final authority of natural philosophy, as the new science did, truly required a revolution.

Greek science arose from roots in polytheistic mythology. Plato (429-348 BC) taught that the visible world had been shaped by the *demiurge*, a deity but one far less powerful and comprehensive than the Biblical Creator. The *demiurge* worked with pre-existing chaotic matter under the constraint of specific Ideas. The visible universe itself is also a divine being, according to Plato. It has an inborn personal disposition or 'nature' (the original root meaning of the Greek word φυσις, the derivation of our 'physics'). For Aristotle (384-322 BC) the Ideas, or Forms, are dominant. There is a strong distinction between the nature of the heavens, where only circular motions are permissible, and the sub-lunar world of the four elements air, fire, water, and earth, in which the natural motion is rectilinear. God, for Aristotle, is the Prime Mover, the final cause, whose immutability is to some extent shared by the earthly Forms. Their behavior is governed by their nature, which directs them towards fulfillment of that nature: bodies fall not because they are acted on by forces but because of their intrinsic 'downness'. Soul pervades the world. This teleological emphasis of Greek science appealed to pious medieval Christian philosophers, and despite falling short of a fully Biblical view of creation, became accepted in a Christianized form by the Church and therefore by society.

In contrast to the personification and deification of nature, and to the accompanying teleological explanations, 'mechanical' science of the seventeenth century sought explanations analogous to the machine. So in Galileo's dynamics (1611), a cannonball could stand for the motion of Venus. Descartes could say "there is no difference between the machines built by artisans and the diverse bodies that nature alone composes." Though Kepler flip-flopped between the older animated nature and the mechanical nature, which is perhaps not surprising since he stands at the fulcrum of the philosophical transition, he could say in 1605 "My aim is to show that the machine of the universe is not similar to a divine animated being, but similar to a clock". The clock metaphor had very wide currency. It stood for something that was uniform, regular, and comprehensible.

The clock metaphor also stood for explanation by immediate cause and effect — secondary, or "efficient", causes. In other words, the motion of one part of the clock, or the universe, is to be explained by the direct (mechanical) action upon it of another. For the seventeenth century natural philosophers, this rapidly came to define what constituted proper explanation. Some parts of this analogy persist today. One of its philosophical implications, for example, is reductionism. Reductionism is the principle of explanation in terms of a hierarchy of components. A complex system is explained in terms of the interaction of a number of simpler subsystems from which it is composed. Those subsystems may themselves be further explained by a lower hierarchy of sub-subsystems, and so on till (in the words of Richard Dawkins *The Blind Watchmaker*[20]) "we reach units so simple that, for everyday purposes, we no longer feel the need to ask questions about them".

Other parts of the mechanical philosophy have not survived as fundamental tenets of modern science. Indeed, twentieth and twenty-first century physics describes the world at the microscopic level not at all in terms of mechanics (forces exerted between mechanical components), nor matter (stuff that fills space excluding other stuff) but in more abstract mathematical terms. Even Newton's *Principia Mathematica*[21], which may be regarded as the culmination of the Scientific Revolution, and which raised its author to remarkable heroic popular stature even in his own lifetime, came under criticism from some rivals precisely because it did not demonstrate mechanical mechanisms for gravity. Newton's famous phrase "hypotheses non fingo" (I do not frame hypotheses) is his explicit statement that he did not feel compelled to put forward a direct mechanical explanation of the law of gravity but only "a mathematical notion of those forces, without considering their physical causes". Although this explanation is part of the *General Scholium*, added by Newton late in his life to the *Principia*'s second edition of 1713, the principle of relying on experiment codified in mathematical terms and opposing purely hypothetical mechanical models was explicitly part of Newton's approach throughout his career. For example, in replying to Ignace Gaston Pardies concerning the researches which demonstrated that white light comprised a spectrum of distinct colors — the work that together with his reflecting telescope first brought him to broad prominence and to fellowship in the Royal Society — Newton said in 1672

> ... the doctrine which I explained concerning refraction and colors, consists only in certain properties of light, without regarding any hypotheses by which those properties might be explained. For the best and safest method of philosophizing seems to be, first to enquire diligently into the properties of things, and to establish those properties by experiments and then to proceed more slowly to hypotheses for the explanation of them. For hypotheses should be employed only in explaining the properties of things, but not assumed in determining them; unless so far as they may furnish experiments.[22]

This is a manifesto that epitomizes the experimental character of the natural science we inherit from Newton. Newton was not himself perfectly consistent in separating the more speculative hypothesis from the experimentally demonstrated "properties". He maintained the corpuscular theory of light, sometimes implying (erroneously) that it was supported by his profound experiments. Nevertheless, he sought rigorous systematic mathematical explanation of the the experimental facts, regardless of whether a coherent mechanical picture of that explanation could be formulated — let alone proved.

Newton's failure to identify the mechanisms of gravity led Leibnitz to accuse him of thereby reintroducing "occult powers" into science. Newton denied it. Not, in his view, because gravity could act without mediation of material bodies, a notion he found absurd, but because gravity was not to be regarded as unintelligible even without that mechanical explanation. In many respects, though, despite Newton's commitment to mechanical principles, the *Principia Mathematica* heralded a second transformation in the archetype of what was taken to constitute scientific explanation. If the first transition of the Scientific Revolution was from animated spirits and innate propensities to mechanical devices, the second was from mechanics to pure mathematics. This second step allowed cogency to physical theories that were mathematically formulated, even if they lacked specific mechanisms. But it did not, for at least two hundred years in physics, discourage the search for mechanisms.

1.4   Characteristics of science

I have sketched in the previous section an outline of the Scientific Revolution. I did that partly to help to explain what I mean by modern natural science, or, for short, simply science. It is the science whose methods and suppositions we inherit from the Scientific Revolution. My sketch serves also as an introduction to identification of two key defining characteristics of science. The characteristics are strongly parallel to the two emphases that were historically influential in science's development, namely experimental or natural evidence, and mechanical or mathematical explanation. However for important logical reasons, I express these two characteristics more abstractly, as *reproducibility* and *clarity*. In succeeding chapters I shall explain these characteristics in more detail and show both that they are intrinsic aspects of modern science and that not all knowledge is susceptible to analysis that takes them as presuppositions. Before I move on to this task, though, let me pause to address some objections to the whole of my explanatory enterprise.

One objection that might be raised at this stage is to ask why one should restrict the designation science to the inheritors of the Scientific Revolution. After all, the argument goes, surely the point is that we should use whatever strategy is available to discover knowledge. Who is to say that we don't now have better, or complementary, methods of discovering knowledge, beyond those that sprang from the experimental and mathematical approaches of Newton? My first answer is immediately to point out that this objection is an example of scientism. It confuses knowledge and science and implies that they are one and the same. I am not at all interested to limit the ways of obtaining knowledge to those that I call scientific. I simply want to be clear in drawing a distinction in terminology to recognize that, as a matter of historical fact, science as we commonly conceive it had, and has, a distinctive characteristic approach to methods of discovering and knowing, to epistemology.

But why insist on this terminology? Here, my second answer goes to the heart of the issue. Science has a well-earned prestige and authority precisely because its epistemological approach leads to knowledge that has proven to be practically important and intellectually convincing. This prestige is, of course, one driving force behind the desire of many disciplines to be considered sciences, whether or not they lend themselves to scientific methods of investigation. This desire goes beyond the attempt to bring to the discipline the kind of confidence that science has. It seeks also the authority of science. And for the purposes of persuasion, of establishing authority, of commanding respect, the aura of science has been unmatched for a long time. To use the metaphor of the market today, it is a question of 'branding'. I think it is inappropriate, a kind of false-advertising, for disciplines that by their structure or subject do not lend themselves to scientific analysis in the style of the natural sciences to try to catch the marketing coat-tails of the natural sciences.

A different kind of objection might also be raised at my seeking to identify characteristics which science possesses. It is this. Suppose we grant that, to avoid confusion, we will use the word science to mean natural science. Doesn't that just mean the study of nature? So should not 'the study of nature' be our working definition of science? And if it is, why should one seek to limit the scope of science by an identification of the characteristics of its methods? Surely one should use whatever methods come to hand to study nature. We should not artificially restrict the methods with which we study it. We should welcome whatever methods work best.

This approach sounds on the face of it very plausible. It promotes the view that science is an open, unfettered intellectual activity, free from the constraints of tradition and authority that the Enlightenment sought to shed. And free from artificial limitations of method, so that gradually, as our systematic knowledge grows, we will unify our scientific knowledge into an all-encompassing whole. Again one can see the tendency for this approach to degenerate into scientism. But there are more fundamental problems. What methods 'work best' begs the question of what we mean by 'work best': best for what purpose or for whom? And regarding 'the study of nature' as a definition simply begs the question: what is nature?

'What is nature?' probably sounds a rather silly question to most people today. We tend to think that nature is self-evident. It is the external world, unmanipulated by humans, the world of forces and matter, of animals and minerals, of sun moon and stars, of laws and regularities, of chance and necessity. But the apparently unproblematic modern view of nature is not self-evident. Prior to the Scientific Revolution, nature was viewed very differently. It was populated with gods and teleological imperatives, with intention and purpose. Even in 1686, Robert Boyle (of Boyles' Law) could identify in his *A Free Inquiry into the Vulgarly Received Notion of Nature*[23] eight different senses of the word nature: 1. The author of nature. 2. That on whose account a thing is what it is: its essence. 3. A creature's inherited temperament and constitution. 4. The spontaneous dynamics of a body. 5. The established order or settled course of things. 6. The structure of a body, or of the universe, its system. 7. The phenomena of the universe. 8. Aristotle's semi-deity, which, in the aphorisms of the Peripatetic philosophers, "conserves itself", "goes by the shortest way", "abhors a vacuum", "cures diseases" etc. Boyle's purpose is to deplore the use of number 8, the semi-deity that underwrote Aristotle's physics, which the Scientific Revolution was in the process of superceding, and to replace it with number 5, the established order or settled course of things.

Moreover, even after the Enlightenment, the romantics such as the poets William Wordsworth and Samuel Taylor Coleridge said that what they were about was the study of nature. Yet no one today would for a moment think to call the poetic understanding of the natural world science. It simply is not adequate to assume that what is meant by nature is obvious. If 'the study of nature' is to serve us to understand what science is, we need a more functional definition of nature.

My approach is that we recognize that we can't simply assume we know what is meant by nature. Instead, we must consider what we mean by natural science. Once we have a clear view of what that is, we will ipso facto have developed a clear definition of what we here mean by nature. Nature is what we are studying in natural science. In other words, we must break into the circular statement that natural science is the study of nature. But the right place to break that circularity is *not* to assert that we know somehow by common sense what nature is. Such an assertion is historically and philosophically unsupportable. Instead, it is to insist, as I do, that the methods of science, on which its authority is based, constitute a definition and delimitation of what is meant by nature in this context. The result of this definition is entirely consistent with what Boyle was arguing for: the established order or settled course of things. He did not propose an explicitly functional definition, and could not have done so in his historic context, but the near equivalence will become clearer as we examine the characteristics of science in the following chapters.

If one accepts this functional definition of nature, then by the same token the meaning of science becomes much clearer, and more useful. Just as we can regard nature functionally as that which science studies. We can most naturally regard science functionally as that which scientists practice. The word scientist has a much shorter history than science. It was unknown prior to the nineteenth century. Before that, what we call scientists were 'natural philosophers'. It therefore inverts history (as well, perhaps, as the frequent preference to base dictionary definitions on abstract concepts) to regard the name of the practitioner: 'scientist', as the definitional entry point for understanding what science is. But for developing an unambiguous understanding, such a functional definition appears to be far superior. And, in fact, in common parlance today, this definition is a much better description of the images evoked by the discussion of science, than the general systematic knowledge implied by its Latin etymology.

Chapter 2
Reproducibility.
What is nature?

Michael Faraday is a fascinating character in the history of science. Born the son of a poor blacksmith, his formal education, such as it was, ended by age 13; but it ended by his becoming apprenticed to a bookbinder and bookseller; his informal self-education was beginning! This unconventional background left him knowing practically no mathematics. But he was an incredibly insightful experimentalist and he had an intuitive way of understanding the world in mental pictures. No less than five laws or phenomena of science are named after him. His experimental discoveries came to dominate the science of electricity, and of chemistry too, for the first two thirds of the nineteenth century. His conceptualization of the effects of electromagnetism in terms of lines of force laid the foundation for Maxwell's mathematical electromagnetic equations, and for the modern concept of a "field", in terms of which much fundamental physics is now expressed.

Figure 2.1: Michael Faraday as a young man[24]

It was said of Faraday that whenever he heard of some new

result or phenomenon, reported in a public meeting or a scientific journal, the first thing he would do was to attempt to reproduce the effect in his own laboratory. The reason he gave for this insistence was that his imagination had to be anchored in what he called the "facts". He understood in his bones that science is concerned with reproducible phenomena which can be studied anywhere under controlled conditions and give confirmatory results. "Without experiment I am nothing," he once said.

Faraday's attitude is a reflection of what is often taken for granted in talking about science, that science deals with matters that show reproducibility. For a phenomenon to be a question of science, it had to give reproducible results independent of who carried out the experiment, where, and when. What the Danish Professor Hans Oersted observed during a lecture demonstration to advanced students at the university in Copenhagen in the spring of 1820 ought to be observed just the same when Faraday repeated the experiment later at the Royal Institution in London. And it was. Here, by the way, I am alluding to the discovery that a compass needle is affected by a strong electric current nearby, demonstrating for the first time the mutual dependence of electricity and magnetism. According to the students present at his demonstration, this discovery was an accident during the heating of a fine wire to incandescence using an electrical current. But Oersted's own reports claim greater premeditation on his part[25].

2.1   The meaning of experiment

Imagine a family trip to the Australian beach. The youngster of the family, three-year-old Andrew, is there for the first time. He is fascinated at all the new experiences. He idly, perhaps accidentally, kicks the gravel on the way down to the sand, and pauses to hear it rattle. When seated in the sun he grabs handfuls of sand, and throws them awkwardly over himself, and anyone else who strays too near. He is fearful and wondering at the unexpected waves, even the gentle ones that surge up the smooth sand towards him. Sarah, the eight-year-old is more deliberate. She is on a trek down the beach to find treasures: smooth pebbles of special shape or color, sand dollars, shells, seaweed, and maybe a blue crab. She returns with her bucket full, and she proceeds to sort her collection carefully into different kinds and categories. Cynthia watches both with motherly affection; her gaze shifts to the surf. She delights in the almost mesmerizing rhythm: rolling in and out. She wonders, at an almost subconscious level, what makes the waves adopt that particular tempo. Dan, the husband, chooses a spot well up from the water for their base, to avoid having to move as the tide comes in. He erects the sun-shade, trying a number of different rocks till he finds the ones that best keep it upright in the soft sand. He lies alongside his wife where the shadow will continue, even as the sun moves in the sky, to protect his fair skin from excessive ultra-violet radiation caused by the antarctic ozone hole.

Humans experiment from their earliest conscious moments. They are fascinated by regularities perfect and imperfect, and by similarities and distinctions. In children we call this play. In adults it is often trial and error devoted to a specific purpose, but sometimes it is simply a fascination that seeks no further end than understanding. We are creatures who want to know about the regularities of the world. And the way we find out about them is largely by experiment.

Induction is often touted as the defining philosophical method of natural science. It takes little thought and no detailed philosophical analysis to recognize that the *de*ductive logic of the syllogism is inadequate for the task of discovering general facts about the natural world. All boggles are biggles, no baggles are biggles, therefore no baggles are boggles, is the stuff of IQ tests, not a way to understand the universe. By contrast, *in*duction, the generation of universal laws or axioms from the observation of multiple specific instances, is both more fraught with logical difficulty and also vastly more powerful. But as a practical procedure it is hardly more than a formalization of the everyday processes of discovery illustrated by our Australian beach.

Francis Bacon (1561-1626) is often credited with establishing the inductive method as primary in the sciences, and thereby laying the foundations of modern science. Here is what Thomas Macaulay, in his (1837) essay thought of that viewpoint.

The vulgar notion about Bacon we take to be this,
that he invented a new method of arriving at truth,

Figure 2.2: Francis Bacon

which method is called Induction, and that he detected
some fallacy in the syllogistic reasoning which had been
in vogue before his time. This notion is about as well
founded as that of the people who, in the middle ages,
imagined that Virgil was a great conjurer. Many who are
far too well-informed to talk such extravagant nonsense
entertain what we think incorrect notions as to what
Bacon really effected in this matter.

The inductive method has been practiced ever since
the beginning of the world by every human being. It
is constantly practiced by the most ignorant clown, by
the most thoughtless schoolboy, by the very child at the
breast. That method leads the clown to the conclusion
that if he sows barley he shall not reap wheat. By that
method the schoolboy learns that a cloudy day is the
best for catching trout. The very infant, we imagine,
is led by induction to expect milk from his mother or
nurse, and none from his father[26].

Bacon thought and claimed that his analysis of Induction provided a formulation of how to obtain knowledge. That's why he
named what is perhaps his crowning work, the "New Organon",
meaning it was the replacement for the old "Organon", the collection of Aristotle's works on logic, which dominated the thinking of
the schoolmen of Bacon's day. Bacon did not invent or even identify
Induction. It had in fact already been identified by Aristotle him-

self, as Bacon well knew. Bacon thoroughly analyzed induction. He offered corrections to the way it was mispracticed, emphasizing the need for many examples, for caution against jumping to conclusions, and for considering counter-examples as importantly as confirmatory instances. He advocated gathering together tables of such contrasting instances, almost as if by a process of careful accounting one could implement a methodology of truth. These methodological admonitions are interesting and in some cases insightful, but they fall far short of Bacon's hopes for them. Scientists don't need Bacon to tell them how to think. And they didn't in 1600. What it seems philosophers did need to be told, or at any rate what is arguably Bacon's key contribution, is captured in his criticism of prior views about the *ends*, that is purposes, of knowledge. He says that philosophy was considered "... a couch whereupon to rest a searching and restless spirit; or a terrace for a wandering and variable mind to walk up and down with a fair prospect; or a tower of state for a proud mind to raise itself upon; or a fort or commanding ground for strife and contention; or a shop for profit or sale; and not a rich storehouse for the glory of the Creator and the relief of man's estate."[27] For the schoolmen and generations of philosophers before them, all the way back to Aristotle, true learning was for the development of the mind, the moral fiber, and the upright citizen, not for practical everyday provisions. The Christianized version was, everyone agreed, for the glory of the Creator. Bacon's innovation was that science must also be for the relief of man's estate; that it must be practical. This insistence on the *practical* transformed speculative philosophy into natural science. Macaulay's summary is this.

> What Bacon did for inductive philosophy may, we think, be fairly stated thus. The objects of preceding speculators were objects which could be attained without careful induction. Those speculators, therefore, did not perform the inductive process carefully. Bacon stirred up men to pursue an object which could be attained only by induction, and by induction carefully performed; and consequently induction was more carefully performed. We do not think that the importance of what Bacon did for inductive philosophy has ever been

overrated. But we think that the nature of his services is often mistaken, and was not fully understood even by himself. It was not by furnishing philosophers with rules for performing the inductive process well, but by furnishing them with a motive for performing it well, that he conferred so vast a benefit on society.

What Bacon was advocating was knowledge that led to what we would call today *technology*. This emphasis has drawn the fire of a school of modern critics of science as a whole (part of the Science Studies movement) whose argument is that science is not so much about knowledge as it is about power. Despite Francis Bacon's many failings of legal and personal integrity, there seems little reason to question the sincerity of his avowedly humanitarian motivation towards practical knowledge. He lived in the court of monarchic power and rose to become the most powerful judge in England before his conviction for corruption and bribery. So he was no naive idealist, and is a natural target for the suspicions of the science critics. But he was at the same time a convinced Christian who would not have been insensitive to the appeal of a philosophy motivated by practical charity, especially since it supported the escape from scholasticism that he also yearned for. Whatever may have been the sincerity of Bacon's theological arguments in favor of practical knowledge, there can be little doubt that they furnished a persuasive rationale that helped to establish the course of modern science, and that persists today.

Technology demands reproducibility. Technology has to be based upon a reliable response in the systems that it puts into operation. Technology seeks to be able to manipulate the world in predictable ways. The knowledge that gives rise to useful technology has to be knowledge about the world in so far as it is reproducible and gives rise to tangible effects. These are precisely the characteristics of modern science.

When we talk about experiments, however, we normally conjure up visions of laboratories with complicated equipment and studious, bespectacled, possibly white-coated scientists; not a day at the beach. The practical experimentation at the beach which is our symbol for the acquisition of everyday knowledge does not draw strong distinctions between the levels of confidence with which we expect the world to follow our plans. At any time we hold to a vast array of beliefs with a wide spectrum of certainties from tentative hypothesis to unshakable conviction; and most often we draw little conscious distinction between them. In most cases, we have no opportunity to do so, since the press of events obliges us every moment to make decisions about our conduct based on imperfect and uncertain knowledge. Establishing confidence in reproducible knowledge, certain enough for practical application, and meeting our expectations for natural science, requires a more deliberate approach to experimentation. This (capitalized) Experiment is a formalization of the notion of reproducibility.

A formal Experiment is generally conducted in the context of some already-articulated theoretical expectation. It can be considered the opposite end of a spectrum of different degrees of deliberateness in experimentation. The idle play of the beach is the other end. And in between are random exploratory investigations, fact and specimen gathering, systematic documentation and measurement, the trial and error of technique development and instrumentation, and the elimination of spurious ideas and mistakes.

At its purest an Experiment is devised specifically to test a theoretical model or principle. Isaac Newton's famous demonstration that white light is in fact composed of a spectrum of light of different colors is often cited as an illustration of experimental investigations leading up to a "crucial experiment". In his letter to the Royal Society of February 1672 he relates in a personal story-telling style his initial experiments with the refraction of light through a prism, and his demonstration by careful measurement that the greater than two degree spread of the refracted colors could not be caused by the angular size of the sun's disc. He talks about various ideas he ruled out as possible explanations of the observations and then says:

> The gradual removal of these suspitions, at length led me to the *Experimentum Crucis*, which was this: I took two boards, and placed one of them close behind the Prisme at the window, so that the light might pass through a small hole, made in it for the purpose, and fall on the other board, which I placed at about 12 feet dis-

Figure 2.3: Newton's drawing of his Experimentum Crucis, published much later in his Opticks (1704).[28]

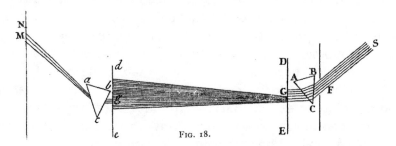

Fig. 18.

tance, having first made a small hole in it also, for some of that Incident light to pass through. Then I placed another Prisme behind this second board, so that the light, trajected through both the boards, might pass through that also, and be again refracted before it arrived at the wall. This done, I took the first Prisme in my hand, and turned it to and fro slowly about its Axis, so much as to make the several parts of the Image, cast on the second board, successively pass through the hole in it, that I might observe to what places on the wall the second Prisme would refract them. And I saw by the variation of those places, that the light, tending to that end of the Image, towards which the refraction of the first Prisme was made, did in the second Prisme suffer a Refraction considerably greater then the light tending to the other end. And so the true cause of the length of that Image was detected to be no other, then that Light consists of Rays differently refrangible, which, without any respect to a difference in their incidence, were, according to their degrees of refrangibility, transmitted towards divers parts of the wall[29].

Even this report and Newton's conclusions were not without controversy. Others seeking to reproduce his results observed different dispersions of the light, presumably because of using prisms with different angles. There followed a correspondence lasting some years, but in a remarkably short time the acceptance of this demonstration became practically universal because the key qualitative features, and by attention to the full details even the quantitative aspects, could be reproduced at will by experimenters with only a moderate degree of competence.

2.2 Is reproducibility really essential to science?

Observational Science

Most thoughtful people recognize the crucial role that repeatable experiments play in the development of science. Nevertheless, there arises, an important objection to the view that science is utterly *dependent* on reproducibility for its operation. The objection is this. What about a discipline like astronomy? The heavenly bodies are far outside our reach. We cannot do experiments on them, or at least we could not in the days prior to space travel and we still cannot for those at stellar distances. Yet who in their right mind would deny to astronomy the status of science?

Or consider the early stages of botany or zoology. For centuries, those disciplines consisted largely of systematic gathering of samples of species; cataloging and classifying them, not experimenting on them. Of course today we do have a more fundamental understanding of the cellular and molecular basis of living organisms, developed in large part from direct manipulative experiments. But surely it would be pure physicist's arrogance to say that botany or zoology were not, even in their classification stages, science.

In short, what about observational sciences? Surely it must be granted that they are science. If they are exceptions to the principle that science requires reproducibility then that principle rings hollow.

Some commentators find this critique so convincing, that they adopt a specialized expression to describe the type of science that *is* based on repeatable experiments. They call it "Baconian Science". The point of this expression is to suggest that there are other types of science than the Baconian model. What I suppose people who adopt this designation have in mind is observational sciences. They think that observational sciences, in which we can't perform experiments on the phenomena of interest at will, don't fit the model of reproducibility. There is some irony in using the expression with this meaning, since actually Bacon was at great pains to emphasize the systematic gathering of observations, without jumping to theoretical conclusions, so he certainly did not discount observational science, even though he did emphasize the motivation of practicality.

However, we need to think carefully whether observational sciences are really exceptions to reproducibility. Let us first consider astronomy. It is an appropriate first choice because in many ways astronomy was historically the first science. Humans gazed into the heavens and pondered on what they saw. The Greeks had extensive knowledge of the constellations and their cycles. And it was the consideration of the motions of the planets, more than anything else that led to the Newtonian synthesis of gravity and dynamics. But astronomy, considered in its proper historical context, is not an exception to the scientific dependence on reproducibility. Far from it. Astronomy was for the pre-industrial age the archetype of reproducibility. It was just because the heavens showed remarkable systematically repeated cycles that it commanded the attention of so many philosophers in attempts to explain the motions of the heavenly bodies. It was because the repeatability gave astronomers the ability to predict with amazing precision the phenomena of the heavens that astronomy appeared almost mystical in its status.

What is more, the independence of place and observer was satisfied by astronomy with superb accuracy. Better than almost all other phenomena, the sky looks the same from where ever you see it. As longer distance travel became more commonplace, the systematic changes of the appearance of the heavens with global position (latitude for example) were soon known and relied upon for navigation. And what could be more common to the whole of humanity than the sky?

Far from being an exception to the principle of reproducibility, astronomy's success *depends* upon that principle. Astronomy insists that all observers are going to see consistent pictures of the heavens when they observe. Those observations are open to all to experience (in principle). And those observations can be predicted ahead of time with great precision.

One way to highlight the importance of reproducibility in the context of astronomy is to contrast Astro*nomy* (the scientific study of the observational universe) with Astro*logy* (the attempt to predict or explain human events from the configurations of the heavenly bodies). Many people still follow assiduously their daily horoscope. Regarded as cultural tradition, that is probably no more harmful than wondering, on the feast of Candlemas, if the groundhog Puxatawney Phil saw his shadow; and recalling that if so, by tradition there will be six more weeks of winter. Astrology, for most people, is a relatively harmless cultural superstition. But surely no thinking person today would put forward astrology as a science. Its results are not reproducible. Its predictions appear to have no value beyond those of common sense. And its attempts to identify shared particular characteristics of people born in certain months simply don't give reliable results. Once upon a time there was little distinction between astronomy and astrology. Their practice in the pre-scientific age seems to be a confusing mix of the two. A major success of the scientific revolution was the disentangling of astronomy and astrology. The most important principle that separates the two activities is that astronomy is describing, systematizing and ultimately explaining the observations of the heavens in so far as they are reproducible and clear to all observers.

There are, of course, unique phenomena in astronomy. Supernovae, for example, each have unique features, and are first observed on a particular date. In that sense they are observations of natural history. On 4th July 1054, astronomers in China first observed a new star in the constellation of Taurus. Its brightness grew visibly day by day. During its three brightest weeks it was reported as visible in daylight, four times brighter than the evening star (Venus). It remained visible to the naked eye for about two years. It is thought that Anastasi Indian art in Arizonan pictographs also records the event. Surprisingly, there seem to be no European records of the event that have survived.[30]

If this were the only supernova ever observed, then we would probably be much more reticent to regard the event with credence. But there are approximately twenty different recorded supernovae (or possibly novae) in our galaxy during the 2000 years before 1700. And with modern telescopes, supernovae in other galaxies can also be observed fairly frequently.

The SN1054 supernova is probably the best known because it gave rise to the beautiful Crab Nebula discovered in 1731. That gas in the Nebula is expanding was established in the early 20th century by observing the line splitting caused by the Doppler effect. The nearer parts of the Nebula are moving towards us and the further parts away from us. In 1968 a new type of pulsing radio emission was discovered coming from the center of the Nebula. This Crab Pulsar is also observable in the visible spectrum. It is now known to be an extremely compact neutron star, rotating at an astonishing 30 times per second.

Figure 2.4: Photograph by the Hubble Telescope of the Crab Nebula.[31]

One can get readily accessible reproducible evidence of the date of the SN1054 supernova. The expansion rate of the Crab Nebula can be established by comparing photographs separated in time. One can then extrapolate that expansion backward and discover when the now-expanding rim must have been all together in the local explosion. This process, applied for example by an undergraduate at Dartmouth College to photographs taken 17 years apart, gives a date in the middle of the 11th century. In 100% agreement with the historic record.[32] [For technical precision we should note that, since the nebula is 6000 light years away, the explosion and the emission of the light we now see took place 6000 years earlier.]

Notice the following characteristics. First the Crab Nebula's supernova, though having its own unique features, was an event of a type represented by numerous other examples. Second, the event itself was observable to, and recorded by, multiple observers. Third, the supernova left long-lived evidence that for years could be seen by anyone who looked, and still gives rich investigation opportunities to experts from round the world, who simply have to point their telescope in the right direction. These are the characteristics of reproducibility in the observational sciences.

What about botany and zoology, in their collection and classification stages? Again, careful consideration convinces us that these do rely on reproducibility. If only a single specimen is available, it remains largely a curiosity. Who is to say that this not simply some peculiar mutant, or even a hoax? But when multiple similar specimens are found, then it is possible to detect what is common to all specimens and to discount as individual variation those characteristics that are not. Indeed, in the life sciences the best option is to have breeding specimens, which guarantee the ability to establish new examples for which the reproducible characteristics are those on which the scientific classification is based.

All right, what about geology then? Its specimens don't reproduce. But again the observation of many different examples of the same types of rock, or formation, or other phenomenon, is essential to its scientific progress. In its earliest stages, before geophysics had more direct physical descriptions of its processes, geology progressed as a science largely by the identification of multiple examples of the same processes at work, that is by reliance on repeatability. As the scientific framework for understanding the earth's formation was gradually built up, the systematic aspects of the rock formations began to become clear. Events could be correlated to produce an ordered series of ages. Then additional techniques such as radioactive dating enabled geologists to assign a quantitative date to the different geological ages, based on multiple assessments of the time that must have elapsed since the formation of rocks identified as belonging to each period. All of this process requires the ability to make multiple observations, observe repeatable patterns, and perform repeatable physical tests on the samples.

So observational science requires *multiple repeatable examples* of the phenomenon or specimen under consideration. It does not require that these can be produced *at will* in the way that a laboratory experiment can in principle be performed at any hour on any day. Observations may be constrained by the fact that the examples of interest occur only at certain times (for example eclipses) or in certain places (for example in specific habitat), over which we might have little or no control. But it does require that multiple examples exist and can be observed.

Randomness

A second important objection to the assertion that science requires reproducibility concerns the occurrence in science of phenomena that are random. By definition, such events are not predictable, or reproducible, at least as far as their timing is concerned.

If science is the study of the world in so far as it is reproducible, how come probability, the mathematical embodiment of randomness, the ultimate in non-reproducibility, plays such a prominent role in modern physics? Here, I think, it is helpful to take for a moment a historical perspective of science. Pierre Laplace is famous (amongst other things) for his encounter with the emperor Napoleon. Laplace explained to him his deterministic understanding of nature. Bonapart is reported to have asked, "But where in this scheme is the role for God", to which Laplace's response was "I have no need of that hypothesis". Regardless of his theological position, Laplace's philosophical view of science was rather commonplace for his age. It was that science was in the process of showing that the world is governed by a set of deterministic equations. And if one knew the initial conditions of these equations for all the particles in the universe, one could, in principle at least, solve those equations and thereby predict, in principle to arbitrary accuracy, the future of everything. In other words, Laplace's view, and that of probably the majority of scientists of his age, was that science was in the business of explaining the world as if it were completely predictable, subject to no randomness.

This view persisted until the nineteen twenties, when the formulation of quantum mechanics shocked the world of science by demonstrating that the many highly complicated and specific details of atomic physics could be unified, explained, and predicted with high accuracy using a totally new understanding of reality. At the heart of this new approach was a concession that at the atomic level events are never deterministic; they are always predictable only to within a significant uncertainty. Heisenberg's uncertainty principle is the succinct formulation of that realization. Quantum mechanics possesses the mathematical descriptions to calculate accurately the *probability* of events but not to predict them individually in a reproducible way. Perfect reproducibility, it seems, exists only as an ideal, and that ideal is approached only at the macroscopic scale of billions of atoms, not at the microscopic scale of single atoms.

Where does that leave the view that science demands reproducibility? Did 20th century science in fact abandon that principle?

It seems clear to me that science has not at all abandoned the principle. The principle is as intact as ever that science describes the world in so far as it is reproducible. For hundreds of years, science pursued the task with spectacular success. Quantum mechanics, shocking though it seemed and still seems, did not halt or even alter the basic drive. What it did was to show that the process of describing the world in reproducible terms appears to have limits, fundamental limits, that are built into the fabric of the universe. The quantum picture accepts that there are some boundaries beyond which our reproducible knowledge fails in principle (not just for technical reasons). Even as innovative a scientist and supple a philosopher as Albert Einstein was repelled by the prospect, famously resisting the notion that the randomness of the world is in principle impenetrable with his comment "God does not play dice". Einstein, like scientists before and after him was committed to discovering the world in so far as it is reproducible, not arbitrary. The overwhelming opinion of physics today, though, is that Einstein was wrong in this epigram. God does play dice, in the sense that some things are simply irreproducible.

But that does not stop science from proceeding to explore what is measurable and predictable. Science does that first by pressing up to the limits of what is reproducible. If individual events are not predictable, it calculates the probabilities of events. Quantum theory provides this reproducible measure in so far as reproducibility exists. The interesting thing about Quantum mechanics is that it is governed by deterministic equations. These equations are named after the great physicists Erwin Schrödinger and Paul Dirac. A problem in Quantum mechanics can be solved by finding a solution of these equations. The equations take an initial state of the system and then predict the entire future evolution of that state from that time forward. This is such a deterministic process that some people argue that Quantum mechanics does not undermine determinism. But such a view misses the key point. The function that is solved for and the future system state that is predicted are no longer the definite position or velocity of a particle, or one of the many other quantities that we are familiar with in classical dynamics (or the everyday world). Instead it is essentially the *probability* of a particle being in a certain position or having a certain velocity. This is an example of science pressing up against the limits of reproducibility. The world is not completely predictable even in principle by mathematical equations, but science wants to describe it as completely as possible, to the extent that it is. So when up against the non-predictability, science invokes deterministic mathematics, but uses the mathematics to govern just the probability of the occurrence of events. Probability is, in a sense, the extent to which random events display reproducibility. Science describes the world in terms of reproducible events to the extent that it can be described that way.

And science proceeds, second, by pressing on into the other areas of scientific investigation that still lie open to reproducible description: describing and understanding them as far as they are indeed reproducible.

The history of nature

A third important challenge to the principle of reproducibility lies in the types of events that are inherently unique. How could we possibly have knowledge of more than one universe? Therefore how can reproducibility be a principle applied to the Big Bang origin of the universe? Or, perhaps less fundamentally, but probably just as practically, how can we apply principles of repeatability to the origin of life on earth, or to the details of how the earth's species got here?

I think these issues all boil down to the question "What about natural history?" Is the history of nature part of science?

It is helpful to think first about the ways that science can tell us about the past. Today, our ability to analyze human DNA has become extremely important in legal evidence. It can help prove or disprove the involvement of a particular person in a crime under investigation. The high profile cases tend, of course, to be capital cases, but increasingly this type of forensic evidence is decisive in a wider variety of situations. Obviously this is an example of a way in which scientific evidence is extremely powerful in telling us something about history — not as overwhelming as it is often portrayed in the popular TV series such as CSI, but still very powerful. Important as this evidence may be, it still depends on the rest of the context of the case which is what determines the significance of the DNA test results. Moreover, the laboratory results themselves are rarely totally unimpeachable. We have to be sure that the sample really came from the place the police say it did. We have to be sure it was not tampered with before it got to the lab or while it was there. We have to be sure that the results are accurately reported, and so on. So science can provide us with highly persuasive evidence, in part because of its clarity and the difficulty of faking it. But when we adduce scientific evidence for specific unique events of history (even recent history) our confidence is, in principle, less than if we had access to multiple examples of the same kind of phenomenon.

To illustrate that difference in levels of confidence, ask yourself how successful a defense lawyer would likely be if they tried to defend against DNA evidence by arguing that it is a scientific fallacy that DNA is unique to each individual. Trying to impeach the principles of science would be a ridiculously unconvincing way to try to discredit evidence in a criminal case. Those principles have been established by innumerable laboratory tests by independent investigators over years of experience and subjected to intense scrutiny by experts. General principles of science, such as the uniqueness of DNA, *need* more compelling investigation and evidence to establish them than we require for everyday events. But they get that investigation, and the support of the wider fabric of science into which they are woven. So, once established, we grant them a much higher level of confidence. What's more, if there is reason to doubt them, we can go back and get some more evidence to resolve the question.

But notice that our confidence in scientific principles is not the same as confidence in knowledge of the particular historical question. We are confident that insofar as the world is reproducible, and can thus be scientifically described, DNA is unique to the individual. But that does not automatically decide the legal case. If in fact there is other extremely compelling evidence that contradicts the DNA evidence, we are likely to conclude that *in this specific instance* there is something that invalidates the DNA evidence and we should discount it.

In summary, then, for specific unique events of history, evidence based on scientific analysis can be important, but is not uniquely convincing.

However, even though it contains some questions about unique events, much of natural history is not of this type. Much is about the broad sweep of development of the universe, the solar system, the planet, or the earth's creatures. In other words, questions of natural history are usually about generalities, not particularities, about issues giving rise to repeated observational examples, not single instances. For these generalities, science is extremely powerful, but continues to rely upon its principles of reproducibility and clarity.

We believe the universe is expanding from an initial event, starting some 13 billion years ago, because we can observe the Doppler shifts of characteristic radiation lines that are emitted from objects over an enormous range of distances from our solar system. We see that the farther away the object is, the more rapidly it is receding from us, as demonstrated by the frequency downshift of the light we see. Anyone, anywhere can observe these sorts of effects with telescopes and instruments that these days are relatively commonplace. The observed systematic trend is consistent with a more-or-less uniform expansion of the universe. If we project back the tracks of the expansion, by mentally running the universe in reverse, we find that our reversing tracks more-or-less bring all the objects together at the same time: the time that we identify as the Big Bang, or the age of the universe. This picture is confirmed by thousands of independent observations of different stars and astrophysical objects. Thus, the Big Bang theory of the origin of the universe is a generality: that the universe had a beginning roughly 13 billion years ago, when all of the objects we can see were far closer together. And it is a generality confirmed by many observational examples that show the same result.

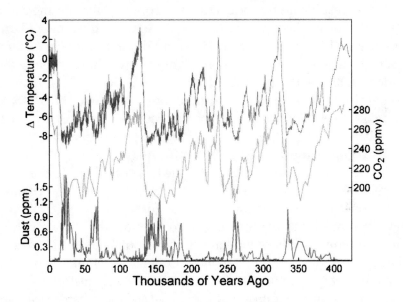

Figure 2.5: Temperature, atmospheric carbon-dioxide, and dust record from the ice cores from Vostok, Antarctica.

What about earth's history? The history of the earth's climate is a topic of great current interest. How do we know what has happened to the climate in past ages? This information comes in all sorts of ways from tree rings to paleontology. Perhaps the most convincing and detailed information comes from various types of "cores" sampled from successively deposited strata. Examples include ice cores, and ocean sediments. Ice cores as long as three kilometers, covering the last three quarters of a million years have been drilled from the built-up ice arising from annual snowfall in Antarctica. The resulting history of the climate is laid out in amazing detail. By analyzing the fraction of different isotopes of hydrogen and oxygen in the water, scientists can estimate the mean temperature. By analyzing trapped gases, the fraction of carbon dioxide can be determined, and by observations of included microscopic particles, the levels of dust in the atmosphere can be

documented, in each case over the entire history represented by
the core. Figure 2.5 illustrates the results from the core analyzed in
1999.[33]

These results are reproducible. If a core is drilled in the same
place, the results one gets are the same. Actually, the longer (3km)
core was drilled more recently (2004) in a different place in Antarctica than the one I have illustrated,[34] but shows almost exactly the
same results for the periods of history that overlap. Moreover,
deep-sea-bed sediment cores from all over the globe show global
ice mass levels deduced from oxygen isotopes that correlate extremely well with the ice-core data for their history, but stretch
back to 5 million years ago. The rapid progress in these observations and analysis over the past decade has enabled us to build up
a remarkable record of the climatic history of the earth. It enables
us to construct well-informed theories for what factors influence
the different aspects of climate, and to say how the climate varied
through time. But these vital additions to our knowledge are still
about broad generalities: the *global* or regional climate, not usually the highly specific questions that preoccupy historians. For
example, the uncertainties in the exact age of the different ice-core
samples can be as large as a thousand years or more. In the scheme
of the general picture of what happened in the last million years,
this is a negligible uncertainty; but on the timescale of human lives
(for example) it is large.

2.3   Inherent limitations of reproducibility

We have seen some examples of the great power of science's reliance
upon reproducibility to arrive at knowledge. These examples are
not intended to emphasize science's power; such a demonstration
would be superfluous for most modern minds. They are to show
the importance of reproducibility. We are so attuned to the culture
of science that we generally take this reproducibility for granted.
But we must now pause to recollect both that this reproducibility is
not obvious in nature, and that in many fields of human knowledge
the degree of reproducibility we require in science is absent.

Of course, substantial regularity in the natural world, and indeed in human society, was as self-evident to our ancestors as it is to

us. But the extent to which precise and measurable reproducibility could be discovered and codified was not. The very concept and expression 'law of nature' dates back only to the start of the scientific revolution, to Boyle and Newton. And in its original usage, it intended as much the judicial meaning of a legislated edict of the Creator as the impersonal physical principle, or force of nature that now comes to mind. Indeed, a case can be made that it was in substantial degree the expectation that law governed the natural world, fostered by a theology of God as law-giver, that provided the fertile intellectual climate for the growth of science. As late as the nineteenth century, Faraday motivated his search for unifying principles, and explained his approach to scientific investigation, by statements like "God has been pleased to work in his material creation by laws". By referring to God's pleasure, Faraday was not in the least intending to be metaphorical, and by laws he meant something probably much less abstract than would be commonplace today.

In drawing attention now to disciplines in which the reproducibility expected in science is absent, I want to start by reiterating that this absence does *not* in my view undermine their ability to provide real knowledge. The whole point of my analysis is to assert that non-scientific knowledge is real and essential. So I beseech colleagues from the disciplines I am about to mention to restrain any understandable impulse to bristle at the charge that their disciplines are not science. I remind you that I am using the word science to mean natural science, and the techniques that it depends upon. If the semantics is troubling, simply insert the qualification "natural" in front of my usage. Let us also stipulate from the outset that there are *parts* of each of these disciplines that either benefit from scientific techniques or indeed possess sufficient reproducibility to be scientifically analyzed. I am not at all doubting such a possibility. I am simply commenting that the core subject areas of these disciplines are not most fruitfully studied in this way for fundamental reasons to do with their content.

In his (1997) graduate text *Science Studies*, introducing various philosophical and sociological analysis of science, David J Hess acknowledges without hesitation the difficulties in applying scientific analysis to other disciplines "Probably the greatest weakness in this position comes when the philosophy of science is generalized from the natural sciences to the human sciences". He says specifically "Many social phenomena are far too complicated to be predictable".[35] In other words, in my terminology, these phenomena are not science. Yet a few pages later he says. "One of the reasons social scientists lose patience with philosophers of science is that we are constantly told that we are in some sense deficient scientists — we lack a paradigm, predictive ability, quantitative exactness, and so on — instead of being seen as divergent or different scientists".[36] This is an argument about titles and semantics. Sociologists today acknowledge that sociology does not offer the kind of reproducibility that is characteristic of the natural sciences. They feel they must insist on the title of science, which I believe is because of the scientism of the age; without the imprimatur of the title they feel their discipline is in danger of being dismissed as non-knowledge. Yet they resent it when the essential epistemological differences between their field and science are pointed out. No wonder there are difficulties in this discussion. As a physical scientist, I need to keep out of this argument, but I will observe that if we disavow scientism, then the whole of this discussion becomes more tractable. It is no longer a problem for sociology to be recognized as a field of knowledge in which reproducibility is not available.

History is a field in which there is thankfully less resentment towards an affirmation that it is not science. Obviously history, more often than not, is concerned with unique events in the past that cannot be repeated. Here is a commentary by a historian on King James the Second's frequent remark to justify his intransigence: "My father made concessions and he was beheaded". Macaulay writes, "Even if it had been true that concession had been fatal to Charles the First, a man of sense would have remembered that a single experiment is not sufficient to establish a general rule even in sciences much less complicated than the science of government; that, since the beginning of the world, no two political experiments were ever made of which all the conditions were exactly alike ..."[37] Macaulay's typical, but confusing, use of 'science' has already been noted, but the point he makes very clearly is that there is no reproducibility in history. No more than a small fraction of its concerns benefit from analysis that bears the stamp of natural science. Yet no thoughtful person would deny that historical knowledge is true knowledge, that history at its best has high standards of scholarship and credibility, and that the study of history has high practical and theoretical value.

Similarly the study of the law, jurisprudence, is a field whose research and practice cannot be scientific because it is not concerned with the reproducible. The circumstances of particular events cannot be subjected to repeated tests or to multiple observations. Moreover, the courts do not have the luxury of being able indefinitely to defer judgement until sufficient data might become available. They have to arrive at a judgement that is binding on the protagonists even with insufficient data. Consequently, the legal system's approach to decision-making is very different from science's.

In Britain in the early 1980s the government of Prime Minister Margaret Thatcher introduced policies in line with Milton Friedman's economic theories, which the press was fond of referring to as the 'monetarist experiment'. Here was what an economist must surely dream about: the chance to see an experimental verification of his theory. What was the result of this experiment? Was monetarism thereby confirmed or refuted? To judge by current economic opinion, it seems neither. Economists don't really know how to assess the outcome unambiguously, because this was a real economy with all sorts of extraneous influences; and what is most important, one can't keep trying repeatedly till one gets consistent results. It may have been an experiment, but it was not truly a scientific experiment. Economics is an interesting case here, because economists have large quantities of precise measured data and usefully employ highly sophisticated mathematics for many of their theories, a trait that they share with some of the hardest physical scientists. Economics is a field of high intellectual rigor. But the absence of an opportunity for truly reproducible tests or observations and the impossibility of isolating the different components of economic systems means that economics as a discipline is qualitatively different from science.

Politics is to many a physical scientist baffling and mysterious. Here is a field, if there ever was one, that is the complete contradiction of what scientists seek in nature. In place of consistency and predictability we find pragmatism and the winds of public opinion. In place of dispassionate analysis, we have the power of oratory. And once again, nothing in the least approximating the opportunity for reproducible tests or observations offers itself to political practitioners. It seems a great pity, and perhaps a sign of wistful optimism, not to mention the scientism that is our present subject, that the academic field of study is referred to these days almost universally as Political Science.

We will discuss more, equally important, examples of inherently non-scientific disciplines later. But these suffice to illustrate that not only is science not all the knowledge there is, it may not be even the most important knowledge. And however much we might hope for greater precision and confidence in the findings of the non-scientific disciplines, it is foolishness to think they will ever possess the kind of predictive power that we attribute to science. Their field of endeavor does not lend itself to the epistemological techniques that underlie science's reliable models and convincing proofs. They are about more indefinite, intractable, unique, and often more human problems. In short, they are not about nature.

Chapter 3

Clarity. The foundation of testability.

The second major characteristic that natural science requires, I refer to as 'Clarity'. I use capitalization to indicate that the word is being used in a specialized sense. Clarity can be thought of as a foundational requirement for the expression and communication of reproducibility; so these two scientific traits are partners. The results of any scientific investigation have to be expressed in terms that are unambiguous. Otherwise it is not possible for other investigators, or indeed even the same investigator, to tell whether repeating the experiment or observation gives the same answer as on the prior occasion.

Lest an immediate misunderstanding should arise, I must call attention to, and partially disavow, the most important historical use of 'clarity' in the philosophy of science. I refer to René Descartes' famous *Discourse on the Method of Rightly Conducting the Reasons and Seeking the Truth in the Sciences*[38], which is not only a foundational text for subsequent philosophy — *cogito ergo sum*, to the dread of freshman philosophy students everywhere — but also the primary source for Descartes' advocacy of the mechanical approach to natural science. He famously writes

> And as I observed that in the words I think, hence I am, there is nothing at all which gives me assurance of their truth beyond this, that I see very clearly that in order to think it is necessary to exist, I concluded that I might take, as a general rule, the principle, that the things which we very clearly and distinctly conceive are true, only observing, however, that there is some difficulty in rightly determining the objects which we distinctly conceive.[39]

What I disavow is the "principle that the things which we very clearly and distinctly conceive are true". I don't at all mean by

Clarity this sort of intuitive certainty, or ability to establish truth. I don't think all ideas that can be clearly and distinctly formulated are, because of that clarity, true. On the contrary, I think one can clearly formulate ideas that are false. That's not really what Descartes meant either. He was, it seems, rather seeking for a way to establish indubitable axioms on which to raise a deductive philosophical structure, giving to all of thought a kind of mathematical rigor. Logical Positivism acknowledges such axioms only in the form of *analytic statements*. Examples of analytic statements might be "all bachelors are unmarried" or "one plus one equals two"[40]; they are considered to be true by definition of the concepts employed. Descartes evidently thought that *cogito ergo sum* was axiomatic because of its clarity. But, no, my use of Clarity is different. I mean instead, and much more colloquially, simply expression of an observation or concept unambiguously, such that its meaning is plain.

3.1   Measurement

The most direct way to ensure this unambiguous Clarity is for scientific observations to consist of *measurements*. The consequent reduction of the main parameters of the observations to *numbers* offers Clarity because numbers are probably the most familiar universal concept of thought. Arithmetic has for thousands of years been an almost universal skill and knowledge — and it is unambiguous. Consequently the expression of scientific observations or principles in numerical form is perhaps the surest way achieve the clarity of expression that is required.

Measurement is more than numbers though. To measure the physical world we need shared scales, references, and common systems of units. When early astronomers were charting the motions of the heavenly bodies, they measured the position in the sky by the angles that their sight-lines subtended to other notable features of the heavens: the constellations. The Zodiac gave agreed points of reference relative to which everyone could understand positions when they knew the relevant angles. Those angles had to be expressed in terms that were understood by everyone. The measurement of angles in terms of degrees, of which there are 360 in a full circle, dates back (at least) to the Babylonians of the second millennium BC. They knew that the perimeter of a regular hexagon is exactly equal to 6 times the distance of its corners from its center, because a hexagon can be made up from six equilateral triangles. The Babylonians used a sexagesimal (base 60) counting system; so they divided each of the 6 arcs corresponding to the hexagon's sides into 60 units: degrees, of which there are 6×60=360 in a circle. That system stuck. Astronomers were able to measure and express the positions of the stars completely unambiguously. Clarity was available. By the way, the measurement of angles is a conceptual facility we might take for granted today, but there is a fascinating history of the increasingly precise instruments invented for making those measurements, for navigation as much as for theoretical star-gazing.

Figure 3.1: The replica K48 of the official kilogram, kept by the Danish National Metrology Institute under two bell-jars.[41]

Mass, length and time are the fundamental quantities whose units, in different combinations, enable us to measure the physical properties of any system or phenomenon. The progress of science closely parallels the development of increasingly accurate standardization of those units, made possible by increasingly precise means of measurement. Today scientific definitions of exquisite precision, better than one part in 10 billion, are required. The unit of mass, the kilogram, is the only remaining unit that is defined by an artifact: an ingot of platinum-iridium kept by the International Bureau of Weights and Measures under special conditions. Because that prototype acquires in a year contaminants with mass as much as a millionth of a gram (one part in a billion of the prototype's mass), there are special cleaning procedures specified before it is used[42]. The unit of time, the second, is the duration of 9,192,631,770 periods of the radiation corresponding to the transition between the two hyperfine levels of the ground state of the cesium 133 atom. The unit of length, the meter, is the length of the path traveled by light in vacuum during a time interval of 1/299,792,458 of a second.

Numbers are not the only unambiguous shared form of expression. Geometry has an equally venerable intellectual history, and of course is part of the definition of angles that I've already cited as an example. Today we know that geometry can be expressed in terms of numbers through coordinate systems and trigonometry. In Newton's day, however, geometry was considered the purer form of mathematics. So, even though Newton had invented calculus in order to be able to calculate with the equations of motion, and quite probably used it in many of his discoveries, he chose not to use it to prove the theorems of his Principia Mathematica. Instead his proofs are geometrical, which makes them far less accessible to mathematicians of today, but presumably made them more accessible, or at any rate more convincing to the mathematicians of his own day.

Some would go so far as to say that the natural sciences must (eventually) be expressed in terms of mathematics. That rubric is achievable in practically all the theory of physics and chemistry, and it certainly provides what I have called Clarity. The problem with this extreme requirement, though, is that much scientific communication is not recognizable as mathematics. In the observational sciences, especially in their initial stages where data gathering is beginning but overall coordinating theories are not yet developed, what is mostly required is *classification*. So the activities in (say) botany in the eighteenth and nineteenth centuries were dominated by the collection of specimens, their identification, and their classification. One might, by a stretch, think of classification as a mathematical process (reflecting set theory), so that the ultimate theo-

Figure 3.2: Sir Isaac Newton, painted by Barrington Bramley in 1992 after the portrait by Sir Godfrey Kneller dated 1689, by kind permission of the Tenth Earl of Portsmouth. Donated by Sir Michael Atiyah, F.R.S., Master of Trinity College, to the Isaac Newton Institute for Mathematical Sciences, Cambridge University.

retical outcome conforms to a strong mathematical requirement. But the collection and identification processes leading up to that classification involve field skills that are highly intuitive and resist expression in mathematical terms. In laboratory sciences too there are practical techniques that are critical to the performance, and to the understanding, of experiments that are not in any meaningful sense mathematical, yet need to be communicated. Going further, not just the techniques in physiology, for example, but also the detailed knowledge gathered through dissection of the workings of animal bodies, while precise and at best unambiguous, can hardly be thought of as mathematical. Thus even the ultimate theoretical description of a subject like physiology has aspects that really don't fit a requirement to be mathematical in the sense most people understand. That is why I adopt a less restrictive terminology.

John Ziman, in his book "Reliable Knowledge" uses the term "consensibility" to mean almost exactly what I call "Clarity". He puts it like this

... scientific knowledge is distinguished from other intellectual artifacts of human society by the fact that its contents are *consensible*. By this I mean that each message should not be so obscure or ambiguous that the recipient is unable either to give whole-hearted assent or to offer well-founded objections. The goal of science, moreover, is to achieve the maximum degree of *consensuality*. Ideally the general body of scientific knowledge should consist of facts and principles that are firmly established and accepted without serious doubt, by an overwhelming majority of competent, well-informed scientists. As we shall see, it is convenient to distinguish between a *consensible* message with the *potentiality* for eventually contributing to a consensus, and a *consensual* statement that has been fully tested and is universally agreed. We may say, indeed, that consensibility is a necessary condition for any scientific communication, whereas only a small proportion of the whole body of science is undeniably consensual at a given moment.[43]

Since few people have ever heard the word consensible, and it is not in the Merriam Webster on-line dictionary (for example) I prefer to use a word, Clarity, whose meaning people do know, even if I run some risk of confusion since I am using it with a meaning that is somewhat specialized. Ziman's other concept, *consensuality*: universal scientific acceptance, is a worthy goal to which Clarity contributes, but not something that in my view is either required by or unique to science.

3.2 Beyond Clarity

Clarity is of course a desirable characteristic in many situations, not just science. But there are many important questions that inherently lack the kind of Clarity that science requires. Consider the beauty of a sunset, the justice of a verdict, the compassion of a nurse, the drama of a play, the depth of a poem, the terror of a war, the excitement of a symphony, the significance of a history, the love of a woman. Which of these can be reduced to the Clarity of a scientific description? Yes, a sunset *can* be described in terms of the spectral analysis of the light, the causes of the coloration arising from light scattering by particles and molecules, and their arrangement and gradient in the sky. But when all the scientific details of such a description are done, has that explained, or even conveyed, its beauty? Hardly. In fact it has missed the point. Many-layered connections and implications are intrinsically part of the significance of these subjects. We appreciate and understand them, we know them, through sharing conceptually in the interwoven fabric of their often only evocative allusions. Removal of ambiguity destroys that significance, because ambiguity is at the very heart of their meaning. One cannot appreciate ambiguity unambiguously. Consequently, matters such as these cannot be encompassed scientifically. Their very nature defeats the Clarity that science demands.

This is not a problem for science. It simply means that science is not able to deal with topics like these. There are more than enough topics that science *is* able to address to keep it busy. But if the amazing successes of science lead to belief that scientific knowledge is all the true knowledge there is, if the possibility of knowledge that is not encompassed by science is ruled out, if, in short, scientism rules the epistemological milieu, then there's a major problem for subjects like these. They have then either to be dismissed from the set of topics offering any real knowledge or they have to be reduced to something like science. Both these reactions or strategies can be observed today.

The first strategy is often at work, for example, when people talk about the distinction between fact and value. In itself, this distinction is harmless enough, and may well be a helpful way to understand and compare the types of topic. However, when scientism places the discussion of value into a category of non-knowledge, of unsupported doctrine, of mere opinion, it fundamentally undermines its significance. Of course, as I've remarked before, scientism rarely operates through an explicitly articulated assessment. Instead a dismissal like this usually works implicitly. The expression "value judgement", for example, may well be an apt one to describe the analysis of some topics that don't lend themselves to the Clarity of science. What is unjustified is the commonplace presumption that the phrase "value judgement" implies the impossibility of forming reasoned and consensual justifications or of acquiring unequivocal knowledge. But it is in this dismissive sense that we most frequently hear it.

The second strategy: reducing the topic to something like science by imposing on it the structures of scientific analysis, is commonplace in many social disciplines, and spills over, for example, into popular journalism. A symptom is the increasing predominance of opinion polls in the press. An opinion poll serves as a mechanism to turn questions of opinion, preference, or other non-scientific understanding, into quasi-scientific, numerical data. Again, in itself, the idea of polling is unobjectionable. Of course the phrasing of questions in many polls accidentally or deliberately biases the results towards a particular outcome. But it is undoubtedly possible to form a realistic assessment of public opinion by well designed polls, and in the political arena such an undertaking is completely justified by the fact that the outcome will in fact be ultimately decided in a democratic society by a poll. What is unjustified is the more subtle presumption that when the poll data are in about a particular question, the *answer* to the question is obtained. For a political election it is; but intellectual questions ought not in general to be decided by popular polls. So why is so much attention in popular newspapers today paid to polling? Scientific questions certainly are not decided by polls. Why should non-scientific? Clearly, if they are questions of knowledge, they shouldn't. But scientism all too often prefers the shallow and in this case inappropriate but apparently 'scientific' numerical poll to the ambiguity and subtlety of the non-scientific discussion.

Music is an interesting illustration of the scientific requirements of Clarity and the fact that not all topics possess it. In contrast to people living before the advent of recording, everyone today is familiar with the fact that music can be captured and represented in a wonderfully reproducible way. The pressure waves impinging on a microphone can be faithfully recorded in analog signals, which these days are immediately converted to digital representation in computer memory and thereby preserved from degradation. Such representations are nothing more than a sequence of values, of numbers, varying in time according to the frequencies and amplitudes of the notes being played. We can regard those numerical values as a scientific description of the music. It is by intention reproducible, so that we can, at will, hear it played through our loud-speakers or earphones, doubtless with varying degrees of fidelity to the sense of our exquisitely discerning ears, but usually with remarkably high precision. Now the question is, to what extent is this scientific description of the music a complete description of it?

Let us set aside any infidelity in the sound. Granted that recordings of classical music don't generally sound as good as a live performance — although when it comes to popular music the opposite is often the case. But possible incompleteness in the sense of inaccuracy is not the point. The reason we don't regard the digital signal, the scientific description, as encompassing the content and meaning of the music is not because of any inaccuracy it might have. It is because music's meaning is bound up in the very act of hearing it.

In the first place, music has an inexplicable direct effect upon the hearer, it evokes emotional responses of sadness, excitement, or pleasure, and so on. It also provokes in musically more sophisticated hearers a conscious intellectual response. They can hear, understand and appreciate the flowing harmony or polyphony, the cadences and the crescendos, the suspensions and the rhythms. They can also appreciate the artistry of the performers, their delicacy, precision, or power, and perhaps almost enter into the performance through an act of sympathetic imagination. Then finally — though these don't exhaust the facets one could discuss — the music connects them through memory to other experiences of their wider lives and those of others, through the evocation of a terrible or a wonderful event, an enemy or friend; or it connects them to the rest of the world through the words of poetry which the mind associates with the tune.

These meanings of music are not captured by the scientific description. They are not present in that description by itself in isolation. They are elicited only by the act of hearing; by the connection of the music to the human. And they obviously don't possess the clarity of being able to be expressed unambiguously in ways that can be conveyed by scientific terminology.

3.3   Reductionism and abstraction

Reductionism's place in science

The explanation of the more complex in terms of the simpler: 're-duction' or 'reductionism', is often spoken of as a distinctive char-acteristic of science. In the middle of thinking about what I might say about this, I went to my bookshelves, which contain a pretty fair selection of books about the history and philosophy of science, to explore what some of these commentators said about it. I began picking up books and looking into their indexes. The most remark-able fact emerged. In none of them did the word reductionism appear. Realism, relativism, reliability, revisability, revisionism, revolution, even religion, but not reductionism. Well, I said to my-self, that's strange. So I picked up a different, but related type of book. Dawkins', *The Blind Watchmaker*, and Michael Ruse's *Can a Darwinian be a Christian*, and lo, there in the index is reductionism. This sampling, though highly 'unscientific', is suggestive. Reduc-tionism has come to the fore largely through the debate about the relationship between science and religion, and notably in the dis-cussion of evolution. Not nearly as much as one might be led to believe has it been considered a distinctive feature of science, wor-thy of special notice. But since it is now such a prominent part of the most prominent public arguments about scientism, and since it does have some relationship to the questions of Clarity, and to a lesser extent reproducibility, it seems important to address it.

Ruse, the philosopher, says "The core belief in reduction is that one is explaining one set of things in terms of another set, and that the thing doing the explaining is more basic or fundamental than the thing being explained. For this reason, the thing explaining is generally taken to be more uniform or less varied than the thing being explained, and reduction typically involves the bigger be-ing explained in terms of the smaller and more standard and/or repeatable. Because of these various aims, we should make a clear distinction. When we are talking about reducing things rather than theories (which raises rather different issues), reduction might be taken at the *ontological* level, where what we are trying to do is to explain the many in terms of the few, ... or reduction might be taken at the *methodological* level, where the bigger is explained in terms of the smaller."[44]

I am not at all convinced that this is an accurate description of the way the distinction between different kinds of reductionism is generally drawn, and Ruse seems to obfuscate the distinction even further when he says about the possibility of a successful Darwinian brain science "No one is then saying that the brain is nothing but a bunch of particles. The methodological reductionist is highly sensitive to order;" "What is important ... and here we see a meeting with ontological reductionism, is that there is denial that the order represents a new kind of thing or substance." In fact, even though Ruse is right in seeing that they should not, many people actually *are* saying that the brain is nothing but a bunch of particles (or words to that effect).[45]

Dawkins' description of reductionism is characteristically more engaging and illustrative, talking about explaining locomotives in terms of fireboxes, boilers, and governors. The 'heirarchical reductionism' he espouses is, he says, "just another name for an honest desire to understand how things work". He contrasts this with the observation that "...'reductionism' is one of those things, like sin, that is only mentioned by people who are against it." This bad sort of reductionist, who is non-existent according to Dawkins, "tries to explain complicated things directly in terms of the smallest parts" rather than in a hierarchical chain of organization in "successive layers".[46]

We should immediately agree that the description of things in hierarchical levels of size and complexity is completely familiar and appropriate, and that it is a habitual and unproblematic part of simple, as well as complex, thought. Certainly, we try to understand machines and artifacts in terms of smaller subunits from which they are made, and the smaller units in terms of smaller still. A car works by having wheels. Wheels work by having tires, bearings and axles. Bearings work by being composed of supporting rings between which rollers (or balls) permit differential rotation, and so on. Equally, and to illustrate that the technique is not at all restricted to engineering or natural philosophy, we make sense of such abstract entities as proofs or arguments by breaking them up into individual propositions, and examining the truth of those propositions. This general strategy, though, has a much simpler name than reductionism. It is precisely what is meant by *analysis*:

the separating of something into its constituent parts in order to understand it.

But Ruse and Dawkins have not identified correctly the reductionism that is "mentioned by people who are against it". It is not the direct explanation in terms of the simplest level that the complaint is against. Nor is it the denial that order represents a new kind of substance. It is the assertion, or more usually unspoken presumption, that when a satisfactory scientific explanation at a reduced level exists, such an explanation trumps, invalidates, or explains away understanding at higher levels: that the higher level descriptions lose their force or relevance. This is certainly what, for example, Donald MacKay in his *The clockwork image* (1974) is complaining about, and why he coined the disparaging but descriptive phrase "nothing-buttery" to refer to ontological reductionism. "Nothing-buttery is characterized by the notion that by reducing any phenomenon to its components you not only explain it, but *explain it away*"[47]. It is definitely helpful to analyze animal bodies in terms of their cells, but it is unhelpful, and fundamentally untrue, to conclude that if one completes such an analysis, then animals are demonstrated to be *nothing but* assemblies of cells. The presumption that reduced level explanations explain away higher level descriptions generally operates inconsistently. It must do so, because science is full of descriptions and explanations that are actually not reductionist in the senses identified by Dawkins and Ruse. Nothing-buttery usually operates in such a way as to discriminate against descriptions that don't conform to the ideals of science. We shall examine later some examples of this process at work, but here we simply draw attention to the fact that it is a trait of *scientism*.

Is reductionism needed in order for reproducibility or Clarity to work? First reproducibility; there really isn't much justification for thinking that reproducibility ultimately requires or encourages reductionism. One might suppose that simpler things behave in simpler ways, which might mean more reproducible ways. It might mean, as Ruse hints, that the smaller components behave more reproducibly, which would ally reductionism with reproducibility. For two centuries it was indeed believed that atoms were governed by simple, totally reproducible, deterministic laws. Unfortunately for this argument, though, it has been utterly overthrown by quantum mechanics. We now know that elementary particles are actually *less* predictable in their behavior than macroscopic systems. They can't even be localized simultaneously in position and velocity because of Heisenberg's uncertainty principle. So at the level of elementary particles, we see the most perfectly statistical, and in that sense most random, behavior of all. It is only at the macroscopic level of assemblies of millions or billions of atoms or electrons that the stable, reproducible, predictable laws of classical dynamics emerge from a ghostly dance of quantum probabilities. No, at the quantum level we have astonishingly accurate and — in the sense of mathematically elegant — simple theories; but in the process of reduction to smaller and smaller units we have discovered a domain that resists the constraints of reproducibility that the scientific description seeks to impose upon it, which remains mysterious and beyond the reach of scientific knowledge.

Second, does Clarity require, or perhaps privilege, reductionism? Well, this is not obvious. Presumably Clarity requires a common understanding. In the case of the mechanical philosophy of Descartes the idea was certainly to attribute phenomena to mechanical causes that were, in a sense, simple and clear. Or if reductionism means explaining the less familiar or less well known in terms of the more familiar and more well known, then it might be argued that this is just what Clarity requires. To be able to express unambiguously the concepts of a scientific discussion requires that the terms of the discussion be well understood; presumably better understood than the concepts they are being used to express. It might be supposed that smaller, more reduced, components are better understood than the larger, more complex, systems which they make up.

A critique of this view of reductionism consists in asking what constitutes the more familiar or well known. It is far from obvious that the notion of personal agency is less familiar than mechanism. From a purely humanistic viewpoint, personality is actually more familiar for example, than impersonality. Children are drawn to explanations in terms of agency arguably because agency, in the form of their parents, predominates in their experience. It takes years of training in science before explanation in terms of a differential equation appears to be "simpler" or "more familiar" than an explanation in terms of agency or of predisposition. And for some people, it is *never* simpler! Yet the removal of appeals to agency, to explicit teleology, is one of the key features of reductionism. I conclude it is not really convincing to regard reductionism as embodying a search for explanations in terms of the *more familiar*.

The Clarity of scientific description is in a sense minimalist, but not necessarily reductionist. There are uncountable different aspects of the circumstances of an observation or the collection of a specimen. The vast majority of these are by preference and design irrelevant. We ought not to care in science whether the experiment was carried out on the Feast of Stephen, on a snowy, frosty day, at the behest of a benevolent despot, or inspired by his inspection of the landscape. Scientific accounts are expected to keep the reporting of such background facts to a minimum. Nevertheless, the place, or time, the temperature, humidity or other aspects of the environment, may well be crucially important for understanding an experiment's significance, or for subsequent attempts to reproduce it.

In even well controlled laboratory experiments of high precision, the possibility may exist for undesirable perturbation by factors such as external vibrations, electrical disturbances, or other environmental influences. In such situations, the significance, or especially the insignificance of particular anomalous results can often be established only by investigation of wider influences; requiring a detective imagination as much as a mathematical insight. For example, perhaps an otherwise inexplicable oscillation in instrumental readings during a particular time period is explained when it is realized that it coincides precisely with the period when an aerobics class meets in the room above! Tracking down spurious influences like these is not an unfamiliar exercise to experimental scientists. Normally it is considered the job of the experimenter to rule out by conscientious trial and error within the context of their own iterations, influences that are definitely extraneous. They thereby preserve the Clarity of their communications from being overwhelmed by excessive detail. But in complex sciences, field observations, and so on, it is not always obvious what is or is not extraneous. So it is conventionally accepted that the observer should err in their judgement of how much detail to include on the side of comprehensiveness rather than of brevity.

In the methods and communication of science, then, it is not really the case that reductionism, as it is commonly understood, predominates. The expression Methodological Reductionism, which has become widespread in the science-religion debate to characterize science's epistemological approach, is therefore unfortunate. The methods of science include aspects that are not reductionist, but recognize and account for the broader connected context of the phenomena. It is true that theoretical models of science are reductionist in the sense of explaining the more specific, and usually more complex, in terms of general universal principles. But it stretches the meaning of the word to regard general principles as necessarily simpler. There is a sense in which they are better understood, at least by trained scientists, and in this sense they have greater Clarity. It is arguable whether there is any meaningful sense in which they are more familiar.

The Web of Science

It is more helpful, instead of focusing on reductionist explanation in science, to think in terms of the integration of new phenomena, specimens, or models into the overall web of scientific description. Human knowledge as a whole, and especially our scientific knowledge of nature, consists of a myriad of cross-connected concepts and relationships. Understanding of the mechanisms or structures of particular phenomena takes place not in isolation, but within the context of that interlocking fabric of prior knowledge. A more helpful recent analogy than that of the spider's web, which generally has connections only to its nearest neighbor nodes, is the world-wide-web, which permits connections to any other place in its content. Indeed, the major power of the world-wide-web, and the conceptual advantage of hyperlinks, consists precisely in embodying and making explicit the connections between different parts of human knowledge. In large measure, it is interconnections which give to scientific knowledge its strength, robustness, and conviction. Another analogy that seeks to express this cross-connectedness is to speak of knowledge as being *interwoven*, like the warp and woof of the weaver's cloth. The threads of fact and understanding have only little strength in isolation, but when woven into the fabric of our overall knowledge they gain mutual support through their connection to the other threads with which they interact, and thus make up a robust whole.

The concepts by which it is considered appropriate to explain novel phenomena are not so much those that are reduced, simpler or more familiar, but rather those that are already part of, or can be readily integrated into, the shared fabric of science or of personal knowledge. A major part of scientific explanation is the recognition of specific new or unexplained phenomena as examples of more general classes of phenomena, for which we already have developed techniques of analysis and prediction. For example, if we see a strangely regular pattern imprinted upon, and apparently molded into, a rock, it goes a long way to explaining the phenomenon if we recognize it as an example of a *fossil*. This is true even it we don't happen to recognize the particular species of which it is the fossilized remains. But the identification as a fossil is not actually the explanation of something in terms of its components. Instead it is a process of *abstraction*; of recognizing a phenomenon as being an example of a general type of thing; of thereby attributing to it a possibly highly complex set of attributes; but attributes which we have already systematized and made part of the matrix of knowledge that we call science.

When Newton, in his *Principia Mathematica* regarded the dynamics of a point mass in a central force as representing the orbits of the planets, he was making what might be called a reductionist move. But this was not to explain planets in terms of their component parts. It was to *abstract* their behavior. Planets are not points; they are finite spheres. Newton was able to show that this did not affect the mathematics. But they are not ideal spheres either; they are only approximate spheres. Nevertheless treating the planets abstractly as examples of point masses moving under the influence of attractive forces one for another was the essence of the Newtonian genius. It incorporated another key abstraction within it: the recognition of the fall of terrestrial objects under gravity (that apple!), and of the acceleration of the moon towards the earth, as examples of the *same* generic phenomenon: universal gravitation.

Notice too, that really major theoretical breakthroughs, like Newton's (or Maxwell's, or Einstein's or a host of others) substantially extend the web of knowledge. So they usually introduce *new* generic abstractions, which often require a sort of reeducation before they can be seen as an explanation in terms of known concepts.

Newton had to do lots of new mathematics in order to show how motion under central forces led to the elliptical orbits and Kepler's other laws. Einstein worked for a decade on the mathematical description of General Relativity before he was able to calculate phenomena. And the scientists who read Newton and Einstein had much hard work to do to understand this mathematics. This additional component in the abstraction process: the working out of some of the immediate properties of the abstraction, is often called the development of a *model*, or *model building*.

Thinking in terms of abstraction, rather than reduction, has a much more flexible and appropriate descriptive value. A measurement may be considered to be the expression of some physical quantity in abstract terms: namely numbers. This is the important sense in which measurement possesses Clarity. In common thought, though, numbers are regarded perhaps as clearer, but not necessarily simpler or more familiar than more qualitative thinking. And actually the act of measurement is a very complicated high-level procedure. We only think of measuring length, for example, as simple because it is familiar to us earlier in our personal experience and in the history of human knowledge. We learn the use of a ruler or other measure very early, for practical more than theoretical purposes. Consequently the expression of physical properties in terms of extent — and likewise in terms of mass and time — as it relates to our everyday experience of those quantities, is in fact an expression in terms that are well understood; so it possesses Clarity; but not really simplicity. The Clarity is founded in part on abstraction: expression in terms of abstract concepts, numbers for example. But comprehending the semantic content of that abstraction requires prior experience and understanding that is personal and, when pursued to its ultimate roots, eventually non-scientific.

Clarity, then, is clarity to scientists. It is under-girded, first, by common-sense knowledge that is personal and experiential, next by the broad education that enables us to understand language, culture and logic, and then by apprenticeship in the field: by the prolonged acquisition of the vocabulary and semantics of science, by the assimilation of the intellectual constructs that the community uses, and the familiarization with the intellectual landscape into which scientific understanding must position new knowledge.

The scientific apprenticeship of course has many features in common with the sort of apprenticeship of a painter, sculptor, musician, writer, or lawyer. Needing to learn the concepts and methods of the craft or discipline is not unique to science. But science's requirement of Clarity functions as a restriction on the scope of its exploratory capability.

I have already pointed out that the practice of the law differs from science very strongly in that the law cannot obtain reproducibility or defer judgement until sufficient evidence is available. It cannot repeat the events and has to decide a verdict in a finite time, whatever might be the extent of the evidence. The discipline of the law is thus not science. There is, however, a strong analogy between jurisprudence and science in the area of Clarity. It is that the courts of law restrict their ambitions to determining not the *justice* of a case, but its *legality*. This limitation is probably a shock to many a budding law school student. I hope, and optimistically believe, that a significant fraction of the young people who are drawn to the study of the law, are drawn by a concern for justice. Certainly the the best intention of legislators ought to be that laws should serve to promote justice, as well as may be possible. Undoubtedly, judges and juries will be influenced by what they see as the justice of the situation. So justice is a major aim of legislation and of many individual lawyers and other participants. But one of the realities that has to be faced early in an attorney's education is that the courts don't decide matters of justice; they decide matters of legality, which is not the same thing. Legality is carefully defined through the formulations of legislation, constitution and precedent, and through the practices imbued by legal apprenticeship and tradition. Legality has a Clarity very like that required in science. Justice, on the other hand, is a concept that lacks the Clarity required for science, and indeed often escapes even the best efforts and intentions of the legal system set up to promote it. This realization does not lead most of us to reject the concept of justice as irrelevant or unattainable. It simply means that the legal system must acknowledge significant limitation of the scope of what it can in fact achieve. It can, in an optimum situation, achieve consistency and adherence to statute, constitution and precedent; it cannot guarantee to achieve justice. In much the same way, science must accept limitations on the scope of its competence that arise because many very important facets of the world (and justice is one of them) cannot be expressed with the Clarity that science demands. Returning to the heart of our discussion, to believe or imply that science is all of real knowledge and that matters outside of science are not matters of knowledge is analogous to denying that justice exists or is a useful concept simply because courts focus instead on legality.

3.4 Purpose

There is another sense of reductionism that is probably more appropriate to apply to science. It is the principle of seeking to describe events in terms of *Efficient Causes*. Aristotle's four causes of a thing were *Material* (what it is made of), *Formal* (its form or pattern), *Efficient* (what acted upon it to start or change it), and *Final* (its goal or purpose). In modern terminology we don't generally refer to the first two, Material and Form, as causes; we might think of them as substance and design. The difference between the last two, however, underlies one of the most important distinctions between modern and ancient science. Aristotle's science depended upon Final Causes, even for inanimate objects. While in modern science the effects follow the causes in accordance with the impersonal, reproducible, dictates of natural laws, not because there is any aim in view but because of a specific microscopic causal chain. Seeking Efficient Causes is the modus operandi of science and it has been highly successful.

Consider this quote from the Nobel prize winning biologist Jacques Monod from his highly popular book *Chance and Necessity*:

> The cornerstone of the scientific method is the postulate that nature is objective. In other words, the systematic denial that 'true' knowledge can be got at by interpreting phenomena in terms of final causes — that is to say, of 'purpose'.[48]

I draw attention to this passage first because it is a classic example of scientism in populist scientific writing. Monod identifies 'true' knowledge with what should be called 'scientific knowledge' because he implicitly assumes that all true knowledge is scientific. In other words his stance is scientism. I don't wish to single out

Monod here. There are many other distinguished scientists whose popular writing is also full of this type of implicit assumption. But this is a wonderfully straightforward example of a compact verbal transition that identifies "scientific method" and "true knowledge"

But secondly, I cite this quotation because I think it *does* correctly characterize science. Science rules out explanation in terms of personality, and hence rules out purpose, from the beginning, as an operational postulate. The way this exclusion works is first by science's insistence on reproducibility. If a cause and its effect are to be truly reproducible, then the cause cannot be a free agent. Free agents' actions are precisely *not* reproducible. That non-reproducibility we take to be one of the evidences of agency. An agent decides based on the integration of a vast range of events and influences, some external: the weather, the time of day, the opinions of others, etc., and some internal: personal preference, opinion, or desire, the state of the digestion, or whim. The combination of these influences we take to be the signature of an agent. An entity that behaves entirely reproducibly is not an agent but an automaton. Not that the action of an agent is totally random, but that it is unpredictable, inscrutable, even often to the agent himself. But of course, purpose presupposes an agent. Only agents have purposes. My little finger doesn't act with its own purposes. It is only the whole of me, the personal agent, that has purpose. My finger can reveal purpose; but any purpose its actions reveal will be the purposes of an agent: me. Since science requires reproducibility, and describes the world only in so far as it is reproducible, it rules out of its scope of description the irreproducible agent, and hence purpose.

There is potential here for substantial terminological confusion, which needs to be avoided. It arises from the fact that the word purpose has two distinct but related meanings. The meaning that Monod and I are using is in reference to *intentionality*. We say that something has purpose if someone *intends* it: if they intend an event to happen because of their plans or desires, or if they intend an object to serve a particular role. Generally the intention of the agent may be embodied in design: their actions are consciously (or more rarely unconsciously) chosen so as to bring about circumstances that cause the intended role to be fulfilled. The rejection from science of Aristotelian teleological explanation, which

Monod is alluding to, banishes the notion that intention, somehow embodied in the nature of objects themselves, is the explanation of their behavior – that goals or ends are dynamic agents in their own realization. Modern science rejects this intentionality.

The other distinct meaning of the word purpose refers to *function*. We might say that the purpose of the heart is to circulate the blood, by which we mean that this role is the function of the heart in the context of the larger organism. Its purpose is the part it plays in the overall system that constitutes the animal. We don't necessarily thereby mean to imply that an agent intended the heart to serve that purpose[49]. Certainly we don't mean that a natural agent did so. Nevertheless, it can be observed that the use of the word purpose in this way, while it occurs frequently in biology, rarely occurs in physics, or in more colloquial discussions of the inanimate world. It would strike us as strange today for a chemist to assert that the purpose of electrons is to enable atoms to form chemical bonds, or an astronomer to say the purpose of gravity is to keep the earth in its orbit, even though those are functions they undoubtedly serve. The reasons for this strangeness are in part that purpose in the sense of function requires a perspective that holds the overall system as superceding the individuality of its components. We train ourselves precisely *not* to adopt this view in physics. But the cognitive dissonance also arises in part, I think, because even purpose in this functional sense still induces mental echoes of the intentionality of an agent. I find it practically impossible even to think about causality in the Aristotelian manner, and I suspect this psychological indisposition is probably almost universal among scientifically educated persons. But until the scientific revolution, and indeed for much of the time since, it was completely natural to identify function in the natural, and especially the biological, world tacitly with design. And that implication still seems to remain within our language. Indeed, a major contribution of the evolutionary perspective to biological thinking is to permit the discussion of function, which had been one of its most fruitful topics long before Darwin, in the terms that had been used all along, but with the implied designer now understood to be metaphorical. The 'designer' that the language seems to imply, is not today banished from the discourse, because talking about function seems to be almost impossible without implying one, but it has become evolution, rather than the Creator. And this is held to excuse even quite extravagantly personified descriptions in evolutionary biology. In respect of purpose, then, science rules out from the beginning, by presumption, consideration of intentionality, but not function.

In addition to the requirements of repeatability, there are aspects of Clarity that exclude agents and purpose. Natural science generally regards introspective observation as lacking sufficient Clarity to be admissible as science. This is one of the most important distinctions between natural philosophy (science) and just plain philosophy. Philosophy traditionally regards the explanation of the internal world of thought as being its primary field. And while some schools of philosophy repudiate the practice, philosophy has historically sought to gain an understanding of the world and of humans from introspection even more than external experiment. Science resists the admission of introspective reports as 'data'. This is true even in the 'science' of mind: psychology. It is dangerous to be very definitive about the methods of psychology, since it is notoriously divided into competing schools, each with its own preferred methods. Moreover, in the early development of psychology, pioneers like Wundt and James considered introspection an important method. Nevertheless, modern psychology, in adopting viewpoints such as behaviorism and cognitive psychology and their descendants has mostly abandoned introspection in favor of experimental psychology. Psychologists work very hard to turn qualitative conscious experience into quantitative passive metrics that can be treated by statistical techniques and rendered as reproducible as statistically feasible. Indeed, it is notable that psychology texts generally spend significant fractions of their space on discussions of 'scientific method', on specifically psychological methods, and on sound approaches to data collection and analysis. This is very much in contrast with texts in the physical sciences, which take the overall scientific approach for granted and focus on results and the theories that explain them.

By now I hope it is obvious to the reader that these trends in psychology are significantly fueled by scientism and the impulse to ensure that psychology is fully 'scientific'. In psychology's case, the criticism internal to the discipline of the scientizing tendency seems even less influential than, for example, in sociology. Whatever may be the merit of these trends of thought, the effect of the process of objectifying psychology is to abrogate the personality of the subject. But common sense tells us that introspective observation can never be fully excluded from knowledge that involves humans, and this is one of the reasons why the status of psychology as natural science is debatable. Persons are not describable impersonally.

There are, then, strong reasons founded in science's reliance on reproducibility and Clarity why science effectively rules out explanations in terms of purpose. Purpose presupposes an agent, a personality. Persons can't be adequately described within the rubrics of reproducibility and Clarity. They are methodologically excluded. And so is purpose.

It should be no surprise, therefore, that science fails to find personality and purpose in the world. It could not possibly do so because it rules them out from the beginning. There can never be a scientific explanation of personality or purpose as such. There can be a scientific description of the material substrate in which personality is embodied; brain science is at the very rudimentary beginnings of such a description for humans; but this does not prove that there is no such thing as personality. It is mere presumption, not based on scientific results, to suppose that a scientific description 'explains away' personality, in the sense of rendering descriptions in personal terms empty or meaningless.

Chapter 4

Demarcation and the philosophy of science

I remarked earlier that there has been an outbreak of new 'sciences' in the past century, many of which share few characteristics with the old natural sciences, and that this is in part attributable to scientism. We now need to consider in more depth the extent to which it is justifiable to criticize this development. We need to address whether there is a clear enough definition or understanding of what natural science is to justify distinguishing it from non-science.

4.1 The History and Philosophy of Science discipline

With roots extending back to the early nineteenth century, but blossoming into an identifiable independent discipline in the mid twentieth, a whole field of academic study has grown up, known as the History and Philosophy of Science. Its practitioners study the particular questions surrounding how science works, what scientists have done and said, and what the influence of science is upon the wider culture. The field encompasses historians who specialize in scientific topics or personalities, philosophers who try to understand and explain the logic, methods and epistemology of science, and sociologists who study the social dynamics of science and scientists. To give an impression of the relative size of the field, the largest academic Department of History and Philosophy of Science (HPS) in the United Kingdom, at Cambridge University, has 5 professors, while the Department of Physics (the Cavendish) at Cambridge[50] has 37. So the professional discipline of HPS, which at Cambridge is taught as part of Natural Sciences, is rather modest in size. Many universities don't have departments but have HPS scholars whose professional homes are in other more traditional departments. Actually, a lot of the published analysis of science, particularly what is written for the general public, is authored not by HPS specialists but by working scientists themselves, and by journalists. This is a situation not unlike, for example, political history, where the books and articles are written by three main groups: historians, the politicians themselves, and journalists. These roles are not mutually exclusive, of course. Politicians can sometimes be historians and journalists, and vice versa; but its is worth being aware of the distinctive emphases of the various perspectives. I write obviously as a working scientist, but in the present context with the hope that what I write is accessible and interesting to a broad audience. I also intend to account fairly for what the academic HPS specialists have discovered, although I don't pretend to their professional focus. I have had the unalloyed pleasure of personal acquaintance with some distinguished historians and sociologists of science, and the more ambivalent experience of being the object of study of others. My first move is now to turn the tables on these folks for a moment and draw some conclusions from simple observations of what they do.

Recall that I have insisted on using the word science not as it was classically derived, referring to any systematic knowledge, but as referring to the study of nature: natural science, what was commonly called natural philosophy prior to the nineteenth century. You might have lingering doubts about the appropriateness of this insistence. And there might be experts in what I have called non-scientific fields who are still smarting at the designation, who feel in it an implied slight. If so, then I want to draw authority from the History and Philosophy of science for my position. Not so much in what HPS scholars *say* is science or non-science, but what they actually demonstrate by their actions is the primary subject matter of their field. If one takes any sample of the writings of a spectrum of HPS academics or of their journals, it becomes immediately obvious that what they mean by science is in fact natural science. Here and there one finds a few studies of borderline fields like psychology, for example, for which considerable hesitation is justified in calling it a natural science; there is also a certain amount of reflexive study of HPS concepts and development itself; but by far the overwhelming bulk of what HPS specialists study is what the common person would call science: physics, chemistry, biology, geology, astronomy, physiology, and so on. I notice that from time to time philosophy of science scholars refer, often with some detectable awkwardness, to 'social science'. They might, apparently somewhat reticently, grant to social science the title. But even if that lip service is rendered, it is almost vanishingly rare that they would actually *study* the field of sociology as scientific knowledge, or *instance* sociological discoveries as examples of science at work. So this is my first conclusion from observation of the HPS field: it supports by its actions the predominant usage of 'science' to mean natural science, and not just knowledge of any systematic type.

4.2 Scientism, sociology and socialism

This state of affairs would undoubtedly surprise the figures of the early nineteenth century who offered analyses of scientific methods that they sought to apply not only to nature but to society. In doing so they addressed the philosophy of science, but also helped to found the discipline of sociology, and through their more indirect influence were instrumental in the birth of various political movements and theories, such as Marxism. Of these figures, Auguste Comte (1798-1857), the founder of what became known as Positivism, is undoubtedly the most notable.

In a study of some of these sociological figures by Nobel-prize-winning economist F. A. Hayek, *The Counter-Revolution of Science* (1952), the English word scientism acquired (from French antecedents) the derogatory implication that is widespread today. At the beginning of the first part, entitled "Scientism and the study of society", Hayek delineates scientism thus

> During the first half of the nineteenth century a new attitude made its appearance. The term science came more and more to be confined to the physical and biological disciplines which at the same time began to claim for themselves a special rigourousness and certainty which distinguished them from all others. Their success was such that they soon came to exercise an extraordinary fascination on those working in other fields, who rapidly began to imitate their teaching and vocabulary. Thus the tyranny commenced which the methods and technique of the Sciences in the narrow sense

of the term have ever since exercised over the other
subjects. These became increasingly concerned to vin-
dicate their equal status by showing that their methods
were the same as those of their brilliantly successful sis-
ters rather than by adapting their methods more and
more to their own particular problems. And, although
in the hundred and twenty years or so, during which
this ambition to imitate Science in its methods rather
than its spirit has now dominated social studies, it has
contributed scarcely anything to our understanding of
social phenomena, not only does it continue to confuse and discredit the work of the social disciplines,
but demands for further attempts in this direction are
still presented to us as the latest revolutionary innova-
tions which, if adopted, will secure rapid undreamed
of progress.[51]

I repeat. This is a definition and assessment of scientism in sociology not by me or by a scientist but by an economist, a world
leading practitioner of one of the most distinguished social disciplines. Hayek's work provides a valuable overview and insight
into the scientisms of the early nineteenth century from which,
however, we shall have space to mine only a few nuggets.[52]

Auguste Comte's apprenticeship, his early thinking and writing, was under the tutelage of Henri Saint-Simon. Saint-Simon, an
adventurer and failed entrepreneur who at the age of 38 turned
to intellectual pursuits, was himself the architect and advocate of
a scientistic approach to the analysis of society that was to regard
"our social relations as physiological phenomena". His intellectual ambitions were adorned, from the beginning, with bizarre
religious overtones. In the "Cult of Newton" he proposed, apparently in all seriousness, that a council consisting of three mathematicians, three physicists, three chemists, three physiologists,
three authors, three painters and three musicians, elected by the
whole of mankind, should become the representatives of God on
earth.[53] Saint-Simon's ability to attract to his coterie dynamic
young thinkers, particularly from the École Polytechnique, opposite which he lived, provided him with an intellectual and literary
depth that he lacked in himself. That symbiosis was handicapped

by many acolytes' eventual estrangement because of Saint-Simon's unsupportive stance toward liberty. Nevertheless, after Comte, a nineteen-year-old, expelled polytechnicien, became his secretary in 1817, much of subsequent Saint-Simonian doctrine bears the strong stamp of Comte; and Comte's most influential *System of Positive Policy* (1824) first appeared as part of Saint-Simon's *Catéchism des Industriels*.

Comte's positive system, in this first incarnation, looks forward to the disappearance of the liberty of conscience from society. Just as such liberty has no place in astronomy, physics, chemistry, etc., it ought not to do so in society. Its disappearance will happen when politics has been elevated to the rank of a natural science: the new science of *Social Physics*. This expectation is in accordance with Comte's most famous dictum, the *Law of Three Stages*. "Each branch of knowledge is necessarily obliged to pass through three different theoretical states: the Theological or fictitious state; the Metaphysical or abstract state; lastly the Scientific or positive state", which of course is what constitutes true knowledge.

Comte's classic work began in 1826 as a series of lectures and extended to six volumes appearing between 1830 and 1842 as the *Cours de philosophie positive*. His task is defined by the Law of Three Stages. Physics, chemistry and biology have passed through the preliminary stages and thus become positive knowledge. Comte is the one who is going to conduct this passage for the *knowledge of society*. Without delving in detail into what this transition was supposed to require, let the following characterization and critique from Hayek's analysis of Comte's scientism stand as a pithy summary of the program.

> ... since the habits of thought which man had acquired in interpreting the actions of his own kind had long held up the study of external nature, and the latter had only made real progress in proportion as it got rid of this human habit, the way to progress in the study of man must be the same: we must cease to consider man anthropomorphically and must treat him as if we knew about him as little as we know about external nature. Although Comte does not say so in so many words, he comes very near doing so, and therefore one

cannot help wondering how he could have failed to see
the paradoxical nature of this conclusion.[54]

The sociological part of the *Cours* expanded to a size exceeding
the sum of the other three volumes which Comte devoted to the
natural sciences. The most crucial part of the sociological analysis,
according to Hayek is

> ... the attempt to prove the basic contention, which
> Comte, as a young man of twenty-six, had expressed in
> a letter to a friend when he promised to show that "there
> were laws governing the development of the human
> race as definite as those determining the fall of a stone."
> History was to be made a science, and the essence of all
> science is that it should be capable of prediction. The
> dynamic part of sociology was therefore to become a
> philosophy of history, as it is commonly but somewhat
> misleadingly called, or a theory of history as it would
> be more correctly described . The idea which was to
> inspire so much of the thought of the second half of
> the nineteenth century, was to write "abstract history,"
> "history without the names of men or even people."
> The new science was to provide a theoretical scheme,
> an abstract order in which the major changes of human
> civilization must necessarily follow from each other.

As Hayek, writing during the Second World War, was increasingly aware, this program's eventual chilling product would be
the rationale for the twentieth century's most despotic totalitarian
regimes. It makes little difference whether the subsequent development set out to be principled, left-wing, academic, and intellectual,
or whether it was employed by manipulative right-wing dema-
gogues to add verisimilitude to their populist mythologies. The
scientistic dehumanization of history and the portrayal of society
as as subject to inevitable laws of dynamics became the suitably
malleable base material from which could be fashioned political
rationalizations bearing the spurious honorific of 'scientific'. From
today's perspective of a post-Soviet and postmodern world, we can
be thankful for the much reduced persuasiveness of this scientistic sociology. But while scientisms are still alive and well, as they

undoubtedly are, it is salutary to recall the consequences, however indirect, of some of the earliest identifiable examples.

I have pointed earlier to the religious character of scientism, its status as a comprehensive world-view, based on prior metaphysical commitments, and as a guiding framework for understanding all of existence and motivating moral decisions. A major objection of secularist advocates to this characterization rests upon the absence in scientism of the clerical hierarchic authority and public rituals that characterize most theistic religions. Whether such features are universal in religion is debatable. And whether scientism today possesses them is also open to interpretation when one thoughtfully considers the ways by which scientific orthodoxy is adduced and enforced, or the ways that academic ceremonies, for example, mimic those of organized religion. But regardless of the current state of scientism, a remarkable feature of the early nineteenth century scientisms was the attempt to embody them in explicit new religions, complete with *all* the trappings of traditional faiths.

The last of Henri Saint-Simon's works published in his lifetime was entitled *New Christianity* and appealed to a divine core of truth focused on "the improvement of the moral and physical existence of the poorest class". It reflected his view, articulated a few days before he died, that "The Catholic System was in contradiction with the system of sciences and of modern industry; and therefore, its fall was inevitable. It took place, and this fall is the signal for a new belief which is going to fill with its enthusiasm the void which criticism has left in the souls of men".[55] His followers, led by Barthélemy-Prosper Enfantin, set out to found the organized religion of this new belief. Their efforts began with a short-lived journal, moved into what might be considered a 'house church' hosted by Hippolyte Carnot (brother of Sadi, the discoverer of the Carnot cycle), and progressed to public lectures on the *Doctrine de Saint-Simon*, and thence to a "Family over which Enfantin and Bazard presided as the two Supreme Fathers — new popes with a college of apostles ... "[56], services, public confession of sins, itinerant preachers, and the founding of local centers throughout the country. It ended in a move to a monastic community complete with menial labor and vows of celibacy.

Auguste Comte quickly disassociated himself in the 1820s with the Saint-Simonian religion. But in his own later writings, the *Sys-*

teme de politique positive (1851-54), and the *Catéchism positiviste* (1852)
he is concerned to move beyond intellectual analysis to "moral re-
generation" which is emotional, imaginative, and subjective. To
do so led him to found his own new *Religion of Humanity* complete with four-fold hierarchic priesthood, and a high-priest, who
was of course Comte himself. Its public worship was to be practiced through commemorative acts in celebration of our beloved
dead. Comte's obsessive prescriptive detail, which led many even
of his supporters to allege mental instability, governs, for example,
the number and length of daily private prayers, his nine personal
sacraments, eighty-one annual festivals, the saints, the icons to be
used in Positive churches, and the stipulation that they should all
face towards the source of their enlightenment: Paris.

The *Religion of Humanity* gained a significant following even
outside France. Although in England the main London church
never had more than 137 contributors, and there were never more
than six or seven English congregations outside London, it did
appeal to some influential figures. John Stuart Mill for example,
whose *System of Logic* (1843) brought Comte's sociology to the attention of the English public, gave support which, though qualified
by his distaste towards the cultic details he regarded as "ridicu-
lous", included financial support. And novelist George Eliot and
her partner Henry Lewes attended Positivist church services, gave
financially, and personally promoted Positivism.[57]

4.3   Scientific method and demarcation

For much of the twentieth century philosophers generally, and
philosophers of science particularly, sought mightily for methodological descriptions or definitions of science. These efforts can be
thought of as being of two types. The more ambitious is to try
to identify and explain the methods that science uses to obtain its
knowledge. One such method is Induction. Francis Bacon's analysis of Induction is a large part of his claim to be the father of modern
science. But in today's terminology, his ideas were an early example of the philosophy of science. Indeed, since Bacon practiced
little or no science himself, it is better to consider him the father of
the philosophy of science, than of science itself. Subsequently In-

duction has been examined logically and historically, in the hopes of being able to articulate a more or less well defined procedure, or set of procedures, that science uses, or should use, to ensure that it discovers reliable descriptions of the world. Nineteenth century philosopher John Stuart Mill, whose 'Mill's Canons' are still considered an important encapsulation of inductive methods, considered Induction the foundation of all knowledge, including the knowledge of logic itself. His view was that the rules of logic are themselves discovered by Induction. In the twentieth century, the logical strengths and weaknesses of Induction, its presuppositions, and the ways that it has in fact been used by scientists have been extensively studied. Other logical and epistemological schemes have also been proposed and subjected to similar critical evaluation, as we shall shortly discuss.

The second type of definition of science is less ambitious. It takes as its objective not a comprehensive description of science's methods, but more modestly a criterion or set of criteria that distinguish science from non-science. This would be a solution to what is called the problem of demarcation: demarcating the boundaries between science and non-science. Obviously if one were successful in the more ambitious program of comprehensively describing science's methods, that would provide a solution to the problem of demarcation. Yet one can imagine a solution to demarcation that does not incorporate a solution of the more ambitious methodological challenge.

To give away the punch line, the current opinion in philosophical circles is that both of these programs has failed. Before discussing more fully this apparent failure however, I want to point out that it gives rise to a paradox. It is this. Despite having concluded that there is no satisfactory working definition of what science is, the History and Philosophy of Science has not collapsed and vanished as an academic field. It is tempting to describe colloquially the apparent failure of demarcation by concluding "HPS does not know what it is talking about". The conclusion I actually draw from the paradox that HPS still seems to be alive and well is different. It is that in fact HPS *does know* what it talking about, but that it is unable to *say* what it is talking about. In other words, there actually are some intuitive ways by which science is identified, as evidenced by the pretty clear boundaries of the topics that HPS does actually study, but that, at least thus far, these intuitions have not been sufficiently clear-cut or logically explicable to survive the rigors of HPS criticism.

What brought a new perspective to the philosophy of science in the late nineteenth century is generally thought to be the modern understanding of logic. George Boole is best known today as the progenitor of Boolean Algebra, the symbolic treatment of logic, in his *An Investigation of the Laws of Thought on Which are Founded the Mathematical Theories of Logic and Probabilities* (1854). Boolean Algebra is an embodiment of the rules of logic, abstracted (from the syllogism, for example) into an algebra, in which statements about sets are represented by symbols and are subject to combining operations such as Or, And, Not, etc. Actually, in Boole's own analysis, the rules of this algebra are not quite in their modern form, which was developed by others in the succeeding 30 years. The rules are somewhat comparable to, but subtly different from, the high-school algebra of numbers we all know. Boole's legacy was not widely known except to mathematicians and logicians until the 1930s, when it was realized (notably by Claude Shannon) that these laws are precisely what is needed to analyze the operation of combinations of switches and relays. Today, because of the importance in electronics of digital circuits, which fundamentally consist of electronic switches, no engineering undergraduate education can be considered complete without at least a passing acquaintance with Boolean Algebra. But, to return to our topic, in the late nineteenth century the development of symbolic formalization was carried further, and with even higher ambitions, by Friedrich Frege. He sought to demonstrate that arithmetic is a branch of logic in his *Basic Laws of Arithmetic* (1893). This path was pushed to what was hoped to be a logical conclusion by Bertrand Russell and Alfred North Whitehead, in their *Principia Mathematica* (1910-13), whose aim was to derive the whole of mathematics from well-defined axioms and symbolic logic.

The undoubted clarification of logic itself through these symbolic mathematical developments, and their apparent[58] success in establishing a firm logical foundation for mathematics, was of great significance for the philosophy of science. It removed much of the mystery from classical logic, for anyone who cared to master the mathematical methods; and it offered a rigorous representational model, an example or paradigm, which it appeared might be extensible to the whole of science.[59]

Logical Positivism was so called mostly because of its ambition to fill this role. It asserts that there are only two types of statement that are meaningful. First, *Analytic* statements, including logic and mathematics, are true, in a sense by definition. Second, *Empirical* statements must be verified empirically; they include, and are best represented by, the statements of natural science. Any other types of statement, especially statements that cannot in principle be experimentally verified, are nonsense — not just false, but meaningless. Thus Logical Positivism not only reinforced the ambitions of the old Positivism to turn all of knowledge into positive science, but it also proffered a definition of what would qualify as science, in effect a demarcation, and ruled out definitively the cognitive value of any undertaking that failed to conform to its standard. If Logical Positivism were right, then every discipline had to be reinvented in its terms. As Rudolph Carnap, the best known of the Vienna Circle that founded Logical Positivism, put it "To pursue philosophy can only be to clarify the concepts and sentences of science by logical analysis. The instrument for this is the new logic."[60] Passing over the elementary, but none the less telling, critique that Logical Positivism is itself neither Analytic nor Empirical, and therefore by its own lights is nonsense, its most serious difficulty is perhaps the whole notion of verification. It rapidly became clear that what counts as verification could not be adequately articulated, and that in any case, acknowledged theories of natural science frequently did not seem to qualify.

Falsificationism (sometimes called Deductivism) is associated primarily with Karl Popper, whose *Logik der Forschung* (1934) followed closely on the heels of the logical positivists, although its English translation, *Logic of Scientific Discovery*[61], did not appear till 1959. Popper's position is critical of the positivists, but still seeks a description of science's methods in terms of logic. Popper's approach is based on the elementary observation that a universal proposition such as "all swans are white" can not logically be proved, no matter how many white swans we see, but can be logically *dis*proved by the observation of a single black swan. He concluded that verification of universal propositions through processes of induction and confirmation is not what science does. Instead, the way science works is by systematic attempts to *falsify* supposed universal laws. When a law successfully survives many such attempts, when it passes the most stringent of potentially falsifying tests, it is regarded as having thereby gained strong corroboration. Although Popper does not advocate a thorough-going scientism like the logical positivists that dismisses unfalsifiable statements as ipso facto meaningless; and he thus avoids their worst excesses of self-contradiction; he does promote falsifiability as a demarcation criterion, as the test of whether a statement is or is not scientific. We shall see in a moment that replacing verification with falsification, while it appeals to a clearer deductive logic, has some serious problems of its own.

Logical empiricism was the term Carl Hempel (1905-97) preferred to describe his position, though he was part of the positivist Vienna circle, and unlike Popper accepted Induction as a process of verification. He was predominantly again a logician, and an advocate of the analysis and identification of science with logic. He is most famous for his *Raven Paradox*[62], which runs approximately like this.

> The statement "All ravens are black" is logically equivalent to "All non-black things are non-ravens". The observation of a black raven is inductive evidence in support of "All ravens are black", and hence of its equivalent, "All non-black things are non-ravens". The observation of a non-black thing that is a non-raven, for example a white shoe, is inductive evidence in support of "All non-black things are non-ravens", and hence of its equivalent "All ravens are black". But it appears unreasonable to regard the observation of a white shoe as evidence that all ravens are black.

This paradox has proven extremely fruitful in the analyses of Induction that it has provoked. It would be inappropriate here to try to list or evaluate all the different types of resolution that have been proposed. However, they all have in common that they invoke something more than the operations of pure logic on the isolated case. Either they quantify the degree of support by appealing to presumptions about the wider context, or else, seemingly more drastically, they abandon Boolean two-value logic, and appeal to other more generalized 'logics'. Let's illustrate with a couple of examples of the appeal to external information. One can argue (in a way that can be formulated quantitatively using Bayes' theorem in probability) that the weight of support given by the white shoe is far less than that of the black raven because we know that ravens are a tiny fraction of all the things there are, whereas the number of non-black things is not. Or one can argue that it depends on one's knowledge of the external structure of the universe whether in fact a black raven observation supports the universal proposition all ravens are black. Suppose we happen to know that we are standing in one of two aviaries of which one aviary possesses just one raven (and it is black) out of ten thousand birds, while the other aviary has one hundred ravens, just one of which is white, out of ten thousand birds, and we see a black raven among the thirty other birds in our field of view. The best guess is then not that "all ravens are black" in our little aviary universe, but actually that, because we see a raven at all, we are probably in the one-hundred-raven aviary, in which not all are black. The observation of a black raven in this situation is evidence *against* the proposition that all ravens are black. Although this example may seem contrived, it illustrates that the evidentiary value of an observation, even whether it is for or against a universal law, depends upon the structure of the 'universe', and our prior knowledge of it. The reason why we don't consider the white shoe evidence that all ravens are black is that we intuitively incorporate into our thinking our background knowledge of the universe, which is not present in the purely logical analysis of the statements.

Hempel's objective was to acknowledge and solve a serious challenge to describing Induction, conceived as a purely logical process, as the foundation of science's method. The predominant view today is that what he succeeded in doing was to clarify the seriousness of the challenge to such an extent that the whole logical positivist/empiricist program became untenable.

Under-determination is a label that gathers together several critiques of simplistic views of the relationship between theory and empirical data. At the beginning of the twentieth century, Pierre Duhem had made the important point "... the physicist can never subject an isolated hypothesis to experimental test, but only a whole group of hypotheses; when the experiment is in disagreement with his predictions, what he learns is that at least one of the hypotheses constituting this group is unacceptable and ought to be modified; but the experiment does not designate which one should be changed."[63] There is no such thing as a simple empirical test of a theory; "hypotheses are tested in bundles". A theory is always tested in conjunction with lots of other auxiliary hypotheses which are necessary to render the results of the theory into experimental form. Acts of observation are not independent of theory, they are 'theory laden', at the very least because even the techniques of observation rely upon theory. Therefore there is no such thing as the unambiguous experimental falsification of a theoretical hypothesis. When a result is observed which contradicts deductions from a hypothesis, either the hypothesis is false, or something in the rest of science used to deduce the falsified result is erroneous, or the observation itself is mistaken. Duhem believed that this meant there could be no such thing as a Crucial Experiment, because theories are under-determined by the experimental data. We have to choose not between two competing hypotheses but among an infinite number of possible hypotheses. Duhem illustrates this with reference to the experiment of Foucault on the speed of light in water that helped to distinguish between the wave and particle theories of light, saying "Light may be a swarm of projectiles, or it may be a vibratory motion whose waves are propagated in a medium; is it forbidden to be anything else at all?" He believed not.

In his celebrated critique entitled *The Two Dogmas of Empiricism*[64], W. V. Quine, in 1951, argued that neither Logical Positivism's distinction between analytic and empirical statements, nor the supposition that individual empirical statements can be reduced to immediate experience were supportable. Instead "... our statements about the external world face the tribunal of sense experience not individually but only as a corporate body." This echoes Duhem's assertion, but extends it to all of knowledge, including logic itself: "The totality of our so-called knowledge or beliefs, from the most casual matters of geography and history to the profoundest laws of atomic physics or even of pure mathematics and logic, is a manmade fabric which impinges on experience only along the edges. Or, to change the figure, total science is like a field of force whose boundary conditions are experience. A conflict with experience at the periphery occasions readjustments in the interior of the field."

Sociology of Science in the form of Thomas Kuhn's seminal *The Structure of Scientific Revolutions*[65], which first appeared in 1962, gave the tottering edifice of logicisms the final shove that brought their ambitions to ruins. However, these particular philosophies of science could hardly be considered more than collateral damage from the bombshell he dropped on the whole enterprise of systematizing science's methods. Kuhn's perspective was based on an observational sociology of science. He treated theorizing about logical structures of scientific warrant as a fruitless form of armchair philosophy, and set out instead to document and analyze what scientists actually do. While both the details and the conclusions of his work have been extensively criticized, many of the scientific traits he identified rang true in the experience of scientists, and he gained such credibility that no subsequent HPS work could ignore it. [Scientists themselves *can* ignore it, and many have done so, just as they have in large numbers ignored the whole of the History and Philosophy of Science discipline; but that is another tale.] Kuhn observed that, in contradiction to Popper, scientists don't in general try to falsify their theories; they defend them. What's more, theories aren't immediately considered defunct if a single example of a falsifying observation arises. Instead, they are shored up by adjustment of auxiliary hypotheses.

This much was not really revolutionary, but Kuhn's more major point concerned those rare but exciting moments of history when a transformation occurs of our conceptions of the universe, or more modestly at least, of a scientific discipline. Such revolutions replace, for Kuhn, the picture of slow, steady, or stumbling, self-correction, which is the more traditional image of science. He regards 'normal' science as being the quiescent period of gradual self-consistent development of the reigning *paradigm*. It leads eventually to an accumulation of explanatory strains arising from the accommodation of perplexing experimental results or theoretical dissatisfactions. Those strains continue to grow, but the paradigm is not overthrown until it can be replaced wholesale by a new one that relieves the strain by a more satisfying explanation of the results that puzzled the prior one. And the process begins over. The formation of paradigms, and the replacement of one paradigm by the other is, by contrast with normal science, a discontinuous and logically inexplicable revolution. In the end, science seems to be little more than opinion, expert opinion granted, but still just opinion. There is, in Kuhn's words "no standard higher than the consent of the relevant community": a situation that has been colorfully characterized as scientific mob rule.

So much so, that Paul Feyerabend seemed to many to represent an extrapolation of the same intellectual path when he argued in *Against Method*[66] (1975) that there is no scientific method; that science is, and should be, anarchic; and that theories are successful because of the no-holds-barred rhetorical tactics of their advocates, not because of any particular correspondence with reality, or conformity with accepted epistemological schemes. Feyerabend is completely explicit that his stand is motivated to a large degree by a rejection of what he dubs the chauvinism of science, "... let me repeat that for me the chauvinism of science is a much greater problem ... Scientists are not content with running their own playpens in accordance with what they regard as the rules of scientific method, they want to universalize these rules, they want them to become part of society at large ...". It is a charge of scientism.

Later sociological studies of science have gone to extreme in developing this theme, arguing that there is nothing special about science, that its knowledge is no more certain than any other type of knowledge, that its knowledge is culturally determined, and that purely cultural analyses of science (e.g. feminist, or third-world perspectives) might lead to sciences with different technical content. We'll explore these postmodern viewpoints later, but I remark here that scientists (and I mean natural scientists) generally regard the notion that there might be a feminist chemistry (for example), having different technical content from our current chemistry, as utterly ludicrous.

Research Programs is the terminology advocated in place of *paradigms* by Imre Lakatos, Feyerabend's contemporary and sparring partner in the metaphorical bout of rationalist (Lakatos in the blue corner) vs irrationalist (Feyerabend in the red corner). A Research Program "... is a series of successive theories with their associated auxiliary assumptions, instrumental procedures, etc." What distinguishes the worthy from the unworthy Research Programs is whether or not they are 'progressive'. All right, but what is progressive? How is that to be measured or assessed? Several plausible measures of progressiveness are offered by the advocates of this viewpoint. *Independent testability* arising from the ability to test auxiliary hypotheses independently, "in *different* bundles"; *Unification*, meaning the successful application of a small family of problem-solving strategies to a broad class of cases; and *Fecundity*, designating the property of theories that open up new and profitable lines of investigation.[67] The vagueness of these 'progressiveness' measures is not just my brevity here. It is the outward evidence that the attempt to define science in terms of mathematically precise logic has been abandoned.

4.4 Demarcation disputes

One might think these increasingly abstruse debates about the status and identity of science an area of philosophical specialization with little practical significance. However, these matters of demarcation have been brought very much into the American public eye in recent years by the role they play in battles about high-school biology. The 1925 show trial of John Scopes for teaching evolution in Dayton, Tennessee, is surrounded by sufficient contemporary and subsequent commentary – and drama – to fill several bookshelves. We shall not expand it further here and will postpone discussion of evolution itself to a later section. But it is appropriate to comment on the influence of the ongoing legal skirmishes upon demarcation.

Although the guilty Scopes verdict was overturned on the absurd technicality that the $100 fine exceeded the judge's authority, anti-evolution law remained on the statutes of Tennessee and several other US states. Text-books worked cautiously around these laws until in 1963 a Pennsylvania court ruled that Bible reading and the Lord's Prayer were not appropriate for public schools but that neutrality between "those who believe in no religion [and] those who do believe" must be observed. Then in 1968 the Arkansas Supreme Court struck down its anti-evolution statute, and was followed in this action by Mississippi two years later.[68] Thereafter repeated attempts by activists to introduce creationism into the curriculum have repeatedly been overturned by the courts based on the opinion that it advanced particular religious preferences and entangled the state with religion, in contravention of the First Amendment clause "Congress shall make no law respecting an establishment of religion, or prohibiting the free exercise thereof;". The logic by which it follows from this clause that religion is to be effectively banished from public school curricula is hard to discern, but that is not our present topic. The strategy adopted by 'Creation Science' activists increasingly, in the face of these reverses, was to portray creationism as *science* and to argue that, as such, it should be taught alongside evolution. A statute worded along these lines in Arkansas was struck down in 1982, after testimony from a host of expert witnesses. Judge Overton's decision was widely reprinted, even in the journal of the American Association for the Advancement of Science (AAAS), *Science*. Louisiana's similar statute arrived by a tortuous legal route at the US Supreme Court on 10 December 1987. Its defenders argued that it was not religious but scientific. Seven of the nine justices were unconvinced. Thereafter, the Intelligent Design (ID) movement[69] went to even further efforts to ensure that their ideas were free from religious taint. A number of local school-board initiatives to include it in the curriculum, or to mandate disclaimers weakening evolution, gained some temporary advantage, leading to the celebrated case in Dover, Pennsylvania, 2005. Judge Jones ruling on that case, identifies ID as "a religious alternative masquerading as a scientific theory" and castigates the school board for precipitating a pointless trial.

The key observation for us here, is that these high-profile legal decisions hinge on the question of whether certain opinions and teachings are or are not science. That this has become the deciding question is a remarkable sign of the dominance of scientism in our culture. Scientism leads to acrimonious arguments about whether opinions are or are not science because the scientistic ethos gives special status to science that it does not give to non-scientific disciplines. The result is that the demarcation of what is or is not science becomes not merely an academic philosophical discussion, but a vital legal matter that decides practical questions of deep importance and emotional significance in the minds of most of the American public.

It is impossible that even academic discussion should escape the influence of this practical significance. In the first place, the various legal verdicts have undergone strong scrutiny by commentators sympathetic to the losing side (the creationists). There is plenty of scope for the criticism that the verdicts are based on an over-simplified understanding of what constitutes science. It is in the nature of legal argument to require sufficient simplification and crispness as to justify the decision. In the process many of the subtleties are inevitably lost. The critics are naturally led to emphasize the difficulty of demarcation,[70] because the broader and the fuzzier are science's boundaries, the easier it is to argue that creationism is inside them. One might have expected the opposite influence upon those who support the verdicts: a preference to regard the demarcation as easier or more definite. However, there does not seem to have been a significant countervailing initiative among philosophers of science to clarify demarcation; although one can perhaps detect a trend away from the more extreme relativism of the sociological critiques of science. Scientists themselves are generally of the opinion that they know science without difficulty when they see it.

4.5   A more modest characterization

Since the program to define science by uncovering its logical methods has thus far failed; since every attempt to identify a process by which one could even establish what is science and what is not science is judged to have been found wanting; since, in fact, it has become a celebrated cause that the problem of demarcation is unsolved; and since this question has become a high-profile legal matter: I am in dangerous waters. I am asserting that there are two identifiable characteristics of science, reproducibility and Clarity. Am I therefore claiming to have solved the demarcation problem?

No, I am not claiming to have solved the demarcation problem. What I am observing is that, despite the difficulties that undoubtedly exist in specific demarcation, there are in fact identifiable *characteristics* of science. These characteristics don't provide algorithms either for the practice or the identification of science, but they are nevertheless truly part of science. They are not exhaustive. They are not *all* the characteristics of science; many others might be identified to differing degrees in different branches of science; but reproducibility and Clarity are vitally important ones. Moreover, and this is the most important point, these relatively non-controversial characteristics on their own constitute a substantial restriction of the scope of science. They don't seek to be definitive enough to resolve all disputes about vexed questions of identifying and demarcating science. They certainly don't resolve all the logical or methodological puzzles about how science actually works. But they are important qualitative elements that are, in actual fact, part of the way that science operates. In short, I am not setting out to provide a comprehensive solution of demarcation, but I am claiming to be able to identify some characteristics of what any solution must look like. Modest answers to parts of problems are sometimes what one must settle for.

Another factor that I want to plead in mitigation of my apparent hubris is that the difficulty of demarcation is substantially amplified by scientism. What I mean is this. First, philosophically, demarcation between science and non-science in the context of scientism, is equivalent to the demarcation between sense and nonsense, rationality and irrationality, knowledge and superstition. If one accepts scientism, the belief that science is all the knowledge there is, then that demarcation of meaningfulness is what one is trying to solve. Many philosophical arguments are about that demarcation. The demarcation of meaningfulness, of all knowledge, is beyond my interests here. I have a much narrower intent which is to identify (some of) those principles which characterize natural science — regarded as a subset, not the totality, of all valid rational knowledge. I think that this problem is soluble, at least in part, and that one should not discount the identifiable characteristics of natural science just because of failures of a wider program. Second, politically, since scientism has embroiled the problem of demarcation in high-profile legal questions that raise emotions on both sides, the difficulty of demarcation is made significantly greater. People see that practical decisions, about which they care very much, hinge on questions of scientific demarcation. No wonder there is great sensitivity about this issue from all quarters. But my whole aim here is to repudiate the scientism that leads to the enhancement of these difficulties. If, as I am saying, science is *not* all the knowledge there is, then the weight that demarcation has to bear is reduced to a scope that is both more manageable and less sensitive.

My ultimate defence is that I am content if necessary to regard the characteristics of repeatability and Clarity as partial *definitions* of what I mean by science. In doing so, I might be ruling out some studies that claim to be, or perhaps even widely are regarded as, science. If that happens, then I say, so be it. This is not simply a semantic stratagem on my part. The characteristics I have identified are possessed by those sciences that are responsible for the high epistemological prestige and compelling explanations of the natural world that we attribute to science. It is those natural sciences which are being implied almost always when science's authority is being cited. So if I have by definition ruled out some disciplines that have a reasonable claim to being scientific in the sense of systematic, I have ruled out only those that are irrelevant to the most significant debates. I recognize that this will sound chauvinistic coming from a physical scientist. But I insist once more that any perception of chauvinism in this position arises from the self-same scientistic viewpoint I am at pains to deny. I find it utterly inconsistent, for example, that toward the end of his splendid introductory book *What is this thing called science?*, philosopher of science, Alan Chalmers criticizes philosophers who emphasize experiment, observing that their consequent failure to provide a "universal account of science" ... "could conceivably be avoided by identifying science with experimental science, but this would hardly serve to appease those who wish to call themselves political scientists or Christian scientists, for example."[71] Yet Chalmer's whole book has been about natural science. I didn't notice a single one of his many instructive illustrative exemplars of science being about sociological, political, or religious topics. If political scientists are offended, so what? Why should these folks have to be appeased? Why should one suddenly regard exclusion of political science as a disqualifying fault in an identification of science's topics, characteristics, or methods?

Finally, and this seeks immediately to soften any harshness of my previous impatient sentences, I need to be crystal clear that I have no intention to discount or disparage academic disciplines that I regard as not being science. That political science is not a science in the way I mean it, does not change its scholarly or practical value. I do not subscribe to scientism. I believe there is deep meaning, truth, relevance, and insight in non-scientific studies pursued with intelligence and rigor. But their merits have to be really their own, not the reflected glow of a terminological anachronism.

In summary, then, the discipline of History and Philosophy of Science does not have simple answers to the questions, what is or is not science? or what methods does science use? Science cannot be, or at least has not so far been, formalized into a purely logical structure. But HPS, like science itself, nevertheless appears to have intuition about what science is, which is definite enough to know what it is talking about. Natural science is what HPS studies. Although strict demarcation is fraught with peril, a peril greatly enhanced in recent debates by a scientism that artificially inflates the stakes, there *are* identifiable characteristics of science. Attempts to turn other disciplines, especially social disciplines, into explicit positive science, after the manner of the natural sciences, have a long history — of failure.

Chapter 5

Evolutionary explanation

5.1 Explanation in physical science

The gold-standard of scientific explanation was set during the scientific revolution. The mathematical description of astronomical orbits contained in Newton's *Principia* became accepted as the model of what it means to explain phenomena by a scientific theory. The unspoken virtues that were recognized in the *Principia* have been the subject of much discussion and analysis in the centuries since its publication, but certainly they include compactness, rigor, precision, agreement with observation, and prediction.

Much of scientific ambition since has been shaped by the belief that, in the end, all of nature will yield to explanation modeled on Newton's dynamics. As a matter of terminology, this belief is often called "materialism". But I find that expression misleading if narrowly interpreted. It was Descartes not Newton who sought to reduce all nature to mechanism. And for Descartes the objective was to reduce it not just to matter, but to machinery; so the Cartesian ideal is not materialism but mechanism. In fact Newton's achievement was precisely not to reduce the celestial motions to *mechanics*, nor to the material (since Newton could offer no material explanation of his forces) but rather to model it with mathematics. It is, I think, the ambition of completing a Newtonian program of explanation that has been behind many people's conception of natural science across the whole spectrum disciplines. That is part of what I refer to as scientism.

Of course many disciplines are still far from completing that program and providing the explanation. That is all right. Patience is necessary during the early development of new fields, while experiments and observations are undertaken, the measurement and analysis techniques are developed, the knowledge is systematized, and so on. Scientists are never happier than when they are working in a field that is in the transitional phase prior to explanation. As the understanding grows, there is a sense of excitement and expectation. Very soon, we sense, the integrating explanatory theory is going to come forth that will show how all the puzzle pieces fit into place. Its arrival is the moment of theoretical break-through. All scientists know that a field of study is not disqualified from being a science just because it has not yet reached the point where mathematical theory *explains* the phenomena in a manner that measures up to the gold-standard. But they also know that the gold-standard is what is being aimed at.

There is, nevertheless, a 150 year old theory, more celebrated and talked about than probably any other scientific theory, which despite its power and scope still does not measure up to the gold-standard. That theory is remarkably compact, and places some important rigorous logical constraints on its explanations, but quite possibly never will give rise to precise agreement with observation or prediction that will justify the more expansive claims of its proponents. I am referring to the theory of the evolution of species by natural selection, popularly known as Darwinism.

5.2 Evolutionary fact

Let's start right away by saying evolution is an established fact. We know, and it was known long before Darwin, that species can be selectively bred; that judicious selective breeding of dogs, cats, horses, cattle, grain, fruit, flowers, and so on, can produce new and sometimes favorable characteristics; and that the extent of the variations that are thereby produced can sometimes amount to effectively different species (strains for which inter-breeding becomes impossible). We also see round about us, today, familiar examples of evolution by *natural* selection. For example, the reason why it is so important to finish my entire course of penicillin is to reduce the chances of evolution of new bacteria that are resistant to antibiotics. One reason why hospitals are such dangerous places is that the environmental pressures on the bacteria there are such that they rapidly evolve resistance to the various anti-bacterial agents that hospitals use. Hospitals are the breeding grounds of resistant bacteria because of evolution. Moreover, the ability to sequence DNA gives us now a very powerful and mathematical description of the molecular genetic code by which characteristics are inherited. So, in a sense, we appear to be close to a "gold-standard" scientific theory of the mechanisms that govern evolution.

So yes, evolution takes place, and yes through the new capabilities of genomics and increasingly detailed understanding molecular biology we are closing in on a mathematical and physical theory of its mechanisms, but still *evolutionary explanations* of the biology of human, animal or plant characteristics are practically all of a type that is distinctively different from the Newtonian gold-standard. The reason for this difference lies in the kind of question that is being asked and in the standards of explanation that are considered to be satisfactory.

Newton was trying to answer such questions as "Why does the arc from the sun to the planet sweep out equal areas in equal times?" "Why do planets move in orbits whose shape is the ellipse?" "Is the fall of an apple towards the earth of the same nature as the acceleration of the moon towards the earth?". By contrast, Darwin was asking such questions as "How do some finches acquire large beaks and some small?" "How did there come to be such enormous variety in plants and animals?" "Why are animals so wonderfully well adapted to their environment?" The difference between the character of these types of questions, and particularly the answers given by the respective theories, can be summarized as being the difference between natural law[72] and natural history. Newton addresses the phenomena of the present, seeking to explain them as consequences of a few key principles or natural laws, in operation simultaneously with the phenomena, and indeed for all time. Darwin, by contrast, seeks to explain the history of how the natural (biotic) world *came to be* what it is. Darwin's theory, in a nutshell, is simply that the competition for survival, combined with genetic variability and inheritance, operating over vast spans of time, has produced both the variety and the adaptation of forms to their environment. In itself that mechanism of natural selection can be formulated as a natural law: "In a reproducing population's competition for survival, variability with inheritance leads to evolution and adaptation". Such a formulation of the essence of Darwin's idea, though, strips it of its real significance. In a sense it becomes a tautology.

You might have seen those much heralded computer simulations of "life", the evolution of mathematical entities in artificial (computer software) environments. The original game by this name was devised by Cambridge mathematician, John Conway, and is played out on a large grid of squares. Whether or not each square is occupied is determined by simple rules that specify how things change from one time-step, or 'generation', to the next:

- For a space that is occupied or 'populated':

   Each cell with one or no neighbors dies, as if by loneliness.

   Each cell with four or more neighbors dies, as if by overpopulation.

   Each cell with two or three neighbors survives.

- For a space that is empty or 'unpopulated'

   Each cell with three neighbors becomes populated.

These days you can play the original game on the world wide web. The game originally came to the public's attention in 1970 through the beloved games column contributed regularly by Martin Gardner to *Scientific American*[73].

Since then, there have been many more ambitious simulations of evolutionary models. Computers are very helpful in solving mathematical equations representing interacting predator-prey populations, for example. These equations are generally strongly nonlinear and give rise to sometimes surprising and counter-intuitive behavior. Computer solution is usually necessary, because analytic, pencil-and-paper solutions of non-linear differential (and difference) equations don't exist in all but a tiny fraction of interesting cases. Computer simulations can show what the mathematical solution really does, and hence validate (or invalidate) the intuitive expectations of the response to selective pressures on populations governed by simplified models.

Useful though these simulations are for understanding the mathematics, they do not validate the Darwinian theory of how species in fact originated. Darwin's *Origin of Species* in its first edition used neither the expression "survival of the fittest" nor even the word evolution. The essence of Darwin's idea is not the principle that the fittest survive and reproduce to pass their genetic characteristics on to the following generations. That is a tautology; since fitness is generally equivalent to survival, it simply says that the survivors survive. No, Darwin's achievement was to make the case for the historical, as well as scientific, claim that this mechanism is in fact sufficient to explain, and does explain, the biology of the earth that we observe, and how it came to be that way.

5.3 Natural Law and Natural History

The distinction between law and history is crucially present in a difference between the Newtonian and the Darwinian model of what constitutes an explanation. For example, the planetary dynamics of Newton depend on the idea that heavenly bodies attract one another as if they were point masses; that is, each behaves as if all its mass were concentrated at a single center of mass. Of course, in fact planets and the sun have finite radius, and approximately spherical shape. Newton took it as an essential part of his task to demonstrate that if every particle of matter attracted every other with the inverse square law of gravitation, then this point-like collective behavior of the total matter of a planet was a mathematical consequence. In other words, he sought to show that the inverse square law of gravitational attraction between planets was the direct consequence of a more general law of attraction of all mass to all other mass. The *Principia* gave the mathematical proof — one of its many remarkable achievements — and that success lent powerful conviction to the theory. Darwin's theory of the origin of species faced analogous key challenges, some of which *Origin* sought to meet: for example, the question of how the eye could have evolved. But the essence of Darwin's resolution of the challenges is very different from Newton's.

For Darwin, and evolutionary theorists since, the nature of explanation is taken not to be to demonstrate that phenomena observed *are a necessary consequence* of the underlying laws or principles — which is the gold-standard that Newton set. Instead it is taken to be to set forth a plausible history of how the observed phenomena *could have been* a consequence of natural selection. This is a profoundly different standard of explanation. It is not my purpose here to argue whether evolutionary theory can or does meet its own standard of explanation. My own impression is that in biology it mostly does so, although there are some very problematic cases, as there are with all theories. What I am drawing attention to, rather, is that what constitutes Darwinian explanation is at best a pale shadow of the explanatory standards of Newton, and virtually all of physical science. What is more, it is precisely because the questions of evolution are mostly about natural *history* that its explanations have so many characteristics in common with just plain history, rather than with the physical sciences.

Failure to account for the important distinction between science as natural law and natural history is at the root of many of the fruitless debates about the status of evolutionary theory. How often in the ongoing debate of the place of evolution and creation in schools do we hear the anti-evolutionists complain "but evolution is only a *theory*" to be rebutted by the pro-evolutionists saying something like "but that's true of all scientific theories; they are just theories". Both are right, but both are omitting the point that is behind the debate. It is that Darwinism is a theory about natural history, not natural law, and that as a result its standards of explanation (and validation) are significantly different from those of much of science, and certainly than the gold-standard of physics.

The evolutionary theory of the origin of species, by virtue of its topic, natural history, is obliged to straddle between history and science. The vehemence with which its proponents assert its status as science, more than history, is an indicator of the influence of scientism. They don't feel it is sufficient that evolutionary histories should be plausible histories (which many of them are). Perhaps without it being recognized, and certainly without it being articulated, the logic is this. If science is the only reliable knowledge, then it is crucial to obtain acceptance of the scientific credentials of evolution. To help gain this acceptance, the real differences between evolutionary standards of explanation and the standards of the physical sciences are discounted.

A biophysics paper was published in late 2004 in the journal *Physical Review Letters*.[74] The journal is one of the most prestigious in physics. It publishes short papers that report breakthrough results, supposedly of wide interest to physical scientists. This paper is an analysis of the dynamics of the semi-circular canals in the inner ear of mammals, which are used to detect orientation and rotation, and provide balance. It focuses on the fact that there is observed to be far less variation in the size of those organs than in the size of mammal bodies as a whole. And it seeks to show on the basis of the properties of the fluids and the hairs that constitute the detection mechanisms of the canals that the rather uniform size of the organs is very close to being the *optimum* size for performing the function that the semi-circular canals do. So much is a question mostly of physical analysis, about which physicists and engineers can debate. Is the size of the organ optimum? If so, optimum for what purposes, and under what constraints? However, the author of this paper goes further in his advocacy of the significance of the results by referring several times to evolutionary selection as having "optimized" the size of the organ. Such expressions are shorthand for the argument that whatever the size of the mammal, if there is survival value in being able more accurately to sense orientation and rotation, then genetic predilection towards having an organ of the optimum size will be preferred by natural selection, and as time passes the species will evolve towards that optimum.

The question that arises, however, is what is the value here of the evolutionary explanation? The overall argument (whose background facts I don't wish here to dispute) is: (1) mammalian cochlear organs show very little variation in size; (2) this is because there is an optimum size determined by physics for their performing their function; (3a) this observation is "explained" by natural selection; (3b) (by implication) this observation serves as evidence to support Darwinian theory. Now I ask, to what extent does the Darwinian explanation (3a) add anything to the scientific understanding? And to what extent does the observation of this optimized organ give support to Darwinism (3b)?

My view is that the Darwinian explanation adds precisely nothing to the understanding of the inner ear as analyzed in this paper. All it furnishes is a naturalistic explanation of why biological systems in general are "optimized", or (to use the more familiar biological word) *adapted* to their environmental constraints, and a broad outline of how the adaptation could have arisen historically by natural processes. What is more, in no useful sense does the observation of an optimized inner-ear support Darwinism specifically. It serves as yet another example of the remarkable adaptation of biological systems. But of course that adaptation (in the sense of fitness) was known before Darwin. Indeed, the main purpose of Darwinism from its beginning was to explain the observed remarkable adaptation, and do it in natural terms. The optimized inner ear may well be consistent with Darwinism, but it is consistent with lots of other theories too, Lamarckianism, for example, or theological explanations based on the intelligence of the Creator. It is, to my mind, equally logical and justifiable for the author to have remarked upon the wonderful providence of God in providing optimized inner ear design for his creatures, as it is to make reference to natural selection.

Contrast this lack of direct connection of evolution to the paper with the significance of the physical theories which the author employs. These theories include elementary concepts of the mechanics of motion such as angular momentum, but also viscous fluid dynamics, and structural mechanics. Even though these are manifestly the natural laws on which the paper's analysis depends, and so, much more directly than evolution, the 'explanation' of the result, they are none of them explicitly mentioned. What's more, to imply that this analysis provides evidence for the validity of those physical theories would not even cross the mind of a competent reader.

Why then, do references to evolution appear in five separate places in this physics paper? It is because Darwinism (or perhaps more precisely neo-Darwinism) is widely regarded as the only credible natural (i.e. scientific) explanation of biological adaptation. It is because, despite the complete irrelevance of natural selection per se to this paper, or this paper to natural selection, the author feels it is important to imply that a complete scientific explanation of the circumstances of the phenomena is available. In short, it is because of scientism.

Since discussions of evolution are so fraught with controversy, let me say again that I do not wish to be interpreted as arguing that Darwin's theory is false. What I am arguing is that it is very different in character from most physical theories. Its explanations are not in the form of demonstrations of what *must happen* because of a law of nature, but more often that there *could be* a natural way that some observed fact of biology arose by natural selection.

Nevertheless, these major differences are frequently glossed over and minimized because secularists wish to promote their philosophy and because evolutionary biologists (and even more so psychologists) wish their speculations to be received with the same level of conviction as the far more rigorous results of physical science.

5.4 Evolution as world-view

There are some Christians who find the idea repugnant that evolution by natural selection is responsible for any aspects of biology. A literalistic interpretation of the Bible such as the infamous time line of Bishop Ussher, who in 1650 traced the creation to 4004 BC, is obviously incompatible with evolution because it simply does not leave enough time for evolution to occur. But the proportion of educated Christians who take this extreme young-earth view, even among evangelicals who hold a high view of scripture, is quite small. A more common position is to accept that the earth is old (3 or 4 billion years is the accepted scientific estimate, based predominantly on geology), interpret the first few chapters of Genesis in a way that harmonizes with an old earth, but then still to view evolutionary accounts of origins with suspicion or often downright hostility.

The reason for this suspicion, even among people who are to a degree flexible in their interpretation of the Bible, is predominantly metaphysics. If evolutionary mechanisms are an important part of how the Creator brought forth animals and humans, there are significant difficulties in making sense of the doctrine of the Fall: that humans are by design eternal beings alienated from God because of sin. Certainly, a naive interpretation of the story of the garden of Eden, as being a single historical event prior to which physical death was absent from the earth, appears ruled out. These theological difficulties do not appear insuperable, but undoubtedly they are a factor making some reticent to accept evolutionary accounts of natural history. But it is not, I believe, *Christian* metaphysics that is the most important cause of suspicion of evolution. It is *evolutionary* metaphysics.

Let me introduce an example from Richard Dawkins book *The Blind Watchmaker*, which has gained him well-earned notoriety as one of evolution's most articulate champions. In the second chapter Dawkins offers a devastating critique of some of the arguments given by the Bishop of Birmingham in his book *The Probability of God*. Bishop Montefiore argues (fallaciously) that the coloration of polar bears can't be explained on neo-Darwinian grounds if they have always been the highest Arctic predators. Dawkins 'translates' Montefiore's incredulity, voicing it as "... I ... sitting in my study, never having visited the Arctic ... have not so far managed to think of a reason why polar bears might benefit from being white". This is a justifiable critique, perhaps, though not without some unintended irony, since a large amount of evolutionary explanation is of just this armchair variety. The only difference being that the Darwinist *can* think of a plausible reason, whereas Montefiore can't. [Again, the standard of explanation in evolution is all too often just that one can think up a plausible Darwinian history.]

Dawkins, after dispensing quickly with Bishop Montefiore's failure to realize that camouflage can be as important to a predator as it can to the prey, and hence that polar bears in the arctic do have a survival advantage if they are white, says... "The polar bear argument turned out to be almost too easy to demolish but, in an important sense, this is not the point. Even if the foremost authority in the world can't explain some remarkable biological phenomenon, this doesn't mean that it is inexplicable."[75]

From a purely rhetorical analysis, here is a remarkable claim. Religious believers are often charged with setting up theologies or cosmologies that are inherently incapable of being falsified. Being unfalsifiable is justifiably considered to be a significant philosophical weakness, at least for a theory that purports to have practical consequences. But here is one of Darwinism's most passionate advocates apparently setting up the same sort of stance for Darwinism. "Even if we found one example that we *couldn't* explain, we should hesitate to draw any grandiose conclusions ...", he says.

It is important to acknowledge that science does not generally proceed by single counter-examples, however convincing. For example physicists were not compelled to move to Relativity by a single outstanding failure of Newton's laws of motion. The evidence for a successful theory is much more complex and interwoven than that. Those theories become part of the fabric of our understanding of the natural world, and as a result don't immediately yield to apparent counter-examples. Therefore it might be simply that Dawkins is pointing to the robustness against anomalous results of scientific theories in general, and hence of Darwinism in particular. But one may be forgiven, I think, for noting that Dawkins appears quite deliberately to be setting forth a view of evolution that makes it immune from any possible falsification. Indeed, Dawkins' aims are so ambitious that it is hardly an exaggeration to call them metaphysical. In his final chapter he says "My argument will be that Darwinism is the only known theory that is in principle *capable* of explaining certain aspects of life. If I am right it means that, even if there were no actual evidence in favor of the Darwinian theory (there is, of course) we should still be justified in preferring it over all rival theories." He ends by briefly addressing religious explanation, one of the rival theories he wishes to dismiss, in this way

> If we want to postulate a deity capable of engineering all the organized complexity in the world, ..., that deity must already have been vastly complex in the first place. ... If we are going to allow ourselves the luxury of postulating organized complexity without offering an explanation, we might as well make a job of it and simply postulate the existence of life as we know it!"[76]

Dawkins' point here is in part the elementary philosophical one that an explanation of the world by invoking God is open to the counter-question, where did God come from.[77] But his metaphysics is the foundation for the argument — and Dawkins is elsewhere quite explicit about this. For him, because of his scientistic metaphysics, explanation means reductionist, scientific explanation: explanation of the complex in terms of the less complex. No other explanation counts. Without that presupposition of the privileged status of scientific explanation, the argument is empty, because, after all, an explanation of biological complexity in terms of molecules is just as subject to the counter-question, where did the molecules come from. This point is illustrated by the story of a future super-biologist confronting God. The biologist proposes to demonstrate that his mastery of the life sciences now equals God's by a challenge: each of them is to create life from inanimate dust. "Ok", says God, "you go first." The hubristic biologist stoops down to pick up a handful of dust. "Hey, wait a minute", says God interrupting him, "get your own dust."

So the metaphysics of scientism permeates Dawkins' argument. God is not a satisfactory explanation of the world because he himself has not been explained scientifically. From scientism's viewpoint that means God explains nothing, and hence does not qualify as an explanation of biological complexity. Evolution through natural selection is the theory that enables Dawkins and many others to feel secure, fulfilled, in their scientistic belief that the physical is all there is. It does so by pushing the questioning regress about origins backward toward a level where they no longer feel the need to ask the question. Scientism, Dawkins' style, is comfortable accepting the *dust* as given. But in no sense is the regress resolved. We may indeed be able to trace biological foundations all the way back to the elementary particles and laws of physics. The stunning progress in molecular biology in the past few decades makes it seem inevitable that the physical basis for life will be understood at the atomic level, in the foreseeable future. But if that reduction is completed, it hasn't terminated the regress other than in ignorance concerning why the laws of physics are what they are, and where did they come from. Scientism might well feel comfortable simply not asking those questions, since they seem to have a non-scientific flavor. But it offers no logical reason for not doing so. And in fact some physicists *do* ask those questions about where the laws of physics come from and why they are what they are. They ask them not just as interested citizens and amateur theologians, but as a motivating factor, and possibly even a technically relevant factor in their research. Admittedly there is so far little consensus on what the answers are, or even what they ought to look like.

In the preface to his book, Dawkins confesses his passionate adherence to an evolutionist world-view, and his adoption of an advocate's approach. His candor is refreshing, since many advocates are not as forthright. And it also serves to explain the confidence with which he and many others approach the popularization of evolutionary theory. Their confidence comes to a large degree from their scientistic presuppositions, which they take to be unchallenged.

5.5 Natural prehistory

As I write, the Smithsonian Institution is opening to the public for the first time the doors of its long-awaited Human Origins exhibit at the Museum of Natural History[78]. Their Human Origins Initiative, which is the driving force behind this exhibit has attracted considerable attention in the public press. The sensitivities of all sides on issues of evolution, especially in respect of humans, make this a hot-button topic. I am not fortunate enough to be in Washington to view the exhibit in person, but the wonders of modern communications enable me to enjoy it electronically through the beautifully-designed web site, whose front-page is entitled "What does it mean to be human?". The pages of the site are artistically and conveniently arranged into six main sub-menus. The last three offer a guide to the actual museum exhibit (which naturally doesn't much help someone not there) and valuable, though elementary, educational resources for schools and for individuals. The first three, which represent the main content of the site, are entitled "Human Evolution Evidence", "Human Evolution Research", and "Human Characteristics". The first of these, "Human Evolution Evidence", is the largest menu. That pop-up menu has a total of 21 click-able links on it. Eleven, over half, of these make up the largest grouping which is entitled "Behavior", under which are "Primate Behavior, Footprints, Stone Tools, Getting Food, Carrying & Storing, Hearths & Shelters, Burial, Recording Information, Making Clothing, Art & Music".

It would doubtless strain your patience if I were to list more details; so I won't. But what I will observe is the peculiarity of the title in respect of the content of this section of the display. Of course, it is completely appropriate for the Museum to put on a display of anthropological artifacts, including tools, weapons, pottery, buildings, graves, ancient writing, clothes, and art. It's all very interestingly and attractively done. But in what possible sense is this "Human Evolution Evidence"? It provides an insight into the undisputed fact that human culture has evolved, in the sense of grown and changed over time, and a glimpse of some of the ways that anthropologists document and seek to understand that prehistory. But in a Museum of Natural History, it is hard not to see the expression "Human Evolution Evidence" as intending to imply much more. If the designers and curators of this exhibit were not deliberately setting out to wave a red rag at the Creationist bull, they had many other choices for their title. Growth of Human Culture, Prehistoric Evidence (or Artifacts), Tools of Anthropology, and so on. In fairness, this menu does also include half-a-dozen links on Fossils and Genetics, which do really bear on evolutionary issues. But still, it is strange that the anthropological links dominate "Human Evolution Evidence".

I do not think the exhibit's curators are deliberately baiting anti-evolutionists. But they are doing something different from offering evidence for human evolution. They seem deliberately to be promoting, and hitching their wagon to, a world-view that conflicts with the world-view of many Americans. The exhibitors' world-view is doubtless a sincerely held one. Moreover, it is possible that they do really think (in contradiction of many evolutionary biologists) that insights drawn from Darwin's theory of the origin of species have important things to say about human prehistorical cultural development. Perhaps they do really think that applying evolutionary arguments to ancient technologies, societies, and individual psychology, constitutes evidence of human Darwinian evolution. If so, they are not the first to think so, although, as I shall discuss shortly, the intellectual weaknesses of sociobiology and evolutionary psychology make them far from the "accepted" theories that their advocates claim them to be. But even if the title was chosen by principled argument, it is hard not to see it also as a branding move, to promote a naturalistic, physicalistic, and especially scientistic (mis)understanding of a topic that is a good deal more history than it is natural, and more development than it is evolution. Anthropological techniques are of course largely what is available to study prehistory, and obviously anthropological analysis of prehistory is completely appropriate in this exhibit. Science and technology provides the basis for many of its techniques, and likewise belongs here. But the spurious implication of the title that its topics offer evidence for human evolution in the sense meant by the natural sciences, is in the same category as "scientifically-proven Wizzo washing powder". In our scientistic culture, branding as science is a synergy of scientism-promotion and populist sales-credential.

5.6 The clash of world-views

The close identification of evolutionary theory and explanation with the metaphysics of scientism is without doubt the dominant reason for the rejection of evolution by a large fraction of the public. In the 2008 polling by the National Science board[79], only 43% of respondents reported they believed the statement "human beings, as we know them today, developed from earlier species of animals". Incidentally, this figure was much higher elsewhere in the world: 78% in Japan, and 70% in Europe and China. The statistics for these and other countries show significant anti-correlation between acceptance of evolution and Christian adherence, although the US anti-evolutionist sentiment is remarkable. This and other deficits in scientific acceptance in the US have become a topic of alarm in scientific societies in recent years. Two types of diagnosis and proposed treatment are common. The first is to regard this as a failure of the US education system, and to call for reform and enhanced funding of education in response. The second is to regard the low acceptance of science as the pernicious influence of religion upon the minds of young people. It identifies the problem as being widespread religious fundamentalism, leading to obscurantism, anti-science, and anti-intellectualism in general. Its prescription in response to this diagnosis is a renewed effort to disabuse religious believers of their errors through scientific arguments and attacks on their views in journals and books. Some of the more popular of these books are very popular indeed, but it does not seem likely that the religious believers make up a large fraction of their readership. More likely the books are preaching, very entertainingly no doubt, mostly to the atheist choir.

I think biologist Kenneth Miller is right when he criticizes these kinds of response as misreading the issue. "[P]ublic acceptance of evolution", he writes, "doesn't turn on the logical weight of carefully considered scientific issues. It hinges instead on the *complete* effect that acceptance of an idea, a world view, a scientific principle, has on their own lives and *their* view of life itself."[80] Americans have a highly ambiguous and apparently contradictory stance towards science in general and evolution in particular. They embrace science as a source of wonder and for the technological development it supports as much as any society in history, and they evidence fascination with dinosaurs, fossils, and movies like Jurassic Park based on evolution. But yet, when asked, they formally reject evolution in large numbers. This is not because of ignorance of the strength of scientific evidence, according to Miller, it is "because of a well-founded belief that the concept of evolution is used routinely, in the intellectual sense, to justify and advance a philosophical worldview that they regard as hostile and even alien to their lives and values"[81].

No less an authority than the National Academy of Science has sought to defuse this confrontation directly. In the Academy's 1998 report *Teaching About Evolution and the Nature of Science*, we read

> At the root of the apparent conflict between some religions and evolution is a misunderstanding of the critical difference between religious and scientific ways of knowing. Religions and science answer different questions about the world. Whether there is a purpose to the universe or a purpose for human existence are not questions for science. Religious and scientific ways of knowing have played, and will continue to play, significant roles in human history.[82]

This concession, principled though it may be, does not seem to do the trick. It does not persuade either side of the ongoing science vs. religion culture war that they can lay down their arms. In part, this is because, with good reason, they don't trust the other side. They know there are irreconcilable differences of world-view between themselves and their adversaries, whatever the National Academy might say. And they both think that science is the battlefield where those differences will be fought out.

The other difficulty with the NAS position and those like it, is that it does not go far enough. It just sounds — to both sides of the argument — like a sop. The problem is that the only other "way of knowing" being identified is religion. In fairness to the NAS authors, of course, they only have a mandate to address the teaching of evolution, and the aim of their report is to help defuse religious sensitivities. But the result of this focus is to make it sound as if religion is being given a special pass to excuse it from the rigors of scientific knowledge. If that is really the case, if religion is unique in claiming other ways of knowing, if the questions of "purpose to the universe or a purpose for human existence" were the only ones that are "not questions for science", then it is hard to escape the feeling that this is special pleading. And that feeling leaves both of the combatant groups unhappy. The atheists are unhappy because they don't see any reason why religion should get this free pass, and the theists because they believe that there are rational — and some would say scientific — justifications for their faith, so they don't need a special pass. I think both sides are right to be uneasy. I don't find it convincing to argue that there are certain (few) ultimate questions that are the province of religion while the rest of our knowledge is scientific. Not only does religious faith address far more directly the everyday questions that people care about than this position allows, but also it seems obvious to me that science is very far from being all the knowledge there is, so religion is far from unique in involving a different way of knowing.

What I think is essential for progress in cooling the faith-science culture war, is to recognize that it is really not an argument between good science and bad science, nor is it at root a war between religion and science. It is a battle of world-views, between a physicalist metaphysical understanding of the world, that thinks that the physical is all there is, and a religious metaphysical understanding of the world. In a very real sense, though, the prime movers on both sides of the battle, are equally mired in scientism. On the physicalist side, I've already characterized many aspects of the rhetoric, but here's another sample

> Modern science directly implies that there are no inherent moral or ethical laws, no absolute guiding principles for human society ... We must conclude that when we die, we die, and that is the end of us ... Finally, free will as it is traditionally conceived — the freedom to make un-coerced and unpredictable choices among alternative courses of action — simply does not exist ... There is no way that the evolutionary process as currently conceived can produce a being that is truly free to make moral choices.[83]

This is the view of William Provine, a biology professor from Cornell, and someone who spent a considerable amount of time in the

1990s debating Philip Johnson, the Berkeley law professor, Christian, and instigator of the ID movement. By Johnson's own account, Provine and he got to know one another quite well and enjoyed friendly relationships despite their debate confrontations. What also became clear to me through their writings and my personal acquaintance with both of them on different occasions is that they have some substantial areas of agreement with each other. Johnson has referred to Provine (and Michael Ruse whom he has also debated) as "associate members of the movement. While they differ from us on the answers, they recognize that we raise the right questions..."[84] In particular, Johnson fundamentally agrees with Provine that an acceptance of evolution as the mechanism for the origin and adaptation of species implies all the consequences Provine cites above. And the reason, it seems to me, is that Johnson, and even more so the ID movement that followed, in effect concede to scientism.

This opinion deserves some unpacking because, to his credit, Johnson in his popular writings such as *Darwin on Trial* is at pains to identify scientism, which he calls scientific naturalism, as the main target of his criticism. In my view, he correctly identifies the *worldview* of scientism as a key driving factor in the evolution versus religion controversy. His analysis shares a great deal in common with what I have been arguing for here; but is accompanied by some important differences, which I believe are debilitating for the ID argument.

He says scientific naturalism is

> a philosophical doctrine called {1}scientific naturalism, which is said to be a necessary consequence of the limitations of {2}science. What {1}scientific naturalism does, however, is to transform the limitations of {2}science into limitations upon reality, in the interest of maximizing the explanatory power of {3}science and its practitioners. It is of course, entirely possible to study organisms {4}scientifically on the premise that they were all created by God ...[85]

This passage is hard to make sense of, because the meaning of science or scientific shifts from phrase to phrase, which is why I have labeled the six occurrences in braces in accordance with what I take to be the different meanings, for future reference. I want to do full justice to Johnson's position; so I provide my detailed analysis of this passage in an extensive endnote [86].

In summary, Johnson repudiates *scientific naturalism*, which is approximately what I call scientism, but then at the end refers to a mode of {4}scientific study that would be free from naturalism's limitations. If that freed mode of study is simply systematic knowledge like the archaic science-definition of the Encyclopédie or of Collingwood, then this is a sudden shift of meaning of the word science from his earlier usage in the modern sense.

I think one can perhaps discern the motivation for this dislocating shift, from Johnson's later remarks: "The monopoly of {3}science in the realm of knowledge explains why evolutionary biologists do not find it meaningful to address the question of whether the Darwinian theory is true." and "the {3}scientific naturalists have the power to decide what that term "evolution" means in public discourse, including the science classes in the public schools."[87] Here I take it that he is referring to the {3}science practitioners. The strategy of the ID movement and its motivation is quite open. They are challenging control of the word science by the {3}science practitioners, because they believe that by doing so they will be able to introduce theistic perspectives as an option into the public schools. Only the word 'science' has the magical power, like the 'open sesame' of the Arabian Nights, of opening the doors of public schools. So they must utter it. It is not enough that there be acknowledgement of systematic knowledge beyond the competence of science. That terminology will not trip the enchanted locks. Therefore, they imagine and advocate this {4}science, which is presumably a scientific approach beyond the methods of natural science. It is completely confusing to call it science, but they are compelled by their legal and cultural strategy to adopt the word.

It is this final terminological move that concedes to scientism. Rather than confronting directly the scientistic world-view, and denying, as I do, that science is all the knowledge there is, they try to change the meaning of the word science to encompass ideas beyond physicalism. I don't say that they do this cynically. But I do say that the result is confusion rather than understanding, and I also say that choosing to fight in this way has the effect of conceding the most important point. It reinforces the idea that science is the knowledge that our students must learn. In effect, it subordinates the religious perspective, which is what its advocates most value, to a test of being 'science'. And by doing so it bolsters scientism.

Johnson's scientism is, therefore, not as explicit or virulent a form as Provine's. In fact one might regard Johnson's as a feigned scientism. He does not really believe natural science is all the knowledge there is, but he thinks that he must speak in scientistic terms if he's to gain the rhetorical victory he seeks. But the logic of the ongoing ID program, and the public debate, is more explicitly scientistic. Its focus, which is to demonstrate *scientifically* that there must be an intelligent designer of the universe, makes complete sense if science is all the real knowledge there is, or if, at any rate, science is knowledge that is uniquely respectable and credible. So both Provine and Johnson essentially agree on scientistic terminology in their debate. After that, it's just about how convincing the evidence for evolution really is. Johnson is convinced that Darwinism's case is {2}scientifically weak, propped up only by the absence so far of {4}scientific alternatives beyond physicalism, and about to crumble under the weight of its own contradictions and inadequacies. If he were right, then a strategy of feigned scientism might be a clever, although hardly a straightforward, rhetorical approach.

Johnson has spent a lot of time as a non-scientist to get to know the details and to probe the rhetoric of evolution. And he is joined by a handful of scientists. He has identified weaknesses in the argument and places where scientism substitutes for genuine science. But, unfortunately, he doesn't have the scientific background and discernment to make a reliable evaluation of the actual scientific status of evolution. The scientists that join him represent a tiny minority opinion in respect of the technical issues in the science. The scientific evidence for biological evolution in the sense of common descent based on genetic variability, heritability, and natural selection, is actually rather strong, and getting stronger. Consequently, he and the ID advocates have an uphill struggle, because they've turned the debate into an argument (to be brutally frank) between good science and bad science. They've chosen a battle they are going to lose. But it's the wrong battle. The real, relevant disagreement is not between Christianity and an evolutionary account of the origin of species, or Christianity and science, but between Christianity and scientism. The irony is that by choosing to fight on a battlefield they call science, the ID advocates have in effect already conceded the relevant debate; they have spoken and acted as if science really is the decider of knowledge; they have, perhaps unintentionally, endorsed the epistemology of scientism and strengthened its hold on both their supporters and their opponents.

5.7 Social consequences

Evolutionary explanations have aspects that are science, and aspects that are history, as I have pointed out. All too often, ever since it became fashionable, and even before it became the predominant theory of natural history, evolution has also been a prolific source of political, social, ethical, and metaphysical opinion. This proclivity is what lies at the root of the visceral reaction of many Christians to evolution. But in their repudiation of Social Darwinism they are joined by a panoply of critics, from all religions, including atheism. Social Darwinism, at its broadest, refers simply to the application of insights purporting to be drawn from an evolutionary understanding of nature to the study and conduct of society. What *exactly* is, or is not Social Darwinism, is a lot more debatable and problematic.

For a start, evolutionary analyses of nature and society fitting the broad definition existed well before Darwin. Charles Darwin's own Grandfather, Erasmus Darwin proposed an evolutionary account of nature in his *Zoonomia; or the Laws of Organic Life* (1794)[88]

> ... in the great length of time since the earth began to exist, perhaps millions of ages before the commencement of the history of mankind would it be too bold to imagine that all warm-blooded animals have arisen from one living filament, which THE GREAT FIRST CAUSE endued with animality, with the power of acquiring new parts, attended with new propensities, directed by irritations, sensations, volitions and associations, and thus possessing the faculty of continuing to improve by its own inherent activity, and of delivering down these improvements by generation to its posterity, world without end!

Jean-Baptiste Lamarck from 1800 onward had elaborated his evolutionary theory of animal progress based upon the inheritance of
acquired characteristics:

> FIRST LAW   In every animal which has not passed
> the limit of its development, a more frequent and contin-
> uous use of any organ gradually strengthens, develops
> and enlarges that organ, and gives it a power propor-
> tional to the length of time it has been so used; while
> the permanent disuse of any organ imperceptibly weak-
> ens and deteriorates it, and progressively diminishes its
> functional capacity, until it finally disappears.
> SECOND LAW   All the acquisitions or losses wrought
> by nature on individuals, through the influence of the
> environment in which their race has long been placed,
> and hence through the influence of the predominant
> use or permanent disuse of any organ; all these are pre-
> served by reproduction to the new individuals which
> arise, provided that the acquired modifications are com-
> mon to both sexes, or at least to the individuals which
> produce the young.[89]

The key ingredient of Charles Darwin's theory to differ from
these "Lamarckian" evolutionary theories was *natural selection*.
Darwin's *Origin* of course drew heavily upon his own extensive
field work, which had undoubtedly convinced him of the fact of
evolution. It was a masterpiece of exposition and explanation, not
least because it addressed a host of anticipated objections to an
evolutionary account of species — many of which remain part of
current debate. But it is fair to say that the primary novelty of
his ideas lay in the idea drawn from demographer, economist, and
clergyman, Thomas Malthus, whose *An Essay on the Principle of
Population* (1798) emphasized "That the increase of population is
necessarily limited by the means of subsistence": human population always grows until the reproductive capacities of the poorest
classes are attenuated — miserably — by lack of food. Malthus's
concerns were social, and he was led from his observations to propose such policies as the gradual repeal of the poor laws. But
Darwin, and simultaneously Alfred Russell Wallace, was inspired

by reading Malthus that the principle of competition for scarce resources could become the driving force of biological evolution through what Darwin called the "Struggle for Existence". Thus Darwin's breakthrough in biological evolution was stimulated by an idea from sociology. The ingredients of Darwin's evolutionary account, then, were: reproduction, heredity, variation, and natural selection of favorable traits by the Struggle for Existence.

Social Darwinism is sometimes taken to include only social theories that conform to Darwin's version of biological evolution, and to exclude what might reasonably be (but never is) called 'Social Lamarckism'. But this focus on the mechanism of variation would cause one to leave out a whole raft of relevant social theories, because many of society's traits are in fact *acquired* in the style of Lamarck, rather than in the random variations of the neo-Darwinian synthesis, today's biological orthodoxy. Such a categorization based on the difference between Darwinian and Lamarckian variation mechanisms appeals to important biological distinctions. However, there are also important philosophical and political distinctions that serve to mark out Social Darwinism — after Darwin — from prior social theorizing. These boundaries cut across the intellectual landscape in a very different direction from the biological ones. Lamarck's perspective was that change takes place from below, as inferior organisms strive to adapt, improve, and progress: "where Darwin saw animals and plants competing for survival, Lamarck saw a more harmonious process of mutual adaptation."[90] The pre-Darwinian perspectives helped to rationalize radical, republican, and socialist political agendas, developing from below. "Clearly Lamarckism had some disreputable associations. It was being exploited by extremists promoting the dissolution of the Church and aristocracy, and calling for a new economic system."[91] (Darwin hesitated long enough before publishing his theory that the decline of the radical Lamarkian influence minimized that taint on his book's reception.) In contrast with the radicals' emphasis on social *progress, change, and adaptation*, the post-Darwinian arguments far more often emphasized the *selection* part of the process, which Herbert Spencer transmuted into the "Survival of the Fittest". This slogan served a much different purpose in politics: rationalizing privilege, imperialism, free competition, and capitalism. Social Darwinism, as it is often bracketed, thus differed from pre-Darwinian evolutionary social theories in the resulting social diagnosis and prescription. Recognition of alternative demarcations to that of the analogy of the biological variation mechanism, persuades me to adopt a fairly broad interpretation of Social Darwinism, even though some authors prefer a primary identification with the post-1860, darker rhetoric, associated with the Survival of the Fittest mechanism.

Mike Hawkins' (1997) study says Social Darwinism is a worldview without a clear ideology. By this he appears to mean that Social Darwinism adopts the guiding principle that Darwinist analyses explain the psychological and social characteristics of humans as well as their biology, but that it does not adopt a unique or stable political or ethical perspective. "Indeed," he says, "the success of Social Darwinism lies in this very flexibility, in the possibilities it contained for transference to a whole spectrum of ideological positions."[92] The flexibility lies in a set of indeterminacies. These concern (1) the mechanism of change (about which I've just commented in respect of Lamarck vs. Darwin, but there are other shades) (2) the cause of organic and behavioral variations (which was resolved at the biological level only in the twentieth century and is not resolved at other levels) (3) what the Struggle for Existence entails, and especially what is the unit of evolution: the organism, the gene, the social group, the meme? (4) the rate of change (5) the direction of change (progress or regress) (6) whether social phenomena are supposed *reducible* to biology, or to evolve with their own processes that are merely *analogous* to those of biology.

Plainly the Social Darwinian world-view is a scientistic worldview, and that is true even in metaphorical versions that don't regard society as directly reducible to biology. It is too narrow to identify scientism as a whole with Social Darwinism. Scientism is much broader. But it may not be too much to say that Social Darwinism frequently serves as the metaphysical handmaiden of scientism. It has often been pressed into service, for the establishment by 'scientific' rhetoric of principles of conduct that were traditionally the province of religion — with results that are less than salutary.

Herbert Spencer

In a paper published in 1852[93], seven years before Darwin's *Origin*, Herbert Spencer was already reviewing a Malthusian population principle applied to organisms from protozoa up to humans, and attributing both the maintenance of the individual's average fitness and society's development to that "pressure of population". But he acknowledges in his autobiography being, prior to Darwin's publication, "unconscious that in the absence of that indirect adaptation effected by the natural selection of favorable variations, the explanation left the large facts unaccounted for."[94] Thereafter in his voluminous writing, while drawing freely from the Darwinian analogy, he sometimes expressed a preference for teleological or Lamarckian explanation, especially in higher animals. Warfare, for example, assisted the pressure on resources, for "The killing off of relatively feeble tribes, or tribes relatively wanting in endurance, or courage, or sagacity, or power of cooperation, must have tended ever to maintain, and occasionally to increase, the amounts of life-preserving powers possessed by men" Optimism in the face of this bleak doctrine was based upon the struggle for survival becoming a more metaphorical "industrial war — by a competition of societies during which the best ... spread most and leave the least to disappear gradually, from failing to leave a sufficiently numerous posterity." Yet the elimination of the unfit must not be interfered with by misguided charity, because "the struggle for life and the survival of the fittest must be left to work out their effects without mitigation."[95]

Spencer's political advocacy, backed up by evolutionary arguments, was for limiting the power and interference of the state, and for economic laissez-faire. It was perhaps his books' promotion of what seemed like rugged individualism, as well as their being received as representative of the "scientific spirit of the age", that brought his writing such astonishing popularity in America. It certainly appealed to those Americans who could thereby justify their own business success — and the failure of others — as the working out of an ineluctable law of nature. Andrew Carnegie was one of the most prominent such Spencer disciples[96]. Spencer's fame in the English speaking world rose with extraordinary speed. But it also peaked quite quickly, in America probably during his visit in 1882, which climaxed at a banquet at Delmonico's famous restaurant. The rapid subsequent decline in popularity of Spencer's individualism is attributed by Richard Hofstadter to "The rise of critical reformism in economics and sociology, of pragmatism in philosophy,"[97] among other influences; yet it left a lasting legacy (which Hofstadter explores) through the intellectuals who absorbed the ethos of his outlook and carried forward the program in their own styles.

Eugenics

In contrast to the meteoric rise — and fall — of Herbert Spencer's popularity, the ideas of eugenics, associated most notably with explorer, scientist, and inventor, Francis Galton, gained acceptance much more gradually. Although Galton was enthusiastic about the subject from 1865 onward, it was only in 1883, the year after the banquet at Delmonico's, that he coined the word eugenics to describe the extension of domestic selective breeding to man[98]. From his earliest commentary, Galton was concerned with what he saw as dysgenic practices: "Many forms of civilization have been peculiarly unfavorable to the hereditary transmission of rare talent. None of them were more prejudicial to it than that of the Middle Ages, where almost every youth of genius was attracted into the Church, and enrolled in the ranks of the celibate clergy"[99]. The eugenics that Galton advocated was to do the opposite: consciously to select, and encourage through state support, the marriage and subsequent fecundity of youths whose children "would grow into eminent servants of the State"[100]. To make this effective it was also advisable to discourage breeding by the less worthy; so "the weak could find a welcome and refuge in celibate monasteries or sisterhoods".[101] This darker side of eugenic selection grew definite only rather slowly in Galton's mind, but in 1907 he wrote privately "Except by sterilization I cannot see any way of checking the produce of the unfit who are allowed their liberty ..."[102] Galton spent the last decade of his life in the promotion of eugenics "It must be introduced into the national conscience, like a new religion. It has, indeed strong claims to become an orthodox religious tenet of the future, for Eugenics cooperates with the workings of Nature by securing that humanity shall be represented by the fittest races. What Nature does blindly, slowly, and ruthlessly, man may do providently, quickly, and kindly."[103] He became president of the Eugenic Education Society in 1908, a year after its founding, and in his will endowed a Chair of Eugenics at University College London.

In Britain, the only legislation that implemented any of the many proposals of the eugenicists was the Mental Deficiency Act of 1913, which allowed mental and moral defectives to be committed to colonies segregated from the public. The procreation strictures the bill originally contained had been blocked by fierce libertarian opposition. By the time the eugenics campaign could subsequently muster the energy in parliament to promote sterilization on eugenic grounds, in the early 1930s, opposition had strengthened, and the darker consequences of the eugenic proposition were beginning to loom on the continent.

In America, federalism permitted more decentralized legislation, and sterilization laws were enacted starting in 1907. By 1917 they existed in 16 states. Most of those laws empowered compulsory sterilization of habitual criminals, epileptics, the insane, and idiots. By 1924, however, only a total of about 3000 people had been forcibly sterilized. Virginia's law was tested by appeals to the US Supreme Court in 1927, and upheld. Justice Oliver Wendel Holmes wrote for the court "It is better for the world, if instead of waiting to execute degenerate offspring for crime, or to let them starve for their imbecility, society can prevent those who are manifestly unfit from continuing their kind." The number of sterilizations in the U.S. rose to 3000 *per year* in the 1930s.[104] Racist procreation laws were also widespread until the Civil Rights movement of the 1960s turned the tide of legal and public opinion.

In Germany, eugenics got its big chance when the Nazis came to power in 1933. Their driving ideology was the superiority of the Aryan race and the need to ensure its improvement and world dominance, and to prevent its pollution by inferior races, especially Jews. A sterilization law was immediately passed, which was praised by some American eugenicists. It was administered by Hereditary Health Courts, leading to the sterilization of an estimated 400,000 individuals. Euthanasia — meaning here the killing of the unfit for society's good, not so much for their own — was practiced quietly on new-borns with congenital defects and adults in psychiatric institutions, but on a much smaller scale than sterilization, at least prior to the Second World War. As that war progressed, though, and Jews from occupied territories swelled the ranks of the "parasites" who represented a drain on the depleting resources of the Third Reich, Nazi leaders wanted cheaper and more effective action. Eventually the "final solution" of the Jewish problem was approved by Hitler in 1942. About 6 million Jews, and perhaps as many again of other races, died in Nazi concentration camps.

The recoil of civilization from the Nazi horror abruptly terminated the 75 year career of eugenics as a social policy in the democracies. Positive preferences to encourage breeding by successful humans had naturally never appealed to popular sentiment, and negative policies had proven how easily they degenerated, or were manipulated, into justification for despicable inhumanity.

Sociobiology

In the now-familiar cinematic cliché of horror movies, the sudden reappearance from off-camera of the monster supposedly destroyed in the previous scene serves both to startle the audience and to prolong the battle scene. Social Darwinism proves just as hard to bury for good as the most resilient of zombies, although its reappearance is generally by stealth rather than by shock. While its critics attribute its resilience to the appeal to science combined with malleability in support of different social agendas, its promoters, in every age, take that resilience to be a sign of its intellectual strength. In any event, after its demise in the reaction to the Nazi horrors, the rebirth of the new forms that Social Darwinism now takes was not long delayed. Sociobiology is the extension of population biology and evolutionary theory to social organization. Though coined in 1945, the term sociobiology exploded into public consciousness through the Pulitzer prize-winning writings of Edward O Wilson, his *Sociobiology: the Modern Synthesis* 1975, and *On Human Nature* 1978. Wilson's stature as the foremost biologist of social insects: bees, ants and so on, was already established. It seemed only natural that the evolutionary arguments that helped to explain the organization of insects whose different roles within the colony gave the appearance and effect of altruistic self-sacrifice, should be applied to humans.

By the way, the association between social insects and the scientistic study of human society has a long history. Hayek drew attention to this impulse, as expressed by the French enlightenment philosophe Nicholas de Condorcet.

> A mathematician like d'Alembert and Lagrange ... [Condorcet] occasionally expressed himself as if the method of the natural sciences were the only legitimate one in the treatment of the problems of society. ... As early as 1783, in the oration at his reception into the Académie, he gave expression to what was to become a favorite idea of positivist sociology, that of an observer to whom physical and social phenomena would appear in the same light, because, "a stranger to our race, he would study human society as we study those of the beavers and bees."[105]

Condorcet's prophetic speculation was coming true, without need for the extra-terrestrial observer, even as Hayek wrote. Alfred Kinsey, who had made a scientific name for himself in the study of another social insect species, gall-wasps, was about to make an even more famous name by publishing his report[106] *Sexual behavior in the Human Male* (1948).

For E O Wilson, to understand the operation of the human mind, and society, "The only way forward is to study human nature as part of the natural sciences"[107] rather than by "ideological or formalistic shortcut". We must abandon the philosopher, the "merely wise", the guru and the legislatures ... "only hard-won empirical knowledge of our biological nature will allow us to make optimum choices among the competing criteria of progress."[108] Wilson is unabashed in his recognition that this is a scientistic view "It is all too easy to be seduced by the opposing view: that science is competent to generate only a few classes of information...", which he says is "obscurantism".

So the basis must be: "human social behavior rests on a genetic foundation". It is "derived in a straight line from neo-Darwinian evolutionary theory that the traits of human nature were adaptive during the time that the human species evolved"[109] [as hunter-gatherers].

But, rather confusingly I think, "sociobiological theory can be obeyed by a purely cultural behavior as well as by genetically constrained behavior. An almost purely cultural sociobiology is possible."[110] "Stern requirements" must be "impose[d] on the infant discipline of human sociobiology" to make "detailed predictions of observable phenomena" so that it conforms "to the canons of scientific evidence and not a new dogma however devoutly wished for."

Wilson implies that his succeeding chapters meet these stern requirements as they discourse on *Incest taboos, Hypergamy, Identical twins, development and learning, cannibalism, aggression, sexual characteristics and behavior, altruism,* and *religion.*

Stern *criticism* met Wilson's opinions, and much of it came from his own biological colleagues. They dismissed the promotional supposition that "we are on the verge of breakthroughs in the effort to understand our place in the scheme of things", saying the biological evidence adduced had "little relevance to human behavior, and the supposedly objective, scientific approach in reality conceals political assumptions." They also took exception to his rhetorical maneuvers.

> 1) ... Thus, for Wilson, what exists is adaptive, what is adaptive is good, therefore what exists is good. However, when Wilson is forced to deal with phenomena such as social unrest, his explanatory framework becomes amazingly elastic. Such behavior is capriciously dismissed with the explanation that it is maladaptive, and therefore has simply failed to evolve. The only basis for Wilson's definition of adaptive and maladaptive, however, is his own preferences.
>
> 2) Another of Wilson's strategies involves a leap of faith from what might be to "what is." ... he ends the paragraph saying "the very opposite could be true." And suddenly, in the next sentence, the opposite does become true
>
> 3) ... One subtle way in which Wilson attempts to link animals and humans is to use metaphors from hu-

man societies to describe characteristics of animal societies. For instance, in insect populations, Wilson applies the traditional metaphors of "slavery" and "caste,"
"specialists" and "generalists" in order to establish a
descriptive framework. Thus, he promotes the analogy
between human and animal societies and leads one to
believe that behavior patterns in the two have the same
basis.

4) ... how can genetic factors control behavior if
social structure within a group can change rapidly over
the course of just a few generations? ... He turns instead
to the "multiplier effect," which is a concept borrowed
from economics. He uses this "effect" in an attempt
to show how small genetic changes can be amplified
enormously in a limited time span. But nowhere does
Wilson present any basis for introducing the multiplier.
A crucial point in Wilson's explanation remains purely
speculative.

5) Many of Wilson's claims about human nature do
not arise from objective observation (either of univer-
sals in human behavior or of generalities throughout
animal societies), but from a speculative reconstruction
of human prehistory.... But these arguments have arisen
before and have been strongly rebutted both on the basis of historical and anthropological studies.[111]

Despite these vociferous criticisms, sociobiology retains a remarkable hold upon a large segment of academia. Wilson himself
argues that it is only a first step to scientize our understanding.
"By a judicious extension of the methods and ideas of neurobiol-
ogy, ethology, and sociobiology a proper foundation can be laid for
the social sciences, and the discontinuity still separating the natural sciences on the one side and the social sciences and humanities
on the other might be erased." Then we must turn to "the second
dilemma: the conscious choices that must be made among our innate mental propensities." Though, unfortunately, "we are forced
to choose among the elements of human nature by reference to
value systems which these same elements created in an evolutionary age now long vanished."[112] In this way, Wilson acknowledges

that if our psyche, our social organizations, and hence our values, are merely the result of evolutionary selection during a period of human existence far different from what it now is, there is not only no absolute basis for ethical or moral value, there is not even an *evolutionary* basis for value within the present environment. How is one then to reassert a meaningful set of values?

Wilson's prescription is "nobility". Although this is almost completely unexplained, it is immediately distanced from its Social Darwinist precursors by an argument that since genius "winks on and off through the gene pool in a way that would be difficult to measure or predict", ... "we are justified in considering the preservation of the entire gene pool as a contingent primary value" — "until such time as an almost unimaginably greater knowledge of human heredity provides us with the option of a democratically contrived eugenics."[113] Universal individual human rights are a primary value also because of the "mammalian plan: the individual strives for personal reproductive success foremost and that of his immediate kin secondarily".

The religious impulse, since it is genetically pre-programmed, cannot be avoided, but it "can be harnessed to learning and the rational search for human progress if we finally concede that scientific materialism is itself a mythology defined in the noble sense." ... "What I am suggesting, in the end, is that the evolutionary epic is probably the best myth we will ever have. It can be adjusted until it comes as close to truth as the human mind is constructed to judge the truth. And if that is the case, the mythopoeic requirements of the mind must somehow be met by scientific materialism so as to reinvest our superb energies."[114] Wilson vacillates on the extent to which his philosophical preference becomes a religion. On the one hand, "it would be reckless to predict the forms that ritual will take as scientific materialism appropriates the mythopoeic energies to its own ends." On the other "Above all, I am not suggesting that scientific naturalism be used as an alternative form of organized formal religion." Yet it will be emotional: "addressed with precise and deliberately affective appeal to the deepest needs of human nature". For Wilson, undoubtedly this ambiguity reflects both a sensitivity to the power and poignancy of mystical yearning, and a horror of the dogma that he identifies with organized religion. But quibbles about whether his scientific materialism is or is not a religion are beside the point. It is an all-encompassing world-view that serves for him, and for others who follow the scientistic path, the purpose of religion.

As a modern illustration of the mythopoeic application of the evolutionary epic, one might consider the almost mystical adherence in modern academic morality to 'diversity' as an over-riding value. My interest is not so much that 'diversity' serves as a suitable euphemism for what used to be called (also euphemistically) affirmative action. What is more significant is that 'diversity' is taken to be morally self-justifying. A big part of that self-justification appeals to resonances with diversity in the natural world which are taken to be products of evolution. It is as if 'diversity' were justified because mother nature has bequeathed a blessed ecological and genetic diversity to the biosphere, and because the supposed evolutionary value of human biological diversity calls for humans to cherish and promote both the diverse genes and their metaphorical and cultural reflection. Like most people today, I find this purported implication of evolutionary metaphysics far more humane and appealing than the implication drawn by the eugenicists (whose conclusion was in many ways the opposite). But I don't find the logic of diversity's arguments any more compelling. And it seems significant to me that evolutionary metaphysicians of adjacent generations have drawn practically opposite conclusions about ethics and social policy, from essentially the same scientific theory.

Richard Hofstadter writing in 1944, summed up his study, by saying Social Darwinism was useless as social science.

> Whatever the course of social philosophy in the future, however, a few conclusions are now accepted by most humanists: that such biological ideas as "the survival of the fittest," whatever their doubtful value in natural science, are utterly useless in attempting to understand society; that the life of man in society, while it is incidentally a biological fact, has characteristics which are not reducible to biology and must be explained in the distinctive terms of a cultural analysis; that the physical well-being of men is a result of their social organization and not vice versa; that social improvement is a

product of advances in technology and social organization, and not of breeding or selective elimination; that
judgments as to the value of competition between men
or enterprises or nations must be based upon social and
not allegedly biological consequences; and finally, that
there is nothing in nature or a naturalistic philosophy
of life which makes impossible the acceptance of moral
sanctions which can be employed for the common good.

These assertions did not settle the matter in the least for those who,
like Wilson, came after. This is, I think, a result of the fact that
actually there *is* something in the "naturalistic philosophy of life",
even if not in nature, which, for those who hold this philosophy,
makes biological analyses irresistibly attractive. Metaphysics has
consequences.

Chapter 6

The case for scientism

Scientism does not logically follow from Darwinism, from the success of modern science, or even from physicalism or scientific naturalism as presumptions.

Few writers today offer explicit arguments in favor of scientistic philosophy. Logical Positivism was probably the last philosophy to do so, and it died in the mid twentieth century. The few who do still offer reasons for scientism, do not use the word scientism, because of its strongly negative connotations. As we've seen, this does not at all mean no one believes in scientism any more. On the contrary, it is a very widespread habit of mind, and one can often read practically explicit espousals of its principles in popular and academic writing, even though offering reasons for those espousals is rare.

The large numbers of people who still adopt a scientistic position presumably do have reasons for doing so. Here we attempt to understand what those reasons are: what the warrant for their position is taken to be. It is admittedly a somewhat speculative effort precisely because of the comparative rarity of reasoned arguments being offered for scientism.

6.1 Explicit scientism and its warrant

Let us draw important distinctions by recalling that this is not an investigation of the warrant for a *physicalist* view of existence.[115] Scientism and physicalism may sometimes seem to be the same thing, but they are not. It is true that physicalism, the belief that everything is physical, is consistent with scientism, the belief that all real knowledge is scientific. But physicalism is also consistent with a belief that there are other important ways of knowing than the scientific, that is, with the denial of scientism. For example, it is perfectly consistent to affirm that we obtain genuine knowledge through non-scientific disciplines or through personal experience, but still maintain that the things known by these methods were at root just physical things, maybe very complicated physical things, but physical just the same.

So physicalism does not logically imply scientism. Nor does scientism imply physicalism. It is logically possible to hold to scientism, even if one denies physicalism — that is, if one thinks that the world contains things that are not physical. Scientism maintains that there is no way other than science to know anything about such things, but it might be willing to accede to their possible existence. One might, for example, adopt a dualist theory of mind, which said that the mind is in part a non-physical entity, soul, or vital essence, even though one thought that it is impossible to establish real knowledge of such things as souls other than by the methods of science.

This logical separation of scientism and physicalism (or naturalism) is possible only if one rejects the functional definition of nature that I have been arguing is part of our modern conception. Because, if one accepts that nature is in effect defined by the methods of science, that nature simply means what is studied by (natural) science, and that nature is physical, then scientism and naturalism — and by extension the physicalism that we are here associating with naturalism — are inextricably linked. Thus, the functional definition of nature means that scientism *does* imply naturalism, and hence physicalism; because if science is all the knowledge there is, and science is about nature, then the only topic we can have knowledge of is nature. In practice, then, those who adopt and defend scientism usually also hold to naturalism and physicalism. And indeed scientism is often used as the philosophical justification of naturalism.

Let us also avoid the pitfall of insisting on an impossible deductive standard. Scientism does not logically follow from science or physicalism, or anything else, for that matter. It can't be deduced from them. But that fact does not mean there is no evidence or warrant for scientism. Many beliefs are warranted even if they can't be deduced from some other known principles. Actually much of scientific knowledge is of this type. It is justified not by deduction but by induction. So looking for deductive proof would be too high a standard. We instead want to understand what are the arguments, reasons, or evidence that lead people to scientism.

Finally, in this list of cautions and qualifications, we must also set aside, for the moment, our interest in the historical, sociological and especially psychological reasons as to why scientism is believed. These are important questions, and the history of beliefs is addressed in various other sections. But we are here not asking how did it come to pass that individuals or schools of thought believe scientism, but rather, what justification there might be for the belief. We want to understand, for someone who takes on board the clarifications of terminology made so far, who is willing, at least for the sake of this discussion, to adopt the terminology we have explained, and who still believes that scientism as so far explicated is at least partially correct, what warrant they might offer for that belief. Here is a list of the main categories of warrant for scientism that seem to be available.

1. Science is Unlimited

One rationale for the view that science is all the real knowledge there is, is to deny any limits for science. Two possible variations of this position hinge on the question of whether there are in fact any identifiable *characteristics* of science and whether, if there are, these imply any *limits* on what is knowable by science.

Denying that limits arise. If one accepts the characteristics of science we have discussed, or for that matter any other specific characteristics, then one can argue that they nevertheless do not constitute significant limit to scientific knowledge. This requires one to argue that science's methods are universal and all-encompassing, in the sense that any claims to knowledge arrived at by other means are spurious. This approach says that whatever insights or intuitions other approaches arrive at, they are not worthy of the designation of knowledge.

Denying scientific characteristics. A different approach is to deny that science has any specific characteristics of its methods. It is to argue that science is simply a no-holds-barred determination to find out about the world, that *any* method that works is allowed, and that, since there is no scientific method, there are no consequent limitations. Areas of knowledge that don't look as successful, at present, as natural science are *primitive* sciences, or *proto* science. Because they are difficult or just in their early stages, they don't yet command the degree of assurance that more mature natural sciences have reached. But eventually they will.

2. Knowledge is one

A common aphorism is "all truth is one" or "all knowledge is one". If this is self evident, then any division of knowledge, and in particular the division into science and non-science is immediately suspect, indeed improper. Since scientific knowledge appears to have attractive and persuasive characteristics of definiteness and utility, it is best to regard it as the archetype, and regard real knowledge as science.

3. Physicalism demands or implies it

This alternative, in contradiction of the caveats with which I began, asserts that not only do we know the world is purely physical, but also that this physicality demands or implies that all real knowledge is scientific knowledge of the natural, physical, world. We can be confident the world is purely physical (it is supposed) because of the explosion of knowledge that has arisen from the pursuit of modern, physicalist, natural science, and by the fact that science is closing in on a seamless physical description of reality. As physical (including biological) descriptions take over succeeding areas of knowledge they displace the prior subjective and superstitious beliefs, which must be repudiated. There may be residual areas of human endeavor like the arts, literature, music, etc., which we value, but in so far as there is understanding of these that deserves the title of knowledge, it is scientific, and indeed at base physical.

4. It works

Science, in this view, is the one epistemological enterprise that gives us indubitable, reliable, objective knowledge. We can see this in the enormously beneficial technologies that it has spawned and its extraordinary ability to produce consensus in the scientific community. Science has progressed inexorably, dispelling ignorance, and illuminating successive areas of study. Scientism is a natural and compelling extrapolation of the past trend of science's successes.

It works. And it works so much better than any other supposed knowledge, that the other is not worth calling knowledge until it has been gathered under science's umbrella.

5. There is no viable alternative

Modern science simply is the only way to get reliable knowledge. It might have its weaknesses, but there is no viable alternative. The proposed or historic alternatives are subjective, dogmatic, super-stitious, obscurantist, and unworkable. They contain metaphysical statements that are unverifiable, or have no definite consequences, and hence are either meaningless or at least useless.

6. The health of science demands it

If we allow the possibility of other, non-scientific, explanations of phenomena, this has a weakening or debilitating effect on science. It breeds a premature satisfaction with a less-than-satisfactory un-derstanding. It halts science's progress and removes the inquisitive impulse by an insufficient or false explanation. Science is so im-portant to society's well-being that we must avoid anything that would handicap it.

My six categories of justification of a conscious explicit scientism might not be exhaustive, but I think they cover the vast majority of the types of warrant that have been offered. Let us recall, though, that more often than not scientism is implicit, not explicit; so the majority of opinions based upon scientism offer *no* warrant for their underlying scientism; they simply assume that scientism is accepted.

In his study of scientism[116], Tom Sorell identifies five claims about science that are characteristic of the broad scientism that Rudolph Carnap called scientific empiricism. They are that science is: 1 Unified; 2 Limitless; 3 Successful; 4 Objective; 5 Beneficial. These claims are present in my categorization of the proposed war-rants for scientism, although my headings do not entirely coincide with his. He cites numerous examples of this sort of scientism from the writings of the Vienna Circle (Logical Positivists). I invite the interested reader to refer to Sorell's first chapter for that background, and especially for examples of arguing for scientism that I won't cite here.

The physicalist argument is not directly addressed by Sorell. However, the case for it has been reviewed by David Papineau.[117] The key question he addresses is why the belief in physicalism is so widespread today. Why, for example, has mind-body dualism fallen into such disrepute in philosophical circles in the past few decades? After all, physics has enjoyed very high intellectual prestige for 300 years, yet physicalism never seemed so strong. Why now? He first notes that a thorough-going physicalism was held in check for the first half of the twentieth century by "the dominant metaphysical view among logical positivists and other scientifically-minded analytic philosophers" phenomenalism — the view that physical objects exist only as perceptual phenomena. "If you think that everything, including physical stuff, is logically constituted out of mental items like sense data, then you would seem already to have ruled out the thought that mental items are in turn constituted by physical items."[118] For him, though, the decline of phenomenalism was not so much a cause as an accompaniment of the physicalist ascent. Papineau's proposal instead is that there is now a previously-unavailable empirical argument for physicalism based upon the "*completeness of physics*, by which I mean that all physical effects are due to physical causes." In the face of the advances in understanding the chemical and physical basis of biology it is no longer plausible to believe in mental or vital "special forces". It should be remarked, though, that the case for the completeness of physics in Papineau's sense (even if there are no special forces), its logical warrant for physicalism, and physicalism's for scientism, are all matters of considerable debate.

6.2   Critical evaluation

Notice that one can regard my first three warrants as foundational, while the second three are pragmatic. In other words, arguments that science has no limits, that knowledge is one, or that physicalism implies scientism, are based upon prior commitments that are essentially philosophical and metaphysical. In contrast, the observation that scientism works, or that there's nothing else that works, or that scientism is required for science and society's benefit, are arguments from results. These last three pragmatic arguments draw on science's prestige, achievements and perceived value, either in an absolute sense or in contrast to the perceived weakness or danger of alternatives.

Foundational Justifications

The alert reader will already have realized that a great deal of what I have said in previous chapters has been directed against the first two of the foundational justifications of scientism: science is unlimited, or knowledge is one. I will expand briefly only on the question of knowledge's unity. Here I think there is frequently a confusion between two different assertions. The assertion that I take to be true is 'the world is one'. In contrast, the assertion that I consider to be a part of an unjustified scientism is 'our knowledge of the world is (or should be) one'. Of course, a nuanced view of 'the world is one' is essential if we are to make sense of it. A realist viewpoint, which is common to most scientists, usually demands some concept of the unity of the world. Realism is the belief that there is something out there that is responsible for the various experiences and impressions that each individual has. That world out there is usually thought to be unified in the sense of being a self-consistent reality, possessing a variety of properties some of which seem to be impersonal and independent of the observer: like continuity, stability, as well as those which reflect human character and perceptual abilities as observers, such as comprehensibility.

The unity of the world does not in the least entail or imply the unity of knowledge in the sense required to justify scientism. To suppose so would be like supposing that the unity of the world requires that there be only one type of human sense organ: that sight is the only valid way to make sense of reality, that smell or hearing don't count. Or it would be like demanding that there be only one perspective or viewpoint from which a landscape could be pictured, or only one valid representation of that view. We can perfectly well maintain the unity and consistency of the world and yet regard both the sight of a young man dressed in a black bow-tie and jacket, smashing together two circular brass disks, and the loud crash of the cymbal sound that we hear during the symphony performance, as equally significant, complementary, yet different ways of knowing that world. The unity of the world is not in the least compromised by recognizing the essential difference between a John Constable painting of a wooded English valley and the valley's description in the writing of Jane Austin. Granted that there is a process of perception, at which humans are quite remarkably skilled, which mentally brings together different perspectives and senses to construct a recognition of a unified world behind the non-unified impressions. But that process of perceptual unification leaves untouched the value of the different modes of knowledge of the event. We do not say that the cymbal crash is *really* just what we see, or *really* just what we hear, nor even that it is *really* just a part of the symphony. Why should we then suppose that it is *really* just the abrupt electromagnetic interaction of the electrons in the respective surfaces of the colliding materials (or some other description in terms of physics). No, maintaining a differentiated understanding of knowledge, does not undermine the unity of the world or even realism in our conception of it.

The stronger unity-of-knowledge claim, which I reject, has appeal, perhaps, as an emphasis on our perceptual unification skills. Our ability to integrate different senses and perspectives (both physical and metaphorical) and form valid assessments of what is happening in the, assumed-unified, external world is a vital part of what we take to be cognition. And it may seem natural to identify that integration, and unification, as the defining character of what we might call philosophical knowledge. Yet I hope that what I have previously said is enough to show both that this semantic move is contrary to common-sense understanding and usage of 'knowledge', and also that it leaves out of account a great deal that we do, as a matter of fact, know.

Pragmatic Justifications

A persuasive warrant for belief that *science* accurately describes (at least some aspects of) reality lies in its success. This is sometimes described as *a posteriori* justification, justification after the fact. The logic of this approach is that we start with a tentative assumption that the world can be described in ways that depend upon reproducibility and Clarity. We then make observations, devise experiments, and construct theories to systematize and explain them. The scientific description of the world that we arrive at provides us with predictions about the future behavior of nature, and with technology for achieving practical ends. These predictions and technologies work. That is proven in today's society by simply looking around us at the achievements of science. The *a posteriori* justification consists of the argument that science works because its assumption is true. If so, then the tentative basis on which we first adopted the assumption that science accurately describes the world has been strengthened. We do more science, with more confidence in our assumption, and we find — perhaps after considerable intellectual effort — further confirmation, and so a virtuous circle of justification is established. It is fair to say that most people find this a convincing argument, although we'll discuss later some opinions that contradict it. But it is important to understand with some precision just what the assumption was that underwrote science's success.

A perverse *a posteriori* logic might say this. I take as my starting tentative assumption that the world behaves reproducibly and that Shakespeare's plays were really written by Edward de Vere, the 17th Earl of Oxford. I make observations, do experiments, formulate theories, and discover that science works. (I also fail to find scientific proof or disproof of Shakespearean authorship.) I therefore conclude that there is *a posteriori* justification for my assumption. Have I thereby justified the Oxfordian theory of Shakespearean authorship? No, of course not. That was an irrelevant part of my original assumption, and is therefore not supported by the success of science. This is an illustration of the important principle that for *a posteriori* justification we must know just what is an integral part of the assumption that leads to the cognitive success, and not claim to have discovered support for irrelevancies.

The assumption that leads us to science's cognitive success is that the world is describable through reproducibility and Clarity. It is not that *everything about* the world is so describable. It is that science leads to knowledge, not that science leads to *all* knowledge, or that knowledge flows *only* from science. Consequently, the *a posteriori* justification is for science, not for scientism.

It might be argued that there is something intrinsic in the idea of a law of nature that requires the stronger assertion. Is not the scientific ideal expressed in terms of a *universal* law, such as Newton's "all masses attract all other masses with a force inversely proportional to the square of their distance"? Does not the universal character of natural laws imply that they always apply, and apply to everything? Perhaps; but it is debatable. Actually, whether what we regard as the laws of physics are the same everywhere has recently become a live debate within physical cosmology. But even if that were so, even if the scientific net were indeed uniform and unbreakable, it would not immediately rule out the possibility of knowledge that escapes the net; perhaps there are fish that are smaller than the two-inch mesh size[119]. So even if natural laws are always obeyed, we can't establish thereby that they are all that one can legitimately claim to know.

Those who have advocated a scientistic position often recognize that science, not scientism, is really supported by argument from success in this weak form; and they try for a stronger version. They allow that there is merit in the weak scientific assumption: the world can be described by science, but they assert that there is greater merit in the stronger scientistic assumption: everything in the world can (eventually) be completely described by science. The greater merit consists largely in the optimism generated by the presumption of the completeness of science. It is, they say, a vital factor in science's success. It underwrites the rationale, the psychology, and the motivation of the science enterprise. It inspires the heroism of the scientist both in prosecuting a scientific research program despite intellectual setbacks or personal or organizational discouragements, and also in confronting the entrenched resistance of anti-scientific interests: political, religious, or superstitious. If, in this way, a scientistic assumption has been the basis of science's success, then an *a posteriori* justification of scientism might logically be claimed. The problem with this logic is that the historic evidence is largely against scientistic motivation as a significant factor. Over history there have been some scientists (as well as those who supported them) whose motivations were scientistic, who believed that science is all the real knowledge there is, who might even fit the heroic iconoclast stereotype of the science versus religion mythology. But there have been even more scientists (I don't say more ideologues), most certainly prior to the twentieth century, who were in fact *not* scientistic in their personal motivations, and a large fraction that were religiously motivated. Kepler, Galileo, Boyle, Newton, Pascal, Dalton, Faraday, Maxwell, Kelvin, and a host of other scientific superstars were deeply religious people, who thought that the foundational reality was not physicalism and scientism but God. Only a gross distortion of history can attribute the success of scientists to their scientism. So much for the justification of scientism by its success.

The argument that there is *no viable alternative to science*, in its most brazen form, is largely a statement of taste. It might often be good taste to prefer scientific to other approaches to knowledge. But the idea that there is no viable alternative has only relatively recent pedigree. Practically no one in the seventeenth century imagined that to study natural philosophy was other than a somewhat unusual preference. During the eighteenth century, the distaste for dogma, and the determination to undermine the religious intellectual power structures and the political system that benefited from their support, came to full flower in a segment (but only a segment) of the French intelligentsia. And, as we have seen, scientism in its youth was recruited to help advocate and empower the struggle. Undoubtedly physics became, in the Age of Reason, a much admired ideal of universal knowledge, one to aspire to; but it can hardly be imagined that even then it was an accepted idea that there was no viable alternative to the methods of natural philosophy or the mechanical arts in the attainment of knowledge. Historically at least, therefore, there were alternatives. The extent to which these no longer appear viable, is a reflection mostly of today's Zeitgeist, not of careful argument.

As representative of today's preference, consider Paul Thagard, someone who directly advocates a scientistic position, based on there being no viable alternative. He says, "What is reality? My answer will be that we should judge reality to consist of those things and processes identified by well-established fields of science using theories backed by evidence drawn from systematic observations and experiments."[120] His argument consists largely in drawing a dichotomy between "evidence-based thinking" and "faith-based thinking" and showing the success of the first and failure of the second. Recognizing that perhaps the contrast between these two might not actually exhaust all the options, he adds a third: "Philosophical attempts to establish truths by a priori reasoning, thought experiments, or conceptual analysis have been no more successful than faith-based thinking has been."[121] So it might seem that we are really offered a "trichotomy". Actually though, what the rejected options share, in Thagard's definitions, is that they are not based on evidence; because as far as he is concerned "Religious faith is a belief in, trust in, and devotion to gods, leaders, or texts, independent of evidence."[122] By defining "faith-based" and "philosophical a priori" reasoning as independent of evidence, he intends to frame the choice as being whether or not we place priority upon evidence. But both these definitions are straw-men. It is just simply not the case that all religious beliefs are independent of evidence, or that all philosophy, even in its most introspective incarnations, is impervious to evidence. Indeed, it is remarkable that Thagard should dismiss "thought experiments" since physics has conducted some of its most fruitful theorizing in precisely such activities, always to be confronted, in due course, with experiments. In reality, both religious thought and philosophical thought depend upon and have recourse to evidence. Where they differ from science, and from each other, is in what they regard as evidence and in the different weight that they accord to different types of evidence. Science insists that evidence must be in the form of clear repeatable experiments. Religious, or philosophical discourse — and for that matter literary, historical, jurisprudential, and artistic scholarship — place more emphasis on the types of evidence that their disciplines expect: testimony, narrative, human nature, personal experience, and so on.

I think there is, nevertheless, a pragmatic reason why the alternatives appear much less viable, in comparison with science, than they did two or three hundred years ago. It is the extent to which science now has a track record of near-universal consensus-formation, while the non-scientific disciplines have a near-universal track record of disputation and controversy. Arguments seem (eventually) to get settled in natural science, but often they don't seem to get settled in other intellectual endeavors. The fact that we now have over three centuries of modern science to look back on, lends this rationale far more cogency than it could possibly have had in the earlier part of the modern era.

The observation of science's ability to gain wide consensus lends some plausibility to the view that science is knowledge while non-science is merely *opinion*. If such opinion is strongly held, and taught as a vital truth for all to embrace, it is often labeled dogma. If it is widely held, but largely innocuous, it is called fashion. If it is a preference of the educated, it is called culture. If it is popularly believed to have some level of efficacy in practical matters yet has no supporting science, it is generally deemed superstition. There is no denying that science has unresolved disputes, or party divisions in its community. Some of its disputes have lasted for centuries. Is light wave or particles? Are there indivisible units of matter? Do continents move? Did the universe have a beginning? It also has its own deep puzzles about topics that few doubt are part of its subject and scope. How are gravity and quantum mechanics to be unified? How did life begin? How do brains work? But the impressive thing about science is its record of eventually resolving even its longest-running arguments, and of maintaining a generally fruitful conversation about even its deepest of puzzles.

There does seem to be something special about science, which enables it to arrive at knowledge that is uniquely persuasive and reliable. That is of course a reason for the high prestige of science in our culture. But science's persuasive and practical power is based on choosing as its topics of study precisely those aspects of the world that are able to be described and systematized into persuasive and practical scientific knowledge. Its insistence on reproducible experimental and observational confirmation, and its insistence on Clarity are the essential foundations of its astonishing successes. For all the justifiable critiques of science's more immodest claims, for all the scholarly disproof of the fables that it has told about its history and certainty, and for all the well-earned condemnations of scientism's ambitions to encompass everything in its hegemony, science still does deserve high esteem. It produces real and valuable knowledge, about the topics it is competent to describe. It attracts into its enterprise those who value the truth that they find there, as well, perhaps, as those who seek the power and wealth that science's technological capabilities can provide. But acknowledging all these sometimes admirable and often powerful characteristics of science in no way establishes that other fields are bereft of knowledge. Non-scientific topics are precisely those that do *not* lend themselves to providing the reproducible and unambiguous answers that characterize science. No wonder that their answers are more ambiguous, more debatable, more uncertain. Yet these topics are, of course, of profound importance in society and in everyday human life, and their pursuit deserves respect when it shows insight, rigor, creativity, and erudition.

Finally, let us consider the argument that the health of science demands that we privilege scientific descriptions and scientific investigations over all others. In fairness, this argument is rarely put forward by serious thinkers, and I don't want to seem to be setting up a straw man. But it does sometimes appear as a rhetorical device in popular attacks on ideas that are considered to be anti-scientific. It is therefore aimed at undermining religion, of course, especially religiously-motivated efforts to influence school curricula. In this context it often takes the form of the charge that religion is a 'science-stopper'[123]. But arguments such as these also appear in defence of science against some of its critics and occasionally its abusers. They also appear in promotional arguments by scientists who are advocating for greater support for science by government and society.

In response to this rather extreme rhetoric, one should comment immediately that, thankfully, science is not so fragile as to be unable to withstand criticism. It is not necessary for science to own the entire field of debate in order for its merits to be appreciated and supported. There does not seem to be any serious evidence that non-scientific descriptions discourage scientific investigation of the same phenomena. Actually, it seems the opposite. Not only are non-scientific interests intrigued by scientific analysis of aspects of their concerns, but also scientists are attracted by the popular attention that offering these analyses often brings. There is a thriving popular literature of scientific investigations of sport, for example. Scientific investigations of physics and physiology related to music are generally received without anti-scientific prejudice, by professional musicians. Physical scientists flatter themselves that they have important insights to offer in such faintly absurd hybrid fields as 'econophysics' or the 'physics of traffic'. Nor is there really any immediate prospect that science will wither away because of some pernicious influence on young people of alternative viewpoints. So, calls to address admitted weaknesses of the education system — especially in science — in the United States (or elsewhere), while undoubtedly often justified, ring hollow if they are based upon a scientistic polemic. Science does not have to disallow the relevance of other disciplines in order to represent and advocate its own positive value. I am not promoting replacements for science in the description of the natural world. Indeed, I have argued that such replacement is logically impossible. I have as strong an aversion to superstition and obscurantism as most scientists. I no more wish than any other to strengthen popular acceptance of astrology or channeling. But what is generally at issue in these types of argument is not just a matter of non-scientific approaches encroaching on the territory of, or devaluing, science; it is as much science (or rather scientism) encroaching on or attempting to devalue other subjects. Territorial disputes are never one-sided. A case can be made, and I'll make it in more detail later, that the criticism of science that has become commonplace in certain academic discourses during recent decades is fueled by a scientistic push toward regarding science as the owner of the epistemic field. If this diagnosis of one of the driving forces of science criticism is correct, then the health of science is in fact jeopardized by scientism, not promoted by it. At the very least, scientism provokes a defensive, immunological, aggressive response from other intellectual communities, in return for its own arrogance and intellectual bullying. Furthermore, since scientism is unjustified, it taints science itself by association.

Chapter 7

Denying science

7.1 Outgrowing the Enlightenment

Opinions are not one dimensional, of course, but at the opposite end of a spectrum of opinion based on the value of scientism — about as far as one can get away from those who explicitly advocate and defend scientism — lies a viewpoint that sees natural science as *socially constructed* to the same extent as any other discipline. In this view, there is no external reality to which science refers and by which science is judged (or at least there's no useful access to it). Instead, what counts as scientific knowledge is little more than the dominant opinion of the self-appointed scientific power-brokers. At its most extreme, this social constructivist position argues that scientific theory is the product of oppressive, Euro-centric, capitalistic, sexist, self-serving prior commitments, and that the very content and findings of science would be (and perhaps will be) different when derived in the context of a liberated multicultural world-view.

To label this viewpoint *postmodern* is certainly to run the risk of misrepresentation by oversimplification[124]; although it is also to invoke such a perplexingly complex and ill-defined temper of recent thought, as to complexify the discussion more than it simplifies. There is, alas, no good alternative; and we must do what we can to portray fairly the arguments of those who promulgate this view.

While there were many strands of analysis predating it, and many opinions that continue to extend far beyond its concerns, *The Postmodern Condition: A Report on Knowledge* by Jean-François Lyotard (1979) is widely considered the defining expression of post-modernism. It serves as a valuable introduction for us, in part because there are some pithy insights in it, in part because it is agreed by all sides to be canonical, and in part because it is mercifully brief. "Simplifying to the extreme, I define *postmodern* as incredulity toward metanarratives. This incredulity is undoubtedly a product

145

of progress in the sciences: but that progress in turn presupposes it."[125] The second sentence in this quotation from Lyotard's introduction warns us of the penchant for unexplained paradox that is a frustrating trait in postmodern texts. The first sentence comes the closest that I know to a compact definition of postmodernism. To understand what it means, one needs a bit more from the previous page

> Science has always been in conflict with narratives. Judged by the yardstick of science, the majority of them prove to be fables. But to the extent that science does not restrict itself to stating useful regularities and seeks the truth, it is obliged to legitimate the rules of its own game. It then produces a discourse of legitimation with respect to its own status, a discourse called philosophy. I will use the term *modern* to designate any science that legitimates itself with reference to a metadiscourse of this kind making an explicit appeal to some grand narrative, such as the dialectics of Spirit, the hermeneutics of meaning, the emancipation of the rational or working subject or the creation of wealth.[126]

We see here that 'metadiscourse', 'metanarrative', or 'grand narrative', which are approximately interchangeable in this parlance, mean roughly a unifying philosophy, justifying rationale, or explanatory world-view that 'legitimates' the practice of a particular approach to understanding, in this case science. Science in seeking such legitimation through philosophy is characteristic of the *modern*, which is superceded by the postmodern. "To the obsolescence of the metanarrative apparatus of legitimation corresponds, most notably, the crisis of metaphysical philosophy and of the university institution which in the past relied on it."

In the context of a discussion of scientism, Lyotard has some salutary and broadly correct criticisms, which parallel some of my present argument. "In the first place, scientific knowledge does not represent the totality of knowledge; it has always existed in addition to, and in competition and conflict with, another kind of knowledge, which I will call narrative in the interests of simplicity..."[127]

Knowledge is not the same as science, especially in its contemporary form; and science, far from successfully obscuring the problem of its legitimacy, cannot avoid raising it with all of its implications, which are no less sociopolitical than epistemological. ...

Knowledge [savoir] in general cannot be reduced to science, nor even to learning [connaissance]. Learning is the set of statements which, to the exclusion of all other statements, denote or describe objects and may be declared true or false. Science is a subset of learning. It is also composed of denotative statements, but imposes two supplementary conditions on their acceptability: the objects to which they refer must be available for repeated access, in other words, they must be accessible in explicit conditions of observation; and it must be possible to decide whether or not a given statement pertains to the language judged relevant by the experts.

What is meant by knowledge is not only a set of denotative statements, far from it. It also includes notions of "know-how", "knowing how to live", "how to listen", etc. Knowledge, then, is a question of competence that goes beyond the simple determination and application of the criterion of truth, extending to the determination and application of criteria of efficiency (technical qualification), of justice and/or happiness (ethical wisdom), of the beauty of a sound or color (auditory and visual sensibility), etc. Understood in this way, knowledge is what makes someone capable of forming "good" denotative utterances, but also "good" prescriptive and "good" evaluative utterances ... It is not a competence relative to a particular class of statements (for example, cognitive ones) to the exclusion of all others.[128]

This is not just a negative rejection of scientism. It is also a positive outline of the alternative, much of which I find very helpful. 'Narrative' is a typical (postmodern) designation of the characteristics of non-scientific disciplines. The 'denotation' of a statement is its literal or definitional meaning. Science, and indeed in Lyotard's vocabulary also 'learning' of which science is a subset, sticks to denotative statements. But knowledge refers to competency broader than determination of truth or falsehood. The prescriptive and evaluative 'utterances' within its wider scope include efficiency, justice, happiness, ethics, wisdom, and beauty.

Of science's relation to narrative knowledge, we read

> I have said that narrative knowledge does not give priority to the question of its own legitimation and that it certifies itself in the pragmatics of its own transmission without having recourse to argumentation and proof. This is why its incomprehension of the problems of scientific discourse is accompanied by a certain tolerance: it approaches such discourse primarily as a variant in the family of narrative cultures. The opposite is not true. The scientist questions the validity of narrative statements and concludes that they are never subject to argumentation or proof. He classifies them as belonging to a different mentality: savage, primitive, underdeveloped, backward, alienated, composed of opinions, customs, authority, prejudice, ignorance, ideology. Narratives are fables, myths, legends, fit only for women and children. At best, attempts are made to throw some rays of light into this obscurantism, to civilize, educate, develop.
>
> This unequal relationship is an intrinsic effect of the rules specific to each game. We all know its symptoms. It is the entire history of cultural imperialism from the dawn of Western civilization. ... it is governed by the demand for legitimation.[129]

Here Lyotard reminds us of the key characteristic of narrative. It does not bother explicitly to legitimate itself. This permits it a hospitable openness to science, which it welcomes as one discourse among many. But this openness is not reciprocated. Science, Lyotard says, rejects the unproven narratives.

Let us pause in the direct explication to comment that Lyotard is here mixing up science with scientism. Scientism generally *does* feel obliged to reject the 'narrative statements' as knowledge, and regularly attributes to them the litany of ills, the fables, legends, ideology, and so on, that he lists. Science without scientism, however, is under no such obligation, and, in so far as the 'narratives' are not setting up a new pretended science that attempts to subvert either the content of natural science or its hard-earned brand-loyalty, science has no compulsion to adopt this aggressive stance. The failure on the part of postmodern proponents to distinguish between science and scientism is the driving force behind their science critiques and a major source of the conflict between scientific and non-scientific academics, which has been elevated in common terminology to the level of 'science wars'. Postmodern science-critiques generally throw the baby out with the bath water. The scientism that many scientists improperly advocate deserves to be washed away. Science does not.

Scientists do become aggressive — with some justification in my opinion — when science is portrayed as *merely* one discourse among many, as if its centuries of hard-won progress and high epistemological esteem counted for nothing, or when that esteem is impugned in the way that Lyotard's charge of cultural imperialism exemplifies. This passage, by the way, is rather mild, as these examples go in their derogatory social deconstruction, attributing science's status to pure political power.

The other trait in postmodern discourse that really riles scientists is the tendency to misappropriate and misrepresent scientific concepts for rhetorical purposes. Lyotard's writing furnishes a (widely quoted) example. It ranges, in a manner that gives the impression of shameless name-dropping and terminology-dropping, over an astonishingly incoherent variety of scientific topics, whose content, when it is explained at all, is treated with an imprecision (to put it charitably) that would scandalize a freshman science undergraduate. In the interests of brevity it must be substantially reduced by selection from a six-page passage[130]:

> The metamathematical research that led to Gödel's theorem is a veritable paradigm of how this change in nature takes place. But the transformation that dynamics has undergone is no less exemplary of the new scientific spirit, ...
>
> Quantum theory and microphysics require a far more radical revision of the idea of a continuous and pre-

> dictable path. ... Jean Perrin ... Knowledge about the
> density of air thus resolves into a multiplicity of incom-
> patible statements; ... Einstein ... Mandelbrot ...
>
> The conclusion we can draw from this research is
> that the continous differentiable function is losing its
> preeminence as a paradigm of knowledge and predic-
> tion. Postmodern science ... is changing the meaning
> of the word *knowledge*, while expressing how such a
> change can take place. ...
>
> ... there is no "scientific method" and [that] a scien-
> tist is before anything else a person who "tells stories".

The passage vacillates between explanation of the science, inter-
preting the science content as some sort of metaphor for its own
development, and drawing larger philosophical conclusions from
it.

Scientists' response to this misuse of science in recent non-
scientific academic discourse is extensively represented by the book
Higher Superstition: The academic left and its quarrels with science by
Paul R. Gross and Norman Levitt (1994). They hypothesize that a
motivating factor of the academic left's quarrels is philosophical revenge. The supposition is that the logical positivism of the first half
of the twentieth century was "devastatingly hurtful to the *amour
propre* of traditional humanists". A good part of the social-science
community responded "with various attempts to introduce quantitative methods, mathematical models, "replicability" and "falsifiability" into sociological work" even though "that craving for
methodological respectability — "scientism" or "physics envy" as
it was sometimes called — must lead to a sterile ... view". "Thus
it probably came to pass that when the brutally skeptical views of
the postmodernists began to gain some currency some years later,
many humanists, and many social scientists as well, were quick to
lay hold of them as instruments of revenge."[131]

The unrelieved disdain that sets the tone of Gross and Leavitt's
writing means it soon becomes tiresome. But no more tiresome than
the nonsense coming from left-leaning perspectivist authors that it
aims to skewer. The hoax perpetrated by physicist Alan Sokal on
the cultural studies journal *Social Text* had, by contrast, the merit of
being funny. He submitted to the journal, as if in all seriousness,

a parody of the pretentious-sounding pseudo-scientific nonsense that is typical of the misuse of science in those circles — and it was published. Hilarious. Enough said. Actually much more was said. The book-length rehash and analysis *Fashionable Nonsense: Postmodern Intellectuals' Abuse of Science* by Alan Sokal and Jean Bricmont documents its sources in excruciating detail[132]. It would be superfluous to reproduce more examples here.

One mitigating factor overlooked by most of the scientists' critiques of speculative, and often irrelevant, citations of scientific results by postmodern commentators is that these citations stand in a long tradition of such extrapolations — written by distinguished scientists! The historian of science, Mara Beller has documented, for quantum theory, that "Astonishing statements, hardly distinguishable from those satirized by Sokal, abound in the writings of Bohr, Heisenberg, Pauli, Born, and Jordan. And they are not just casual, incidental remarks. Bohr intended his philosophy of complementarity to be an overarching epistemological principle — applicable to physics, biology, psychology and anthropology. He expected complementarity to be a substitute for the lost religion. He believed that complementarity should be taught to children in elementary schools."[133] There may be some differences in the pronouncements of these heroes of quantum physics from those of the postmodernists, but it takes some detailed analysis to separate them, and Nobel-prize-winning physicist, Steven Weinberg, in an exchange concerning his 1996 review of the Sokal hoax book, betrayed an embarrassment with the scientists when he said of their extrapolations "we know better now"[134]. (Actually, contra Weinberg, there does not seem to be strong evidence, in science popularizations, of repudiation of these analogical extrapolations; in other words, it is not clear that we do know better now.) Except that the physicists generally avoid egregious technical misrepresentation, it is hard to see much difference in the content of their statements. Both the physicists and the postmoderns appeal to science as a source of insight into matters which don't seem to have anything to do with the science. The physicists are apparently motivated by a scientistic belief that their science is the route to all knowledge. The postmoderns disavow such a viewpoint. They think that science is no more special than any other discourse, which means that science is as much game for their reference and quotation as any other topic, whether they understand its technical content or not. And they can't help being drawn by science's intimidatingly strong image to use scientific allusions and name-dropping to lend an aura of intellectual depth to their ruminations.

A critique of the social constructivist view of science more civil than that of Gross and Leavitt, or Sokal, is a two part review by Cornell Physics Professor, David Mermin, of the book *Golem: What everyone should know about science* by Harry Collins and Trevor Pinch (1993). It appeared in 1996 in the monthly magazine of the American Physical Society sent to every member of the Society, *Physics Today*, (which later published Beller's article). Mermin outlines the way that *The Golem* goes about making the case that "Science works the way it does not from any absolute constraint from Nature, but because we make our science the way we do", that is, because of the way the scientific community constructs its consensus. Speaking to his fellow physicists, Mermin says the collective import of Collins and Pinch's message is "You and I may think it works because, by a long and arduous process, scientists have become better and better at formulating questions that extract useful information from the natural world while avoiding questions that lead nowhere. This view is an expression of our naive realism, but it is important that we believe it. The conviction that we are trying to learn an objective truth is a powerful sustaining myth that drives us onward in our efforts at consensus building." But Mermin identifies "The pertinent issue in assessing the claims of *The Golem* is not whether scientific truth is determined by constraints from nature or by social construction, but whether Collins and Pinch strike a satisfactory balance between these two aspects of the process. I believe their book furnishes an instructive demonstration of what can go wrong if you focus too strongly on the social perspective." His more detailed diagnosis of the cause of their misrepresentation is that the authors have not properly understood that the strength of scientific knowledge lies in its collective, multi-stranded, interwoven nature. "The method of Collins and Pinch is to follow one strand of an enormous tapestry of fact and analysis. They note that the strand is quite thin in places. Often they can demonstrate that the contribution of that particular thread to the whole picture has been greatly exaggerated. But they pay only perfunctory attention to everything else that holds the tapestry together." He works out this problematic attention to a single strand in a detailed analysis of the portrayal of the Michelson-Morley experiment, which is one of the key evidences for the theory of relativity.

In a response letter, also published in *Physics Today*, Collins and Pinch reveal some of their background motivation as follows "Many scientists, especially those who have become spokespersons, are evidently scientific fundamentalists. They think of science as the royal route to all knowledge; they think of it as able to deliver the kind of certainty that priests once delivered; they think of it as a complete world view or quasi religion. ... Where we sociologists think of ourselves as trying to gain social and historical insight into science, the fundamentalists see heresy. ... [Mermin's] reaction has the whiff of the offended priest. It seems that it is not so much the book as a whole that has touched a raw nerve in Mermin; the trouble arises mainly from our having defiled the holy of holies; relativity." "... the history of science is difficult to reconcile with scientific fundamentalism unless a body of perfectly respectable interpretations are censored. It is such uncensored stories that are told in *The Golem*"

To this brickbat Mermin replies, still characteristically genial, that their comments "nicely illustrate how our views of science and scientists differ. They think I used the example of relativity because I was offended by their defilement of a sacred text. I think I did it because I understand relativity better than the other subjects they discussed in their book, so I'm better able to see where they got it wrong. They overlook the obvious explanation because the rightness/wrongness axis is not a relevant dimension in their kind of sociological analysis of science."

Mermin had, perhaps, earned this priestly characterization by his review's contrast between questions that extract useful information from the natural world, and those "that lead nowhere". This might be interpreted as a put-down for any questions not designed to extract information from nature. Collins and Pinch are helpfully direct about the "scientific fundamentalism" that they are aiming to combat, the "royal route to all knowledge" — scientism. But the way they set about trying to combat it isn't going to gain the appreciation even of as open and broad-minded a scientist as Mermin if it implies that scientists don't really know what they think they know about nature. As long as scientism and science are undifferentiated, there's no way to approach a meeting of minds between the two cultures. The scientists are going to say that science really is the royal route to knowledge. They are going to be basing that on the observation that it really is the royal route to knowledge *of nature*, and they may be extrapolating to *all* knowledge (or possibly may not if asked the right questions and given credit for what they really do know, at least that's my hope). The social critics are going to say, in response, science is not the route to all knowledge, and mean a wider scope than nature. And then, to try to prove it, they are going to try to undermine science's claims to know nature, by a deconstruction of science's route to knowledge or some other detected shortcoming. The scientists are then going to respond defending the reality of science's knowledge of nature. This sort of exchange occurs with dreary predictability. Another example, which I will not trouble you by relating[135], arose in the New York Review of books from Weinberg's review of Sokal.

The 'science wars' have cooled in the past ten years. The differences between the scientists and those who study them have been aired in more collegial situations than the pages of magazines, with results that are sometimes more illuminating[136] but, admittedly not generating so much interest, perhaps because public confrontation and mud-slinging is in one sense more fun. What I find interesting in the rapprochements is that they hardly at all address directly the scientism that, it seems to me, lends the passion to this debate. Instead, the social critics (in the rapprochements it is usually sociologists of science) fervently disavow an intention to undermine science. They justify the relativism of their stance in respect of the truth-claims of science as being adopted as a principle of sociological analysis. This principle, they say, stems from a methodological requirement called *symmetry*; so that "we try to avoid explaining the emergence of truth by reference to its truthfulness because such explanations are circular."[137]. The scientists still see it as misleading the public. It is not clear whether, on their part, the sociologists' charges of scientific fundamentalism are really dropped or not. Neither side seems convinced that the ceasefire is really peace.

7.2 Shattering The Mirror of Nature

To understand postmodern attitudes to science and scientism, it is helpful to engage with philosopher Richard Rorty. He is a good choice for several reasons. First, among postmodern writers, he is one of the clearest; second, his thinking is deep, original, and nuanced and consequently receives wide recognition; and third, Rorty gives important rational arguments. This final remark is not a dismissive put-down of postmodernists. The point is that one of the tenets of postmodernism is that reasons given to justify beliefs are frequently rationalizations; so rational argument ought not to be privileged above other rhetorical methods in postmodern discourse. A commentator is therefore being true to postmodern principles if they adopt a more varied, possibly irrational, literary style, which deliberately avoids giving rational arguments. And a lot of them do.

Rorty's signature study, *Philosophy and the Mirror of Nature*, critiques the whole enterprise of epistemology as founded on erroneous understanding of how the mind and knowledge works. At the risk of oversimplifying Rorty and yet still mystifying you, dear reader, I will attempt a summary of the book's main burden[138]. The *Mirror of Nature* of the title refers to Rorty's view that "The picture which holds traditional philosophy captive is that of the mind as a great mirror, containing various representations — some accurate, some not"[139]. Associated with this picture, is the conception of "knowledge as accuracy of representation", and a view of the mission of philosophy (distinguished since Kant from the natural philosophy that was turned into science by Descartes and Locke) as the "guardian of rationality"[140] and referee in the assessment of truth construed as representative. If we drop this metaphorical Mirror of Nature, says Rorty, then various vexed problems of philosophy, such as mind-body dualism, simply dissolve. The traditional view that there is a Nature out there, which the Knowledge of our minds is supposed to mirror, confronts us with the question of how to attain this knowledge and how to know that we have attained it. Philosophers have thus sought foundations in the form of indubitable truths on which to construct this knowledge. Candidates for these foundations include sensory experience and 'analytic' statements. A wide variety of philosophical endeavor can be interpreted as attempts to explain how this foundation for knowledge works. But the mirror metaphor, or its alternative historical metaphor as impressions on a wax tablet, arose within a different view of what constitutes knowledge. "Locke did not think of knowledge as justified true belief. He did not think of it as a relation between a person and a proposition. He thought, as had Aristotle, of "knowledge of" as prior to "knowledge that", and thus of knowledge as a relation between persons and objects rather than persons and propositions."[141] Thus knowledge could *impress itself* upon the knower, yet the metaphor allowed one to imagine rationally looking upon and examining the impressions, in order to formulate knowledge. "It is precisely the choice of ... ocular imagery which makes both Aristotle and Locke attempt to reduce "knowledge that" — justified true belief in propositions — to "knowledge of" construed as "having in mind". Since Locke views himself as an up-to-date scientist [of 1690] he would love to cash the "tablet" metaphor in physiological terms. Since he cannot, shuffling [vacillation] is his only option." "This is the shuffle that Kant detected as the basic error of empiricism"[142].

The crisis of twentieth century philosophy is that there appear to be no privileged perspectives, no foundations on which to build knowledge. However, since the mirror metaphor that demanded these problematic foundations simply arose as part of a particular historical tradition, and since the results haven't been particularly fruitful, we should simply get rid of the metaphor and hence dissolve the problems it engendered. In its place, Rorty recommends pragmatic philosophy represented by philosophers such as Dewey, Wittgenstein, Heidegger, Quine, Sellars, and Davidson, who have a "commitment to the thesis that justification is not a matter of a special relation between ideas (or words) and objects, but of conversation, of social practice." ... "The crucial premise of this argument is that we understand knowledge when we understand the social justification of belief, and thus have no need to view it as accuracy of representation."[143] Instead of epistemology, which the Mirror of Nature made into the main concern of philosophy, we will turn to *hermeneutics*. The terms of this contrast are these

> the view that epistemology, or some suitable successor-
> discipline, is necessary to culture confuses two roles

which the philosopher might play. The first is that of the informed dilettante, the polypragmatic, Socratic intermediary between various discourses. In his salon, so to speak, hermetic thinkers are charmed out of their self-enclosed practices. Disagreements between disciplines and discourses are compromised or transcended in the course of the conversation. The second role is that of the cultural overseer who knows everyone's common ground — the Platonic philosopher-king who knows what everybody else is really doing whether *they* know it or not, because he knows about the ultimate context ... The first role is appropriate to hermeneutics, the second to epistemology.[144]

Instead of treating epistemology and hermeneutics as "dividing up culture between them" giving epistemology the cognitive part and giving hermeneutics the rest — a residual which is then "stigmatized as merely "subjective"", one should

... construe the line between discourses which can be rendered commensurable and those which cannot as merely that between "normal" and "abnormal" discourse — a distinction which generalizes Kuhn's distinction between "normal" and "revolutionary" science. "Normal" science is the practice of solving problems against the background of a consensus about what counts as a good explanation of the phenomena and about what it would take for the problem to be solved. "Revolutionary" science is the introduction of a new "paradigm" of explanation, and thus of a new set of problems.[145]

Logical-empiricist philosophy of science, and the whole epistemological tradition since Descartes, has wanted to say that the procedure for attaining accurate representations in the Mirror of Nature differs in certain deep ways from the procedure for attaining agreement about "practical" or "aesthetic" matters. Kuhn gives us reason to say that there is no deeper difference than that between what happens in "normal" and in "abnormal" discourse. That distinction cuts across the distinction between science and nonscience.[146]

Rorty sees the distinction as paralleling only in a "somewhat strained" sense what, in German, are referred to as *Naturwissenschaften* (studies of nature) and *Geisteswissenschaften* (literally studies of spirit).

> Nature is whatever is so routine and familiar and manageable that we trust our own language implicitly. Spirit is whatever is so unfamiliar and unmanageable that we begin to wonder whether our "language" is "adequate" to it.[147]
> ... hermeneutics is, roughly, a description of our study of the unfamiliar and epistemology is, roughly, a description of our study of the familiar.

And he is willing to go so far as to relinquish claims to knowledge for hermeneutics [presumably provided that everyone else will agree to relinquish it too] and replace it with pragmatic "coping".

> Hermeneutics is not "another way of knowing" — "understanding" as opposed to (predictive) "explanation". It is better seen as another way of coping. It would make for philosophical clarity if we just *gave* the notion of "cognition" to predictive science, and stopped worrying about "alternative cognitive methods". The word *knowledge* would not seem worth fighting over were it not for the Kantian tradition that to be a philosopher is to have a "theory of knowledge", and the Platonic tradition that action not based on knowledge of the truth of propositions is "irrational".

The descriptions of Rorty and Lyotard (published the same year, notice) appear to be complementary. Lyotard is arguing for narrative. Rorty is arguing for hermeneutics, which is, of course, exactly the practice required to investigate and understand narrative. These seem to me very appropriate unifying concepts for many non-scientific disciplines. But neither Lyotard nor Rorty is satisfied for science to escape the narrative net. They are not willing, it seems, even for science to be based on a distinctive type of narrative. It must not be seen as distinctive. Rorty seems to acknowledge that these distinctions have been drawn in the past, and he hints that science appears to attain a degree of certainty that is not possessed by other fields. But he is at pains to soothe away these apparent differences by definition: science is the routine, familiar, and manageable, while Spirit is the unmanageable; and by analogy: science is like Kuhn's 'normal' or familiar and non-science is the 'abnormal' or unfamiliar[148]. If hermeneutics applies to the unfamiliar, still this is not a distinction of topic, but just of state. The tightrope balancing act that Rorty walks, between granting science's strength and clarity and not granting to science any distinctive epistemology, I take as testimony to his fairness and truthfulness. There are plenty of postmoderns who do not scruple to dismiss science out of hand as no more certain than any other discipline, a position that most scientists, not to say most thoughtful observers, regard as preposterous.

I hope it is clear, though, that, while the recommendations of Rorty and Lyotard appear to me to provide ideas that are helpful in understanding non-scientific knowledge, I feel none of the compulsion they do to force science into this same mold. They wish to deny to science a unique epistemology. They argue that such epistemology is the cause of insoluble philosophical problems, and that twentieth century science studies have shown science not in fact to have any identifiable method that could serve to sustain its unique status. They are perfectly comfortable doing without *any* epistemology, and without claims to knowledge, provided that science will go along, and become one of the gang. I find the argument unconvincing. Science — natural science I mean — really does have distinctive methodological requirements of reproducibility and Clarity. These provide to science a degree of confidence in its justified scientific assertions that is greater than most other fields of knowledge. It leads to technology, for good or ill, that works. But the requirements bring also *intrinsic* limitations of scope. They limit science to those aspects of the world that happen to possess these characteristic requirements. This is not just a terminological distinction between what happens just now to be manageable or unmanageable (even though Rorty's distinction-that-is-not-supposed-to-be-a-distinction comes close to mine). It does not explain science's success by a tautological definition of science as the routine and familiar — in a sense the successful — without making it different.

Of course science is still a construction of human culture in the sense that its knowledge is discovered by a social process that is as appropriate for social analysis as any other. Careful and insightful studies like Kuhn's will reveal about science's social dynamics some traits that are unfamiliar, that contradict some of the accepted mythology, that challenge popular philosophies of science, and that may discomfort scientists. Even the wilder, anarchistic, iconoclastic flights of a Feyerabend perhaps serve useful purposes in the formation of our assessment of science's social status and in discouraging scientists from taking themselves too seriously. But as long as we can repeat the measurement, observe again the phenomenon, compare our results with the published ones, solve mathematical models that give precise agreement, predict the future, and develop technology, scientists are going to say that science provides abiding unambiguous knowledge; and all but a few of them are going to say, with total conviction, that the knowledge is in some sense about a reality that is independent of any cultural construction.

If the price of entry into the hermeneutic salons of discourse is an abandonment of claims of knowledge, the scientists will tender their regrets, no matter how gracious the invitation; and so will not be charmed out of their self-enclosed practices. Indeed, even if the scientists are welcomed with open arms at no charge, and with no pre-conditions, wined and dined, charmed with erudite conversation, and even if they don't detect their postmodern hosts' knowing glances and barely perceptible smiles (at the naivety of scientists maintaining their epistemological pretensions), the scientists will deliberately remain 'naive' to that extent. On the evidence of history, the practice of science does not, in fact, require a philosophical understanding of its foundations, true or false. Scientists can get on with the business of science regardless of whether their activities receive the endorsement of philosophers. And they will. What's more, if they are forced into defensiveness by poorly informed attacks on science, or even by what just appear to be attacks, they will be even less likely to move away from a scientistic prejudice.

7.3 Freeing the oppressed

I have so far given what, for a scientist, is a relatively sympathetic representation of the postmodern stance. I am genuinely sympathetic because I believe that a great deal of what fuels the postmodern impulse is a fully justified rejection of scientism. I think that the diagnosis offered has important insights, although I think the recommended course of treatment misses the mark when it fails to distinguish science from scientism. But now I need to turn to parts of the postmodern analysis that become progressively more radical, with which I find myself far less sympathetic, and whose advocates prescribe as treatment the metaphorical equivalent of bleeding the patient.

We begin by returning to the issue of grand narratives or metanarratives, resistance to which, according to Lyotard, is the hallmark of postmodernism. Why are these so fiercely to be resisted? For a postmodern it cannot be as simple as that they are false. Who is qualified to make that judgement? The postmodern explicitly denies that anyone is so qualified. Rather it is that they are 'totalizing'. By offering a perspective that purports to be universal, metanarratives cannot help operating as justification for oppression, violence, exclusion, and injustice. They serve to legitimate "the vested interests of those who have the power and authority to make such universal pronouncements"[149]

This theme of knowledge being 'power' and 'interest' predates the emergence of postmodernism as an identifiable movement. Philosopher Jurgen Habermas published in 1968 an important study *Knowledge and Human Interests* which argues for the identity of knowledge and (self-) interest. According to Habermas, *theory* in the philosophical school of *phenomenology* (of which Edmund Husserl was considered the founder) purported to undermine the "objectivist illusion" by which the positivist sciences deluded themselves "with the image of a reality-in-itself". But, while it brings to consciousness the "interlocking of knowledge with interests", phenomenology "succumbs to another objectivism" constituted by the way "it derived *pseudonormative power* from the *concealment of its actual interest*"[150]. Habermas became a fierce critic of postmodernism, charging that it too was motivated by interests that it kept concealed; in effect, according to Habermas, it was itself a 'totalizing perspective'. And for our present study Habermas offers an identification of scientism (although with a broader-than-natural meaning) as follows. "The glory of the sciences is their unswerving application of their methods without reflecting on knowledge-constituting interests." This self-ignorance has a "protective function". It avoids the "risks that appear once the connection of knowledge and human interest has been comprehended..." But "As soon as the objectivist illusion is turned into an affirmative *Weltanschauung* [world-view], methodologically unconscious necessity is perverted to the dubious virtue of a scientistic profession of faith."[151] Thus, according to Habermas, all knowledge is constituted by interest. Science, like all other knowledge is constituted by interest; it does not escape into a supposed objective reality. It is fine for scientists to pursue their knowledge without concern for its philosophical foundations and background interests, with a naive illusion that it is "pure theory". But if science develops into a "positivistic self-understanding" [what I call scientism] this leads to the "substitution of technology for enlightened action".

What has happened in more recent decades is that this critique of science has been radicalized. The movement in Western thought toward the empowering of individual *perspectives*, has taken hold in the academy and society. The obvious examples spring to mind: feminism has given rise to *Womens' Studies*; the civil rights movement with its critique of racism has led to departments of *African Studies*. Developing nations have asserted the significance of their anti-colonial perspective. Environmentalist priorities are one of the growing emphases of the moment. Every different *interest group* asserts the special value of their opinions and perspectives. The main qualification for being accorded this special perspective status is the ability to point to some historic persecution, exploitation, or disadvantage experienced by the interest. The clamor by every group to establish its victim-hood is the result. Science has enjoyed a high status in the academy and in society for so long that it becomes a natural target of the critiques of the perspectives. It therefore joins Christianity as one of the most reviled 'totalizers'. Despite a few recent fitful and unconvincing attempts, science has not succeeded in acquiring a victim-hood aura to protect it from attack as the ascendant interest groups do, by rendering 'immoral' any criticism of its interests or of its arguments. The fact that science has not descended to the strategy of relativism and victim-hood is heartening to most scientists. In our more optimistic moments, we think that our knowledge is robust enough, even in today's intellectual maelstrom, to be sustained by stronger pragmatic and factual realities. But the understandable feeling of being embattled has the unfortunate effect of deafening the ears even to well-grounded criticisms. So scientists are perhaps even less open to a renunciation of scientistic tendencies when they sense that all of science is under attack.

My present purpose is not to attack science; it is to understand it and distinguish it from the totalization that is very definitely present in scientism. But to do so in the existing intellectual climate risks being seen as allied with the radical perspectivism of the age. That's one reason for citing some examples here of what I regard as unfounded multicultural science critiques.

Most of these extreme perspectivist critiques are in the form of sociological analysis, and appear to reflect a view that "... it makes good sense to think of the natural sciences as a sub-field of the critical social sciences"[152]. It hardly needs to be said that to most scientists this opinion is laughable. There is, no doubt, much to learn and gain by sociological study of the sciences. Moreover there is probably something (but I suspect not very much) to learn from explicitly perspectivist studies of science. The radicals suppose, though, that the very content of science is determined by the oppressive sociological forces of the past and present, and that the future incorporation of the victimized perspectives will change that content. Here is an illustration from feminist Sandra Harding's *Whose Science? Whose Knowledge?* (1991).

> Women need sciences and technologies that are *for* women and that are for women in *every class, race, and culture*. Feminists (male and female) want to close the gender gap in scientific and technological literacy, to invent modes of thought and learn the existing techniques and skills that will enable women to get more control over the conditions of their lives. Such sciences can and must benefit men, too — especially those marginalized by racism, imperialism, and class exploitation; the new

> sciences are not to be *only* for women. But it is time to
> ask what sciences would look like that were *for* "female
> men," all of them, and not primarily for the white, West-
> ern, and economically advantaged "male men" toward
> whom benefit from the sciences has disproportionately
> tended to flow.[153]

This example is typical of the rhetorical progression of such critiques. It advocates for a representative inclusion of the interest
group in the practice of science "to close the gender gap"; and it
thinks that this will lead to different scientific outcomes "modes
of thought ... techniques and skills" that empower and benefit the
group. It asserts that empowerment of this group will benefit all
worthy victimized groups by breaking the hegemony of the powerful, who are white, Western, economically advantaged, male, and
so on.

Although scientists see this critique that "Science is politics by
other means"[154] as overdrawn, they generally do accept justifiable
criticism of the scientific culture and they have sought practical
ways to do something about it. However, scientists are first aston-
ished and then dismissive when the critics proceed to the stage of
hinting at a desirable transformation of the content of science itself,
as do questions like "what sciences would look like that were for
...?" The sociological critiques detect bias not just at the social level,
but infesting the entire hierarchy of scientific research and understanding: "Androcentric biases can enter the research process at
every stage, as critics have shown. They enter in the concepts and
hypotheses selected, in the design of research, and in the collection
and interpretation of data."[155]

Scientists see this as silly. They consider pure fantasy the idea
that the laws of biology or physics are what they are because of
an ethically deficient social organization of science, or that natural
laws could and would be different if that deficiency were corrected.
Yet that is what the more extreme perspectivist critics are alleging.
Sociological criticism of science has a substantial history, long predating its recent guises. For example Marxist critiques of science
as the servant of capitalism were predominant in the first half of
the twentieth century. The recent perspectivist critiques often echo
some of the same themes, but with an extremism that goes beyond

their historic roots. Here is an illustration of this sort of argument from the perspective of the developing world.

> ... the principal laws of science, like the second law of thermodynamics, arose out of industrial experience. The law of entropy resulted from efforts to improve the working of the steam engine so as to advance industry. ... Seshadri [C.V.Seshadri "Development and Thermodynamics" (Madras: Murugappa Chettiar Research Centre, 1982)] finds the second law ethnocentric, and therefore outside science. Because of its industrial origins, it has presented a definition of energy in a way calculated to favor the allocation of resource for the purposes of big industry, often depriving the rest of the population of them.[156]

> ... The efficiency criterion stipulates that the loss of available energy in a conversion becomes smaller as the temperature at which the conversion is effected is higher above the ambient. Therefore, high temperatures are of high value and so are resources such as petroleum, coal, etc., which can help achieve such high temperatures. In this sense, the law of entropy provides a guideline for extraction of resources and their utilization.

However sympathetic one might be to the needs of the third world, including the need for culturally appropriate technology, it strikes a scientist as absurd to argue that the second law of thermodynamics is ethnocentric because of the historical situation in which it arose. Alvares, the author of this critique, says further that "Colonialism added a new burden on modern science: it was compelled to claim a monopoly in knowledge in order to retain its claimed superiority. This monopoly is based on the premise that all other forms of acquisition or accumulation of knowledge, all other epistemologies, are worthless, antiquated, magical, and must be eliminated."[157] His criticism of a scientistic claim to a monopoly in knowledge may be justified. Indeed, I am arguing it is. But his diagnosis that colonialism forced scientism upon science, is unconvincing, and his supposition that the content of science would be different without it, is incredible.

In the same volume we learn from Vanda Shiva "The fact, however, is that reductionist science itself often resorts to misinformation and falsehood in order to establish its monopoly on knowledge."[158] And that "Reductionism, however, is not an epistemological accident. It is related to the needs of a particular form of economic organization. The reductionist worldview, the industrial revolution and the capitalist economy were the philosophical, technological and economic components of the same process." So that by a leap that defies common sense "Stripped of the power the state invests it with, such a science can be seen to be cognitively weak and ineffective in responding to problems posed by nature. As a system of knowledge about nature, reductionist science is weak and inadequate; as a system of knowledge for the market, it is powerful and profitable." This is just about the direct opposite of what idealist scientists have thought. For most of its history, science has been practiced by amateurs, leisured gentlemen, clerics, and relatively impoverished professors. Their dedication was inspired not by power or profit, but by the chance to find out something lasting and true about nature. The military industrial complex of the last sixty years has exploited that knowledge. It turns out, somewhat to the surprise of the pure scientists of yesteryear, to be immensely powerful. But whether they have been subverted by the promise of power and wealth or not, scientists as a rule honestly believe that knowledge is the source of power, rather than that state power is the source of scientific status or the alternative to knowledge.

7.4   Gathering the threads

We have seen in this chapter that what motivates a great deal of postmodern anti-science or science criticism is, *by its own account*, a view that science is a *totalizing metanarrative*, ensnared in the promulgation of its own *legitimation*, which improperly excludes the perspectives, the narratives, of other non-scientific discourses. In my terminology, this is a critique of scientism, not really of a properly-understood science. But the critics do not distinguish between science and scientism. Quite possibly, if offered the invitation to make that distinction, many critics would refuse, and continue to indict science. Such a combative stance is consistent with the rhetoric of many scientists who likewise refuse to draw the distinction. The extent to which this refusal on both sides is a principled stand or a tactical ploy is not something that anyone can really disentangle except by speculation. My observation is that failing, or refusing, to make that distinction, and continuing to identify scientism with science, is the main fuel of the science wars. In this sense one can regard postmodernism as a justified rejection of scientism, distorted by misidentification on both sides of the discussion into an unjustified rejection of natural science.

Postmodern characterizations of non-scientific topics helpfully attribute to them the traits of *narrative*, and to their systematic study the character of *hermeneutics*. If one disavowed scientism, one would have no need for hesitation in calling the valid outcomes of this study *knowledge* — and I do so.

Chapter 8
The Technological Fix

A society dominated by scientism is a society that looks first, and sometimes only, for a technological fix for every challenge that confronts it.

8.1 Science and technology

As we've seen, science is intimately related to technology in the first place because science is precisely the kind of knowledge that gives rise to technology. Technology requires that the world respond to the application of controlling and manipulating influences in a reproducible way. The basis of technology is just this reliable response. And technology is the most convincing demonstration of the reality of scientific knowledge. Science is persuasive in the modern world not because of some theoretical argument that shows it to have particular methods or approaches that are guaranteed to yield objective knowledge, but because it gives rise to understanding that works. Nothing so convincingly demonstrates human understanding of compressible fluid dynamics as to fly in a Boeing 747. A laser pointer that can shine with exquisite focus for hundreds of meters is a palpable demonstration that we really understand light, and the quantum mechanics that governs its emission. There is no more convincing proof of our understanding of bacterial diseases than to experience the dramatic cure by penicillin of an otherwise fatal infection. No intellectual argument has anything like the impact of useful technology.

The intimate relationship between science and technology has existed since the scientific revolution. Before it, the technologies, 'Arts' as they were called, existed primarily in the craft guilds who practiced and made their livelihoods from technical skills that were passed on largely by apprenticeship and inheritance. Although we today might think of their knowledge as a kind of science — and it was frequently systematic and reliable by the standards of the day

— it was generally not an intellectual enterprise. Bacon's vision of intellectual science as enabling the relief of man's estate helped to justify the rejection of the sterile arm-chair philosophizing of the schoolmen. And it helped to bring together the intellectuals and the craftsmen.

The relationship is not, and has never been, a one-way street. Science gives rise to technology, but just as importantly technology has always been an enabler as well as a motivater of science. Galileo made his name as a scientist and made the case for the Copernican solar system not by his world-leading understanding of dynamics, but by being an early-adopter of the latest technology: the telescope. He did not invent it. But he did construct telescopes that outstripped the power of any others of the day, and he was the first to turn them on the heavens and interpret what he saw in physical terms. The leading edge of today's astronomical and cosmological knowledge is likewise completely dependent upon technology, for example on the power of space flight to place in orbit, above the obscuring blanket of the atmosphere, telescopes that detect ultra-violet radiation, x-rays, and gamma rays, as well as light. Thus, even the least applied of subjects, such as astronomy, has always depended on technology for its progress.

The reciprocal dependence, of technology on science, though hardly requiring much argument to establish it today, was actually far less obvious until fairly recently. The inventors who brought profitable techniques to practical industry, and the philosophers whose aim was to understand the world of nature, were historically different breeds and different classes. In nineteenth century England, Michael Faraday, chemist and electrical scientist, was highly unusual in being from a working-class background. His public lectures at the Royal Institution made him more of an entertainer than a technologist, though he was consulted by the Admiralty about lighthouses. William Thompson, gentleman Professor at the University of Glasgow and a founding father of thermodynamics and the principle of conservation of energy in the mid nineteenth century, made handsome profits investing in transatlantic telegraph cables, for which his scientific expertise proved invaluable. But applications such as these were still almost incidental to scientists' activities, and the professionalization of science itself was only beginning to move it from the domain of the gifted amateur gentleman or professor to the focused professional. Engineering remained a discipline largely independent of natural science, and was held in a degree of disdain by the pure scientists, even in the early twentieth century.

A part of the self-image of science was disinterested objectivity, a picture that science was *pure* knowledge, free from commercial self-interest, based upon a virtuous commitment to rationality, whose content was purely factual, but whose applications might be good or bad. It maintained that image by portraying the application of science to industry, commerce and warfare, as a separate, subsequent step, in which clearly value-judgements *were* made, while science itself was morally neutral, simply opening up possibilities. During and after the Second World War, the power of science to bring to pass new technologies that could remake the world became more widely accepted. Governments adopted policies that explicitly supported scientific research precisely because it led to technological development. And academic engineering increasingly began to focus on Engineering-Science, technology based on science. That process has led now to the acceptance of a very intimate relationship between science and technology, which hardly recognizes the distinctions of an earlier age.

8.2 Technological critiques

Critiques of science and technology have progressed through a long development. They first began with the industrial revolution, as protest against its displacement of workers from agricultural to urban employment, and from individual craftsmanship to factory production. The critics of the industrial revolution included not only the Romantics, who regretted the alienation from 'nature' that it brought and who represented an anti-scientistic viewpoint; but they also included those who were thoroughly scientistic. Marx, for example, thought his social science could identify the oppressive capitalistic traits of those who controlled the means of production, and point the way toward a full liberation of the workers in a future communist organization of society. The Luddite movement, of 1811 onward, was more directly aimed at technology. In this case, the mechanization of the textile industry was the target, and the Luddites broke into factories and destroyed their machines. Actually, the mechanization had been taking place for at least half a century prior to that time, but the increasing introduction of power looms and similar technology provoked impoverished workers to fear further degradation of their working and living conditions. The popular movement was quelled only by harsh laws that made the destruction of textile machinery a capital offense.

The Luddites lent their name, of course, to the supposed *irrational* rejection of technology. It is uncertain the extent to which their hardship can really be attributed to the technological changes, and it is certain that there were many other important influences, such as the economic exhaustions of the Napoleonic Wars. Unfortunately the charge of irrationality became entrenched in all arguments about the adoption of technology, even till today.

The twentieth century saw increasing reaction against not merely the displacement of the poor, but the dehumanization of all of society. However, it was accompanied by an even more widespread countervailing enthusiasm for technology, as shiny new labor-saving machinery appeared in the household as well as in the factory.

Perhaps the epitome of the critique of technology came in Jacques Ellul's *La Technique* published in French in 1954, whose English translation appeared as *The Technological Society* in 1964. As John Wilkinson wrote in his translator's introduction "*The Technological Society* is a description of the way in which an autonomous technology is in process of taking over the traditional values of every society without exception, subverting and suppressing these values to produce at last a monolithic world culture in which all nontechnological difference and variety is mere appearance."[159]

Ellul attributes the emergence of the full-scale industrial revolution to the joint occurrence of five factors

> (1) a very long technical maturation or incubation without decisive checks before the final flowering; (2) population growth; (3) a suitable economic milieu; (4) the almost complete plasticity of a society malleable and open to the propagation of technique; (5) a clear technical intention, which combines the other factors and

> directs them toward the pursuit of the technical objective.[160]

The subsequent development has led to a new overwhelming culture of technique that possesses five characteristics. The first, Ellul dubs *automatism*, by which he means the "technical movement becomes self-directing" towards the most efficient methods. "The human being is no longer in any sense the agent of choice." "...everything that is not technique is being eliminated. The challenge to a country, an individual, or a system is solely a technical challenge."[161] The second characteristic is *self-augmentation*, with the result that "1. In a given civilization, technical progress is irreversible. 2. Technical progress tends to act, not according to an arithmetic, but according to a geometric progression." and then "technique, in its development, poses primarily technical problems which consequently can be resolved only by technique."[162] The third characteristic is translated *monism*, by which he means that "it ought never to be said: on the one side, technique; on the other the abuse of it." "... all techniques are inseparably united". Technique does not evolve with an end in view of human good. "It evolves in a purely causal way: the combination of previous elements furnishes the new technical elements. There is no purpose or plan that is being progressively realised."[163] Self-augmentation and monism combine to provide the fourth characteristic, *the necessary linking together of techniques*, by which organizational technique of necessity emerges from prior techniques and comes to dominate economics, commerce, society, and the state through military, police, administration, and politics. Finally we arrive at the fifth characteristic, *technical universalism*, whereby technology spreads to all geographic regions and subverts all cultures until it has "taken over the whole of civilization"[164]

Together this leads to a self-sufficiency of technique that constitutes the usurpation of humankind's highest aspirations. "Since [technique] has put itself beyond good and evil, it need fear no limitation whatever. It was long claimed that technique was neutral. Today this is no longer a useful distinction. The power and autonomy of technique are so well secured that it, in its turn, has become the judge of what is moral, the creator of a new morality."[165] In our technical age "Everything today seems to happen as though ends disappear, as a result of the magnitude of the very means at our disposal." And though "Comprehending that the proliferation of means brings about the disappearance of ends, we have become preoccupied with rediscovering a purpose or a goal", this is "merely a pious hope with no chance whatsoever of influencing technical evolution."[166] Jacques Ellul, remarkably for a theologian, offers no solution, nor any hope for one.

Neil Postman, almost forty years later, in *Technopoly, the surrender of culture to technology* echoes many of the same substantive charges, although with a very different style. His neologism 'Technopoly' has gathered even less currency as a popular term for the excesses of technology than scientism has in respect of science. But, in short, his meaning and the distinction with the more familiar word 'technocracy' is as follows. Culture was in the state of technocracy when "two opposing world-views — the technological and the traditional — coexisted in uneasy tension." But "With the rise of Technopoly, one of those thought-worlds disappears. Technopoly eliminates alternatives to itself..." "It makes them invisible and therefore irrelevant. And it does so by redefining what we mean by religion, by art, by family, by politics, by history, by truth, by privacy, by intelligence, so that our definitions fit its new requirements. Technopoly, in other words, is totalitarian technology."[167] This description parallels in the technical realm what I have been calling scientism. But Postman and Ellul both perceive a degree of compulsion in Technopoly that goes beyond the intellectual, and beyond science.

For both these commentators, and many others, a key feature of the critique of technology revolves around what is often called (elsewhere) the *technological imperative*: "The idea that if something could be done, it should be done" or perhaps, from Ellul's perspective of the automatism of technology: if something can be done, it *will* be done.

I have emphasized the fact that the traffic between science and technology has always been both ways. Each has enabled and, to a degree, motivated and justified the other. It would be a mistake, historically and even logically, to identify one as the progenitor and the other as the progeny. For much the same reason, I refrain from identifying scientism as either the parent or the child of Technopoly. A more accurate metaphor might be to regard them as mutually supportive siblings. Postman and Ellul, from their stance as critics of Technopoly, speak of scientism as a facet of Technopoly. Without wishing to contradict their perspective, in this study of scientism, I treat Technopoly instead as a facet of scientism. Postman summarizes his view of scientism, a word he uses mostly in the same way as Hayek, thus

> It is not merely the misapplication of techniques such as quantification to questions where numbers have nothing to say; not merely the confusion of the material and social realms of human experience; not merely the claim of social researchers to be applying the aims and procedures of natural science to the human world. Scientism is all of these, but something profoundly more. It is the desperate hope, and wish, and ultimately the illusory belief that some standardized set of procedures called "science" can provide us with an unimpeachable source of moral authority, a suprahuman basis for answers to questions like "What is life, and when, and why?"[168] ...

Although I recognize the *moral* dimension of scientism, which Postman is at pains to point out. I see scientism as the broad intellectual foundation of Technopoly. If from the perspective of Postman and Ellul, scientism is *theoretical* Technopoly, then from my perspective, Technopoly is *applied* scientism. My discussion is aimed more at examining and understanding the theoretical underpinning of the technological domination of modern society, rather than setting forth the empirical results. It may seem now that Technique is in practice sufficiently automatic, sufficiently self-propelled, that it needs no theoretical justification. Yet theories have consequences, and if we understand scientism, we have the intellectual equipment to contradict and undermine Technopoly's foundations.

Unlike Ellul, Postman is willing, however tentatively, given the immensity of the task, to offer suggestions for solutions. These are of two types. The first, for the individual, is to be a loving resistance fighter. The second, for society, is to reform education.

Postman, who thinks that America is the only country so far to have succumbed to Technopoly, says that to be a loving freedom fighter "you must always keep close to your heart the narratives and symbols that once made the United States the hope of the world". And the resistance is expressed as aphoristic traits. The freedom fighters are those, for example, who "refuse to accept efficiency as the pre-eminent goal of human relations", "refuse to allow psychology or any "social science" to pre-empt the language and thought of common sense", "take the great narratives of religion seriously and who do not believe that science is the only system of thought capable of producing truth", "who admire technological ingenuity but do not think it represents the highest possible form of human achievement"[169]. His curriculum reform would be configured around the theme of "The Ascent of Humanity", drawing inspiration from Jacob Bronowski's approach (but side-stepping the political-incorrectness of the title of his early 1970s TV series). Its content "must join art and science. But we must also join the past and the present" so that "all subjects are presented as a stage in humanity's historical development; in which the philosophies of science, of history, of language, of technology, and of religion are taught; and in which there is a strong emphasis on classical forms of artistic expression."[170]

8.3   Energy and environment

My physics research interests are motivated by the attempt to make fusion energy available on the human scale. Nuclear energy is a million times greater per unit mass than the electromagnetic chemical energy that we derive, for example, from hydrocarbons or sunlight. As a result, it offers the possibility of generating energy sustainable for many millennia, while generating only tiny amounts of waste. Present nuclear power is derived from *fission*, the breaking up of heavy nuclei like uranium, which releases energy that is used to drive electricity generators. The stars are powered instead by *fusion*, the combining together of light nuclei like hydrogen to form heavier ones, which also releases energy. Fusion reactions require very energetic collisions between the reacting nuclei, so as to overcome their mutual electrical repulsion. The high temperatures, fifty million degrees Celsius or so, required to cause such energetic interactions are present in the center of the sun and stars. But such temperatures require an immaterial form of containment.

Any solid container would be immediately vaporized. Creation's remarkable fusion reactors, the stars, are based on gravitational confinement of the ionized atoms, the 'plasma', that is their fuel. But gravity is such a weak force that it requires stars to be very large. To make a fusion reactor on the human scale calls for a different, stronger force of confinement. For this purpose we use magnetic fields to confine the plasma. Figure 8.1 illustrates the configuration we use. Fusion energy on the human scale has proven far more difficult than fission. The first fission reactor was operational just a few years after nuclear fission was discovered. Fusion research during the past 60 years has succeeded in releasing 16 megawatts of power for a second or so, but is only now on the threshold of a scientific demonstration of a controlled fusion reaction, and still many years from engineering practicality.

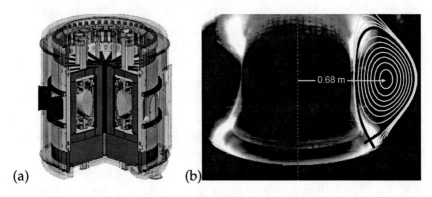

(a)   (b)

Figure 8.1: Cut-away diagram of the 'tokamak' plasma confinement device (a). The plasma is the light toroidal (doughnut-shaped) region surrounded by a vacuum chamber and various circular and rectangular magnetic coils. They are supported by a heavy steel structure to withstand the magnetic forces. In (b) a wide-angle video frame of the plasma itself is shown. Only the edge radiates in visible light. The center is too hot; it radiates predominantly x-rays. On the frame are superimposed a section through the magnetic surfaces which confine the plasma, one inside the other like the layers of an onion. This MIT experiment is relatively compact, having a radius of just 0.68m.

I mention my research interests as background to matters that have in recent years acquired increasing prominence in public concern and discussion — energy and the environment. In the west, everyone is now sensitized to the challenge that our modern technology has brought. What to do about the environmental impact of the technologies of modern society. The usage of fossil-fuel energy, the foundation of the industrial revolution and modern society, is, we now realize, causing the accumulation in the upper atmosphere of carbon dioxide and other greenhouse gases. The prospect we now face is of global climate change with consequences that, while uncertain, may well be disastrous for life on earth. In a sense this is just one of many environmental impacts of our scientifically and technologically advanced and empowered society. But it is a particularly significant impact because, unlike the pollution of many industrial wastes, it is not local, but global. It afflicts the whole planet, not just the societies that caused the (perhaps unintended) pollution and enjoyed the (intended) technological benefits. So a question that faces industrialized societies is how to preserve the benefits that the availability of abundant energy has brought, without doing untold harm to the Earth.

For the vast majority in undeveloped nations, however, the emergency is different. For them, who subsist on a tiny fraction of the consumption characteristic of the developed world, who use as little as one hundredth of the energy per capita of the west, the challenge is how to obtain access to their basic needs: clean water, food, shelter, and a meager level of energy for cooking and light. For developing and industrializing nations, the issues are different again. They are how to obtain the capital to construct the technical infrastructure: roads, dams, electric power plants, and so on; and how to develop the human capital, in the form of education and social coherence, that will enable them to obtain the benefits of being a competitive part of a global technical economy. For the developing world, the environment is a concern, but they don't have the luxury of a detached policy debate about how to avoid global warming. Their overwhelming immediate priorities are different.

When most westerners think about energy and the environment, most often the question they are asking is something like "what technologies are going to contribute to solving this problem". In other words, they are looking for the technological fix.

From my parochial perspective as a scientist in energy research, that's good for me. It means that one of the few unopposed priorities within recent policy debates has been government support of science and technology which holds promise for clean energy. But while I do think it is useful and appropriate to do research in energy, and I've done it most of my career, I am concerned about the unrealistic expectations that our society has for future technology.

This is based on simple arithmetic applied to the global situation. Right now the average per-capita energy consumption of the world is less than one fifth of the US rate. So if a global population of six billion (optimistically) were to achieve the rate of consumption of the US, it would require five times as much global consumption as at present. Such a consumption would not be sustainable even if by some extraordinary (and unexpected) breakthrough we were able to replace all but 10% of the fossil fuels with non-emitting sources. Even the most ambitious and unrealistic of political hopes, to replace 80% of US fossil energy with sustainable forms by 2050, is not enough. It would not lead, of itself, to a sustainable global energy scenario compatible with the basic aspirations of the rest of humanity.

In this sense, there simply is no technological fix for energy.

But it is worse even than that. Every technological innovation of significant scope has foreseen or unforeseen consequences. The side-effects or even direct effects are themselves the cause of new challenges. It is not just that technology can be used for good or ill. It is that even the good effects themselves may lead to new challenges, and that they may be accompanied by unexpected consequences. Take as an example the health benefits that result from the understanding of the causes of disease. The demonstration by Louis Pasteur in the mid nineteenth century that a whole spectrum of diseases and decay arise from germs, not from spontaneous generation, led to new strategies of public health and disease prevention and treatment that eventually transformed the survival prospects of humans in the west. Mortality rates dropped dramatically, and much suffering was obviated. As a result of this and other technical and social developments, which resulted in increased food supplies, the population of England, for example, *quadrupled* during the nineteenth century. The population growth, and the growth of consumption that accompanies it, is the primary cause of the adverse environmental impacts in the form of urbanization, pollution, and deforestation. Thus the environmental challenges of today are a direct result of past technological development. And the problems arise not from the failures of unnecessary technologies, but from the successes of technologies devoted to basic human needs of food, sanitation, health, and so on. Every technological *solution* leads to new technological *problems*. Often the new problems appear to be greater than the older ones, and if this is so, then we have a vicious spiral in which ever greater technological resources are chasing ever growing technological problems, with the new solutions leading to even greater challenges. Each 'fix' just winds the spiral higher into greater problems. Just as the successes of health technologies have led to greater problems, so the successes of energy technologies, of every kind, have provided the ability to affect the environment ever more powerfully, and ever more difficult challenges have arisen.

This pessimistic scenario is not pre-ordained. In terms of a mathematical analysis of the dynamics of the system, what I have described is an unstable 'diverging' situation, with ever increasing demand. It is also possible that there might be a stable 'converging' situation, where the new problems caused by each 'fix' are smaller than the prior problems, in which case the system will soon stabilize and the perturbations die away. Unfortunately there is no sign that technological fixes lead to stable solutions for society as a whole. What's more, economists have spent a hundred years proclaiming that growth (the unstable case) is good; indeed their doctrine is that economic growth is the most important goal that government ought to promote.

In essence the problem of environmental sustainability is that the world has too many people wanting too much stuff. Technology cannot fix that. And more often than not it makes the problems worse because of the additional power that it provides. A sustainable world is one in which the reasonable aspirations are not for the life-styles of the rich and famous or indeed of the developed west, but for a globally 'middle-class' economic level characterized by bicycles, buses, nourishing food, and adequate housing and communications. For the west, such a sustainable future will certainly mean reduced consumption, but it need not mean a less satisfying life. It will require a change of *values* away from the the consumer-driven culture. Values are not a matter of technology or science. The types of changes we are going to need to achieve sustainability are not technological.

I do not mean that there are no technological improvements, or that technological improvements are useless. Technological improvements can be very beneficial, and the science that enables them is worth-while. It is just that those technological benefits are insufficient in themselves and may serve as a distraction from more fundamental issues. It is that not all the important solutions are technological. Many of the most intractable challenges of society are not technical, they are human, and moral. Technology is of little use for those challenges. Just as it is an erroneous scientism which supposes that all the real knowledge is science, it is an erroneous technocentrism which supposes that all the efficacious solutions to our challenges are technological. But the one error leads to the other. The search for the technological fix follows from the scientistic world-view.

Chapter 9

Scientism and religion

9.1 Militant atheism

The relationship between religion and the natural sciences, as we have noted in some previous chapters, is currently of great social significance. It is the subject of ongoing legal battles, the focus of concern about education, and a topic that provokes passionate debate. There has over the past decade been a spate of aggressive atheist polemic books arguing that religious belief is disproved by science, explained away by science, and in any case intrinsically evil. The phrase recently used most widely to denote these polemics is 'the New Atheism'. We'll have a little bit more to say about the extent to which their arguments are new; but certainly they are immoderate, dismissive, disdainful, and discourteous. Some have called them 'hysterical atheism', but let's settle for a more neutral adjective, 'militant'[171]. These militant atheist arguments are notable for their assertive scientism. We will examine a few examples.

Science disproves religion

Richard Dawkins' *The God Delusion* is perhaps the best known of the militant atheist books of the early twenty-first century. In it Dawkins is pretty much as direct as he can be. About the existence of God he writes "Either he exists or he doesn't. It is a scientific question; one day we may know the answer, ..."[172] Or again, "Contrary to [T.H.] Huxley, I shall suggest that the existence of God is a scientific hypothesis like any other. ... God's existence or non-existence is a scientific fact about the universe, discoverable in principle if not in practice."[173] Actually Dawkins' book does not "suggest", or even argue, it assumes, and repeatedly asserts that the question is a scientific question. For example he later states "The presence or absence of a creative super-intelligence is unequivocally a scientific question ..."[174] It then goes on at length to try to show that, regarded as a scientific question, the existence of God has poor evidence in its support. The question of the strength of the evidence is important but that's not what I want to focus on. I am drawing attention to the remarkable fact that Dawkins asserts that the existence of God is a scientific question. Why so remarkable? Well, if there were ever any meaningful distinction between "scientific" questions and other possible types of question, surely the distinction between scientific, *physical* questions (about nature) and *metaphysical* questions (about God) is the most obvious and traditional one. But Dawkins does not even bother to acknowledge the possibility of such a distinction. Instead he castigates those who regard themselves as agnostics as failing to pay attention to the scientific evidence (or lack thereof) in forming their theological opinions.

But since the existence of God has, from time immemorial, been considered *not* to be scientific question, or, to express it less anachronistically, not a question of natural philosophy, how can Dawkins get away with a bald assertion to the contrary? It is because he is relying on the widespread acceptance of his scientistic outlook, even among those who disagree with his theological views. The reference to "scientific fact" betrays his implicit assumption that all significant "facts" are scientific. Otherwise, it would be just as sensible to assert that the existence or non-existence of God is a *historical* fact, or a *legal* fact, or a *sociological* fact, or a *religious* fact.

In criticizing evolutionary paleontologist Stephen Jay Gould's avowed agnosticism and "Non Overlapping Magisteria" approach to the relationship between science and religion, Dawkins betrays himself further. He is at pains to oppose Gould and other scientists who draw back from using science to dictate metaphysical conclusions, because he thinks their reticence is motivated by the attitude "theologians have nothing worthwhile to say about anything else; let's throw them a sop and let them worry away at a couple of questions that nobody can answer and maybe never will."[175] Then he is overtaken by his own rhetoric in questioning Gould's *de facto* atheism by asking "On what basis did he make the judgement, if there is nothing to be said about whether God exists?"[176] Again this is elementary scientism at work. Actually, although Gould betrays his own substantial scientism by implying that religious matters are not matters of fact, he never asserts "there is nothing to be said about" God's existence. Gould's position appears to be that *science* does not prove or disprove it. Dawkins' "nothing to be said" reinterpretation of Gould is a distortion of his position, one that could be overlooked only by someone who completely takes for granted that the only sound basis for judgement is science. In other words, Dawkins' whole viewpoint is sustained by overriding scientism; without it his arguments are utterly hollow.

About questions of the historicity of Biblical events such as the resurrection, Dawkins says "There is an answer to every such question, whether or not we can discover it in practice, and it is strictly a scientific answer. The methods we should use to settle the matter, in the unlikely event that relevant evidence ever became available, would be purely and entirely scientific methods." Well, actually, no. These are questions about history. Natural science is almost completely powerless to answer historical questions about unique events of human history. If you insist that there is no useful evidence except that of "purely and entirely scientific methods", then of course there is not going to be such evidence. But that's not all the evidence that historians consider for these or for any events of history. Only a blatant scientism would insist on "purely and entirely scientific methods" for historical matters.

Science explains the mind

The evolutionary psychologist Steven Pinker is a more multidimensional figure in the scientistic front line. His book *How the Mind Works* is a an eclectic smorgasbord of ideas and opinions ranged artistically around the main course consisting of the advocacy of the computational theory of mind and of evolutionary psychology. Pinker contradicts many of the more mechanistic approaches to psychology such as Behaviorism. The "big picture" he says is "that the mind is a system of organs of computation designed by natural selection to solve the problems faced by our evolutionary ancestors in their foraging way of life." The computational theory of mind is that "beliefs and desires are *information*, incarnated as configurations of symbols. The symbols are physical states of bits of matter, like chips in a computer or neurons in the brain... the symbols corresponding to one belief can give rise to symbols corresponding to other beliefs ... The computational theory of mind thus allows us to keep beliefs and desires in our explanations of behavior while planting them squarely in the physical universe. It allows meaning to cause and be caused."[177]

"Beliefs and desires" as information is innocuous enough. Something like this 'computational' description (vague though it is) may well turn out to reflect reality, though science is a very long way from demonstrating that it does. More positively, Pinker clearly acknowledges that beliefs and desires can't possibly be excluded from a description of the actions of humans (or animals) without making nonsense of what we know introspectively to be the case for ourselves, and what we routinely use with great success to explain the behavior of others.

The evolutionary part of the argument, which is its major subject, is less persuasive. Pinker echoes Dawkins in saying "Natural selection is the only explanation we have of how complex life *can* evolve..." and dismissing teleological explanation with "One of the reasons God was invented was to be the mind that formed and executed life's plans. The laws of the world work forwards, not backwards: rain causes the ground to be wet; the ground's benefiting from being wet cannot cause the rain. What else but the plans of God could effect the teleology (goal directedness) of life on earth? Darwin showed what else."[178] This forwards-causality argument sounds plausible. But let's dig a bit deeper. Consider irrigation; it is precisely an example of the ground's benefitting from being wet causing the 'rain'. Irrigation does not happen to concrete patios, rocky outcrops, or lakes. Neither theist nor atheist attributes crop irrigation to something supernatural. It is attributed to the intentionality of the human agents that implemented it. But Pinker's argument dismissing God could equally well be applied as follows "One of the reasons human mind was invented was to be the mind that formed and executed life's plans. The laws of the world work forwards, not backwards: rain causes the ground to be wet; the ground's benefiting from being wet cannot cause the rain." Does Pinker really mean to imply, as his argument does, that we are in error when we speak of human intentionality as a cause? Presumably not, since he has allowed "beliefs and desires" as explanations. But then why is the intentionality explanation disallowed when God is referenced? Perhaps the Darwinian theory removed the *necessity* to posit a Creator, at least in respect of biological diversity, but it hardly rules one out. It disabled the argument from design as far as it is based on biological adaptation. Perhaps, by Dawkins' memorable overstatement, "Darwin made it possible to be an intellectually fulfilled atheist", but he did not make it impossible to be an intellectually fulfilled theist.

It seems that if Pinker, and those who argue in the same way, concede that humans and their intentionality are part of nature, then as a consequence there *can* in nature be such a thing as "backward causation", call it teleology, purpose, or intentionality. Either that or he must reverse his opinion that human intentionality is a process of the physical universe. He's trying to have it both ways. But either explanation in terms of intentionality is permitted by natural science, or else *human* (as well as divine) intentionality is ruled out in scientific explanations. Both Pinker and I think that intentional teleological explanations are not part of science's methods, that the laws of science do "work forwards, not backwards". My position is that intentionality is nevertheless a perfectly acceptable (indeed obvious) way to understand many phenomena, but that it is part of non-scientific knowledge and explanation. Pinker however is trapped in a contradictory scientism. Scientism's argument against God amounts in summary to the following.

> Purpose and personal agency is deliberately omitted in science's descriptions of the world. All real explanations are scientific explanations. Therefore all real explanations are impersonal; God, being personal, is not a real explanation. Impersonal evolutionary explanation remains.

But this argument, whether Pinker likes it or not, applies equally to any explanation in terms of *human* agency. It rules out human purpose as a valid explanatory factor, which seems to me, and to many, as a disqualifying fault.

A key weakness of evolutionary psychology is that it makes even fewer specific predictions than biological evolution. It is generally content instead with composing stories that are purported to explain some fact of psychology in terms of a hypothesized evolutionary history. In most cases such stories are independent of other phenomena. They are not integrated into a scientific explanatory web that would make them a robust part of theory; they are subject-specific, and regularly sound like special pleading or mere speculation. In this respect they contrast with evolutionary explanations of biology and physiology, some of which do gain strong plausibility from serving as consistent integrated explanations of multiple phenomena. Evolutionary psychologists often cite successes of evolutionary explanation in physiology or physical biology as arguments in favor of evolutionary psychology. This seems a non-sequitur. It is perhaps appropriate to explore the degree to which evolution can be extended to explain psychology, but sometimes the evolutionary enthusiasm of the advocates gets the better of them. For example, Pinker sets out to counter the claim that "natural selection is a sterile exercise in after-the-fact storytelling" by quoting Mayr

> The adaptationist question, "What is the function of a given structure or organ?" has been for centuries the basis of every advance in physiology. If it had not been for the adaptationist program, we probably would still not yet know the functions of thymus, spleen, pituitary, and pineal. Harvey's question "Why are there valves in the veins?" was a major stepping stone in his discovery of the circulation of the blood[179].

And Pinker immediately goes on "... everything we have learned in biology has come from an understanding, implicit or explicit, that the organized complexity of an organism is in the service of its survival and reproduction."

Pinker's escalation of Mayr's already hyperbolic claim is based on a fundamental confusion. He is confusing the search for *function*, which has indeed been a vital principle of biology for millennia, with *Darwinian* adaptation. Notice that when Mayr wrote about what had been the case "for centuries", it was only 123 years after Darwin's "Origin" was published. His example of the circulation of the blood dates from Harvey's notes in 1615. So Mayr could not justifiably have meant Darwinist when he said adaptationist. He presumably meant nothing more than that organs have valuable functions and we learn most by looking for their function. Certainly adaptation, in the sense of fitness to the environment, was noted long before anyone thought to address it in terms of evolution. But for the purpose of his argument Pinker makes the further unjustified leap that all biological knowledge comes from a focus on survival and reproduction, on a Darwinist program. He's implying in effect that, even before Darwin, biology proceeded only by a closet ("implicit") Darwinism. That is a ludicrous attempt to have it both ways. Darwin's ideas made a big difference to the progress of biology, but you can't prove it by saying that centuries before his time scientists were dependent on those ideas by some mysterious 'implicit' process.

The sort of psychological explanation that Pinker favors, which would escape the just-so-story criticism, is when predictions are made on the basis of evolutionary arguments, and prove to be correct. To cite such occasions is a principled approach to trying to demonstrate his case. How convincing is it? Here's one example concerning the question "How do parents make Sophie's Choice and sacrifice a child when circumstances demand it? Evolutionary theory predicts that the main criterion should be age ... right up until sexual maturity." In order to try to validate the 'prediction' based on life expectancy, that parents would not sacrifice an older child when a younger one is born (actually a postdiction, since this is already an observation in all existing cultures) he offers this. "When parents are asked to imagine the loss of a child, they say they would grieve more for older children, up until the teenage years. The rise and fall of anticipated grief correlates almost perfectly with the life expectancies of hunter gatherer children."[180] This "almost perfectly" is an almost perfectly gratuitous claim of numerical correlation that can't possibly be backed up. Grief can't be unambiguously quantified or measured. It obviously does not possess the Clarity required for such quantification. That's quite apart from the fact that the life expectancies of hunter gatherer children from prehistory are thoroughly speculative. Pinker refers to them (strangely) as "actuarial tables", although he appears to mean three numbers derived from guesses at mortality rates. Pinker devotes two pages to birth-order arguments like this, which by the way, even his own sources acknowledge to be considered by the majority in the field as a "mirage"[181]. Just pause for a moment from the evolutionary enthusiasm and consider the possibility that parents feel the way they report, not because of some evolutionarily programmed survival calculus, but because they realize that their love for their children grows through the shared experiences of their years together. This seems a far more sensible explanation, but of course it doesn't have the honorific of being scientific, or evolutionary. I suppose that is why Pinker prefers his actuarial tables.

When it comes to religion, Pinker no longer offers anything even as feeble as this in support of his opinions. "What we call religion in the modern West", he opines, "is an alternative culture of laws and customs that survived alongside those of the nation-state because of accidents of European history."[182] A profoundly ill-informed remark like this about the roots of western culture hardly constitutes an argument. It is of a piece with his purely rhetorical litany of the evils and self-interest of religion. Referring to witches, shamans, ancestor worship, the Bible, rites of passage, and so on, we are informed that although "Religion is not a single topic", it "cannot be equated with our higher, spiritual, humane, ethical yearnings". Clearly Pinker wants to leave the field free for ethics and 'spirituality' without having the unpleasantness of religion. We get the picture. He's against religion. But it would have made his diatribe more an integral part of his exposition of evolutionary psychology if he'd actually offered some evidence relating the two. Without it, we are in a position analogous to that of the two Victorian parishioners discussing the week's sermon:

"What was the sermon about?"

"Sin."

"And what did the Vicar say?"

"He was against it."

Pinker is of course completely at liberty to advocate his opinions about what people believe and why they believe it. In the case of religion he doesn't seem to think that he needs any justification for those opinions. In the case of many other beliefs, his book offers evolutionist stories in justification, or explanation, of his opinions about them. In all too many cases those justifying stories appear to be just-so stories, plausible sometimes — sometimes not — but hardly compelling, falling far short of what most scientists consider demonstration demands, yet all too often spuriously portrayed as some kind of scientific consensus, rather than what they are: his opinions.

Evolutionary psychology seems to draw much of its momentum from a fundamentalist scientism, which regards naturalist explanation as the only explanation worth having — even of the human mind and society. It has appeal as a way to incorporate consciousness and culture into a scientistic world-view, especially for those who want a stick with which to beat religion. But it falls far short of the convincing explanations science offers of the physical world, of nature. And it must do so, because much of psychology does not possess the characteristics that are required for scientific analysis.

Science explains away religion

Daniel Dennett, even though he is a philosopher, not a scientist, does try to offer evidence that relates evolutionary psychology to religion. Indeed, his *Breaking The Spell. Religion as a Natural Phenomenon* sets out to argue that religion is convincingly explained by evolutionary arguments about human psychology, and that it is thereby debunked.

Right from the outset, Dennett wants to draw on, and exploit indirectly, descriptions of the natural world for his argument. Religion is to be understood as analogous to a parasite invading our brains, causing us to set aside our personal interests in order to further the interests of an *idea*: religion. For his purposes, Dennett defines religions as "social systems whose participants avow belief in a supernatural agent or agents whose approval is to be sought"[183]: a definition, as he readily admits, crafted to avoid the "delicate issue" that the scientism that permeates his views is arguably a religious commitment and certainly a metaphysical commitment. Let's pass quickly over the difficulty that his definition excludes Confucianism, Buddhism, most Deism, and sundry other obviously religious teachings from its scope.

"Eventually", says Dennett, "we must arrive at questions about ultimate values, and no factual investigation could answer them". But it is "high time that we subject religion as a global phenomenon to the most intensive multidisciplinary research we can muster..."[184]. Even though (three pages later) this "might" *break the spell* of religion, we must carry out a "forthright, scientific, no-holds-barred investigation of religion as one natural phenomenon among many."[185] Wait a minute, though, what just happened to "questions about ultimate values", or "multidisciplinary"? Well, any *scientific* discipline is allowed, I guess. In Dennett's view the neglect of this scientific program has been because of a "largely unexamined mutual agreement that scientists and other researchers will leave religion alone"[186], but now we need to "set about studying religion scientifically". The study of religion as a natural phenomenon, Dennett asserts, is no more presupposing atheism than is the study of *Sports as a Natural Phenomenon* or *Cancer as a Natural Phenomenon*. The metaphor gets a bit out of hand when sports "miracles", by a strange transition, become the topic. But a miracle, and presumably by extension all of religion, requires us to "demonstrate it scientifically" Was Gould right that there is a boundary between two domains of human activity? Dennett shows his identification of "scientific" with "factual" by saying, "That is presumably a scientific, factual question, not a religious question"[187].

Dennett shares in the disingenuousness of most of the militant atheist writers when he bemoans the neglect of this project as caused by academic distaste begotten by biased prior studies, and portrays himself as representing a small band of "brave neuroscientists and other biologists who have decided to look at religious phenomena"[188]. The embattled potential-martyr self-portrait — even though he's not the first to paint it — is not particularly convincing for a best-seller author on the fashionable anti-religion band-wagon.

Dennett spends significant effort confronting the [supposed[189]] "worry that such an investigation might actually kill all the specimens" [of religion]. In the process we learn that "music is another natural phenomenon ... but is only just beginning to be an object of the sort of scientific study I am recommending", by which he means for example "why is it beautiful to us? This is a perfectly good biological question."[190] It does not appear to cross Dennett's mind that there might be structural or methodological reasons why scientific study of non-scientific topics like music and religion are circumscribed. His concern is to combat what he thinks is simply the "propaganda ... from a variety of sources" that religion is "out-of-bounds".

Dennett thinks that goods (moral and physical), for which he instances deliberately problematic cases: sugar, sex, alcohol, music, and money, can anchor their value only in "the capacity of something to provoke a preference response in the brain quite directly."[191] A co-evolutionary "bargain that was struck about fifty million years ago between plants blindly "seeking" a way of dispersing their pollinated seeds, and animals similarly seeking efficient sources of energy" explains "sharpening our ancestors' capacity to discriminate sugar by its "sweetness." " All values "started out as instrumental", as a biologically programmed preference conferring survival value, and "The same sort of investigation that has unlocked the mysteries [sic] of sweetness and alcohol and sex and money" needs to be applied to religion.

The argument here becomes puzzling and self-contradictory, which makes it hard to summarize. On the one hand a biologically costly activity (like religion) can persist only if "it somehow provokes its own replication ... to ask *what pays for* one evolved biological feature ... nicely captures the underlying balance of forces observed everywhere in nature, and *we know of no exceptions to this rule*"[192]. [Emphasis his. Actually organs like the human appendix are such exceptions if they are truly vestigial, as one major evolutionary argument maintains.] On the other hand, the spectrum of possible evolutionary explanations of religion includes both those that maintain there are benefits to religion, and also those that "we may call the *pearl* theory: religion is simply a beautiful by-product." By pearl theory, Dennet means that "religion is not *for* anything, from the point of view of biology; it doesn't benefit any gene, or individual, or group, or cultural symbiont." This description appears to be almost the same as what Gould and Lewontin call a *spandrel*. The word refers to the tapering triangular surface region that occurs where the bases of arches meet, notably in St Mark's Cathedral in Venice, where they are exquisitely decorated with mosaics that exploit their geometry. The spandrel might be thought the reason for the surrounding architecture, but this would invert the proper interpretation. The spandrel is a by-product of the overall architectural design. It is then used opportunistically by the mosaicists for their purposes[193]. In evolution, argue Gould and Lewontin, some things are not justified by an adaptationist story, they are just opportunistic by-products. Incidentally, their article exemplifies some penetrating criticism by biologists of evolutionary explanations in anthropology and psychology (E.O.Wilson being an author cited, and cannibalism the topic!). In fact their criticism is precisely of the position adopted by Dennett's "we know of no exceptions". Their whole point is that there *are* exceptions. I am tempted to

Figure 9.1: The spandrel referred to by Gould and Lewontin.

speculate that inventing a new metaphor (pearl) rather than adopting the one already in common currency (spandrel) is motivated
by Dennett's realization of this fact, and his desire to avoid promoting the ideas of two of the strongest critics of sociobiology and
evolutionary psychology: Gould and Lewontin.

Returning to the evolutionary explanation of religion, at times
it seems that Dennett is going to settle for the *pearl/spandrel* theory,
seeing religion as a result of "our overactive disposition to look
for agents"[194]. But it serves his approach better to remain non-
committal and follow a speculative and eclectic narrative pathway
that allows different (and sometimes incompatible) stories to serve
for different phenomena.

Dennett's ideas and those of E. O. Wilson and Pinker, which
he freely draws from, have been directly subjected to withering
criticism from many quarters. The more pertinent of these criticisms have come not from religious advocates, but from atheists
and agnostics. Perhaps the most telling are from evolutionary
biologists, such as Richard Lewontin and H. Allen Orr, from experts in cognitive psychology and computational linguistics such
as Stephen Chorover and Robert Berwick, and from philosophers
of science such as Philip Kitcher[195]. Pinker attributes this criticism

to left-wing ideology,[196] which he dates to the strong repudiation (in 1975) of Wilson's book *Sociobiology* in a review by 17 authors, including five Harvard professors[197]. But the more plausible reading is the one given originally in the critiques and re-expressed in a response to Pinker: "To us Darwinian fundamentalism is a form of irrationalism that, left un-checked, erodes the very theory of evolution it embraces."[198]

Experts who understand evolution, psychology, and the philosophy of science quite well, and who see the weakness of applying simplistic adaptationist arguments to society and religion don't want biology to be tarnished by the association.

It would not be very interesting go into greater detail and rebut the individual assertions that Dennett makes, or to dissect the logical argument, in so far as there is one. What I have been trying to do, though, is to draw attention to the all-pervasive scientism that informs his position. I see no reason to deny there is such a thing as human nature, or that human nature has been influenced by biological evolution as well as cultural evolution (meaning cultural development). It is not that discussing religion (or music, or anything else for that matter) from a scientific, or even a specifically evolutionary, perspective is improper or out-of-bounds. Rather, the fallacy is to imply that by doing so one is discovering their *real* explanation, the *scientific facts* that render superfluous all other descriptions, that *debunk* other claims of significance or knowledge. Actually it is even worse than that, and this is a feature of evolutionary argument that, I must admit, drives this physicist crazy. When Dennett says "The only honest way to defend" an explanation of religion in terms of God's actions is to consider "alternative theories of the persistence and popularity of religion and rule them out"[199], he is privileging so-called scientific explanation to the extent that in order to displace non-scientific explanation, even in non-scientific fields, it only has to meet the standard of *not being ruled out*. Since when has not being ruled out been enough to sustain a theory in science — or in any other discipline? This astonishingly lowered standard of what will count as a sufficient scientific demonstration and explanation is one reason for the low esteem in the natural science community, and elsewhere, of the specific theories of evolutionary psychology. Not only that, but since music is in fact well explained to the satisfaction of its professionals in ways that actually provide useful predictive knowledge but are expressed in non-scientific, musical terms, would it not be folly to discard those explanations in favor of a scientific analysis of music? If so, why would one think this way for religion? On what basis does it make sense to rule inadmissible religious explanation of the things of religion, and prefer a list of alternative, unsupported, speculative, *possible*, 'scientific' explanations? Only on the basis of scientism.

Summarizing the Militant Atheist Arguments

The popular militant atheist writers of this century spend a great deal of effort to retell anti-religious arguments which have a long history, dating from the nineteenth century and in some cases much earlier. That is only natural. However, the strong impression is given by writers that I've already cited and others such as Christopher Hitchens, and Sam Harris, that there is new knowledge that supports their arguments. It seems nearer the truth that there are some new twists on the old arguments. It is worth trying to gather them systematically, in the light of our discussion of scientism. In broad strokes, the case made by the militant atheists consists of three assertions: (1) God is a scientific hypothesis that has been essentially disproved[200] by science. (2) Evolution explains religion as nothing more than a natural phenomenon. (3) Religion is demonstrably evil.

(1) The existence of God is, in my view, a *factual* question. Either he exists or he doesn't. I see no reason to dispute this. But insisting that God's existence is a *scientific* question is a leap further that only scientism justifies.

To identify factual with scientific — with knowledge gained through the methods of the natural sciences — is the fallacy I am addressing. It is so much a part of modern thought that even Michael Polanyi falls into it in the midst of his systematic repudiation of scientism. In his book *Personal Knowledge*, Polanyi's intent is to describe knowledge as founded on personal commitment, more than a supposed objectivity. He says "We owe our mental existence predominantly to works of art, morality, religious worship, scientific theory and other articulate systems which we accept as our dwelling place and as the soil of our mental development. Objectivism has totally falsified our conception of truth, by exalting what we can know and prove, while covering up with ambiguous utterances all that we know and *cannot* prove, even though the latter knowledge underlies, and must ultimately set its seal to, all that we *can* prove."[201] This is an important thread of Polanyi's argument. It is that scientific knowledge depends for its existence upon much knowledge that is completely informal, unspecified, and unscientific, for example our understanding of the meaning of language. But Polanyi, most unhelpfully, identifies fact and natural science, for example when saying

> Ever since the attacks of philosophers like Bayle and Hume on the credibility of miracles, rationalists have urged that the acknowledgment of miracles must rest on the strength of factual evidence. But actually, the contrary is true: if the conversion of water into wine or the resuscitation of the dead could be experimentally verified, this would strictly disprove their miraculous nature. Indeed, to the extent to which any event can be established in the terms of natural science, it belongs to the natural order of things. However monstrous and surprising it may be, once it has been fully established as an observable fact, the event ceases to be supernatural. ... Observation may supply us with rich clues for our belief in God; but any scientifically convincing observation of God would turn religious worship into an idolatrous adoration of a mere object, or natural person.[202]

I completely concur with this important recognition that miracles, by their very character, cannot be scientifically proved. The main reason is that they are, practically by definition, not reproducible. If they were reproducible, they would instead be part of natural science, as Polanyi notes. But I find it most unhelpful and confusing when he implies that resting on "factual evidence" is equivalent to being "experimentally verified", or that being "established in the terms of natural science" means the same as "established as an observable fact". Polanyi wants to draw some fine distinctions: "The words 'God exists' are not, therefore, a statement of fact, such as 'snow is white', but an accreditive statement, such as ' "snow is white" is true'... " And the way he sees it is that God exists but "not as a fact — any more than truth, beauty, or justice exist as facts"[203]. Yet he immediately afterwards tells us that religious conviction depends on factual evidence. I want to be clearer than this. As far as I am concerned, there are scientific facts, and there are non-scientific facts, such as facts of history, jurisprudence, politics, personal acquaintance, and religion. Just as science is not all the knowledge there is, scientific facts are not all the facts there are. This is where I contradict the presumptions of the atheists.

A crucial recent move of the militant atheists is the argument that evolutionary explanations are intrinsically more satisfactory than others because they explain the complex in terms of the simple. Complex life is explained in terms of simpler chemical and physical laws of nature. In contrast it is argued that explaining anything in terms of God is to explain the simpler (things in the world) in terms of the *more complex* (God). We've dispensed with that argument in section 5.4.

(2) Explaining away religion as a natural phenomenon is not new. Seeing religion as a product of human psychology is as old as religion itself. Religions recognize the religious impulse as a universal part of human nature. They have not regarded the universality of spiritual yearning *per se* as a disproof of its truthfulness; on the contrary, they argue that a universal religious tendency is just what one might expect if God really exists. Unbelievers doubtless have thought religion was merely natural. Seeing religion as having developed over human history is a similarly ancient understanding, and is similarly accommodated by most faiths. For example, the Bible portrays God's self-revelation as developing through a sequence of events of history. Explicitly Darwinist explanations of religion are, practically speaking, as old as Darwin, even though the *Origin of Species* was at pains to avoid that hot issue. So there's nothing new in the idea that religion is a universal part of human nature or in atheists arguing that religion is *nothing but* a natural phenomenon. What is taken to be the recent arguments' additional plausibility is based upon the 'progress' in evolutionary psychology and sociobiology in recent decades. I have pointed out the controversial standing of these disciplines within the science community.

For the most part, the arguments that are offered to explain away religion are not scientific. We do not require any evolutionary theory to tell us that humans can deceive themselves, are prone to wishful thinking, exercise commitment to ideas, or have heightened ability to detect agents. These traits might lead to stubborn belief in the supernatural, which might be mistaken. But the ideas surrounding them are not scientific. They are pop-psychology to which is being attached a spurious honorific as if they were derived from scientific analysis. Yet, trite as they are, these are essentially the explanatory options that evolutionary psychology supposes itself to have 'discovered'. What's more, the polemicists have no basis for making specific choices between the options, so they leave them open. For their purposes, it does not matter which of the dozens of different evolutionary explanations might be correct. Provided we can be persuaded that *some* natural explanation or combination of explanations is going to work, their point is made. It does not matter to them whether the explanation is of the type that variously sees religion as having actual survival value for the group, or is of the type that sees it as a by-product of some other trait with survival value for the individual. The by-product theories include for example, "children are native teleologists and many never grow out of it"[204], "Could irrational religion be a by-product of the irrationality mechanisms that were originally built into the brain by selection for falling in love?"[205], "irrationally strong conviction is a guard against fickleness of mind", "hiding the truth from the conscious mind the better to hide it from others", "a tendency for humans consciously to see what they want to see."[206]. And if these biological-evolution explanations don't seem persuasive, one can always fall back on the concept of "memes", those hypothetical entities which "evolve" as viruses of the mind, providing the aura of scientific explanation to anthropological analysis of cargo cults, for example, but working just as well or as poorly, as far as I can see, for pretty much any fashion of the moment.

A truly scientific explanation ought to be different. It ought to be uncomfortable with the myriad of possible explanations (with no way to decide between them) not, like the polemicists, seemingly happy to pile up more and more possibilities as if their multiplicity somehow made the argument weightier. In any case, psychological analyses, whether evolutionary or not, do not decide whether the content of the beliefs analyzed is true. Dawkins might say that I believe in God because I was taught to do so by my parents, or because it comforts me to do so, or because I was programmed by evolution to do so. I might say that Dawkins disbelieves because he was taught so by his parents, or because it serves his desire for personal liberty to do so, or because he was programmed to disbelieve by evolution. The arguments on both sides are, I suppose, as convincing or unconvincing as one another, but they don't settle the question of whether God exists one way or the other. That's quite apart from the self-defeating logical status of psychological determinism. If one supposes that the ideas humans have are fully explained by a physical analysis of the brain, or by a behaviorist analysis of training, or an evolutionist description of inherited predispositions, or some combination of these or other 'scientific' analyses, then presumably the very belief that this is the case is determined just by these influences. If that were so, then why should we suppose the content of the belief to be true? In short, if our beliefs are determined by evolution or psychology, why should one believe so?

(3) The assertion that religion is evil is not really part of the scientism discussion, but for completeness I offer a few observations. The fact that religious organizations and individuals do evil is amply demonstrated by history. Blaize Pascal, a convinced and

$$1$$
$$1\ 1$$
$$1\ 2\ 1$$
$$1\ 3\ \ 3\ 1$$
$$1\ 4\ \ 6\ \ 4\ 1$$
$$1\ 5\ 10\ 10\ 5\ 1$$
$$\cdot\ \cdot\ \cdot\ \cdot\ \cdot\ \cdot\ \cdot\ \cdot\ \cdot\ \cdot\ \cdot\ \cdot\ \cdot$$

Figure 9.2: Pascal's Triangle. It is a table whose n^{th} row contains the coefficients of algebra's "binomial expansion" of $(x + y)^n$. Each entry is the sum of the adjacent values of the row above. The number of rows is unlimited.

earnest Christian, as well as a remarkable mathematician and scientist, said it in the mid seventeenth century "Men never do evil so completely and cheerfully as when they do it from religious conviction."[207] What Pascal recognized was, first, the simple point that people do evil intending and thinking that they do good when they do it from conviction. Second is the more complex point, that religious conviction has no monopoly on truth, yet is conviction's strongest form. In Steven Weinberg's memorable atheist aphorism, the claim becomes "With or without it, you'd have good people doing good things and evil people doing evil things. But for good people to do evil things, it takes religion." Weinberg's punch line is either patently false, since obviously many non-religious people who are otherwise 'good' do evil things, or else, if we charitably seek a serious meaning for the aphorism, it is an extrapolation of Pascal to the point of asserting that people do evil they take to be good only by *religious* conviction. But even that is false unless you remove the word religious, and say "only by conviction". The convictions that have led people to what one might term 'principled evil' have almost all *not* been religious during the past couple of hundred years. Realizing that, one is left only with the practically tautological first part of the meaning of Pascal's pensée: people do evil they take to be good only by conviction.

When it comes to assessing how good is the track record of Christianity in its influence on society and history, it is not enough simply to point to the evil that it may have inspired, demanded, or permitted. One must ask, how good compared to what? From this perspective, the recent militant atheist writings betray themselves. They recount the now familiar list of evils of religion, but largely ignore the evils of the atheist alternatives, which in the twentieth century have inflicted suffering and death on an unprecedented scale. By the simple measure of executions, for example, atheist regimes have already outstripped the body-count of Christianity for its entire history by an enormous factor[208]. Perhaps sensing the weakness of their position on this score, the militant atheists try to minimize the extent to which religion inspires good, and maximize its responsibility for evil. Mother Teresa is scurrilously attacked by Christopher Hitchens, and if Dawkins is to be believed, Martin Luther King's "religion was incidental"[209]. They argue "Individual atheists may do evil things but they don't do evil things in the name of atheism. ... Religious wars really are fought in the name of religion, and they have been horribly frequent in history. I cannot think of any war that has been fought in the name of atheism."[210]

This is double-think, which can immediately be refuted. No war has ever been fought in the name of generic 'religion' or 'theism'. Wars have been fought in the name of specific religious beliefs and groups. Similarly no war has ever been fought in the name of a generic 'areligion' or 'atheism'. But many have been fought in the name of specific atheistic beliefs and groups. The atheists' argument is: when religious people do good, their religion is incidental, but when they do evil, their religion is to blame; when atheists do good it is because they are enlightened, but when atheists do evil, they do it as individuals, and their atheism is not to blame, or if it looks as if they are motivated by shared conviction, then this conviction is a kind of 'religion', so religion is (still) to blame. The inconsistency and special-pleading is palpable.[211]

9.2   Rocks of Ages: A niche for religion

One of the better-known attempts at a kind of reconciliation of science and faith of the past decade or two comes from a person active on the evolutionist side of the school textbook debate, Stephen Jay Gould. In his (1999) *Rocks of Ages* Gould puts forward his "central principle of respectful noninterference ... the Principle of NOMA, or Non-Overlapping Magisteria"[212]. He summarizes this simple approach by saying "Science tries to document the factual character of the natural world, and to develop theories that coordinate and explain these facts. Religion, on the other hand, operates in the equally important, but utterly different, realm of human purposes, meanings, and values — subjects that the factual domain of science might illuminate, but can never resolve."

Gould cites the example of Thomas Burnet (1635-1715) whose *The Sacred Theory of the Earth* is now dismissed as trying "to reimpose the unquestionable dogmas of scriptural authority upon the new paths of honest science". Incidentally, this is the same Burnet who played a vital role in the accession of William of Orange to the English throne and whose *History of his own time* served as one of the major sources for Macaulay's *History of England since the accession of James the second*, which I've cited earlier. Gould gives several examples from twentieth century textbooks of unrestrained condemnations of Burnet's concordist approach to natural history.

The *Sacred Theory* is largely an attempt at harmonization of the Bible with the science of the day. In Gould's view Burnet was unfairly castigated because, though he practiced both magisteria, he kept them separate. Gould quotes from Burnet as saying

> 'Tis a dangerous thing to engage the authority of scrip-ture in disputes about the natural world in opposition to reason; lest time, which brings all things to light, should discover that to be evidently false which we had made scripture assert.[213]

Gould's fairness and scholarship are evident in many places, for example his discussion of the reasons for Darwin's loss of faith, largely as a reaction to the problem of suffering, brought into sharp personal relief by the untimely death of his daughter. But Gould's attempts to argue that T.H.Huxley also practiced NOMA and is unfairly portrayed as being anti-religious, ring hollow. Or perhaps rather, one should say that they reveal the very limited qualities of what Gould allows as religion. The shallowness of Gould's and Huxley's permissible form of religion is epitomized by this quote from Huxley's letter to Kingsley, saying that he is led

> ... to know that a deep sense of religion was compatible with the entire absence of theology. Secondly, science and her methods gave me a resting-place independent of authority and tradition. Thirdly, love opened up to me a view of the sanctity of human nature, and im-pressed me with a deep sense of responsibility ... I may be quite wrong, and in that case I know I shall have to pay the penalty for being wrong. But I can only say with Luther, "Gott helfe mir, Ich kann nichts anders".[214]

What Huxley (and it becomes clear Gould too) values, then, is a "deep sense of religion" totally devoid of doctrinal content, or in-deed apparently any factual content. The authority that remains is science and her methods. Huxley's image of himself is the em-battled hero, standing, like Luther, before a modern-day Diet of Worms, willing to sacrifice his immortal soul for what he believes. For all the ironic oratory, Huxley as martyr is not exactly a con-vincing portrait. Though perhaps it is more convincing than the similar self-portraits of the militant atheists of the early twenty-first century.

For Gould the second magisterium seems to consist of matters of value. He says that it is "dedicated to a quest for consensus, or at least a clarification of assumptions and criteria, about ethical 'ought', rather than search for any factual 'is'..." and includes "much of philosophy, and part of literature and history" as well as religion.

He rightly denies to science the ability to say anything about "the morality of morals", citing as an example that the possible anthropological discovery of adaptively beneficial characteristics of infanticide, genocide, or xenophobia doesn't at all justify behaving in that manner.

Gould is at his best when supporting the idea of NOMA by deflating the excessive portrayal of warfare between science and religion. He summarizes the arguments of Mario Biagioli[215] to the effect that the Galileo affair was more a matter of court intrigue than intellectual contest. And he discusses the openness of the Roman church to evolution, as represented by Popes Pius XII (*Humani Generis*, 1950), and John Paul II (1996). He devotes substantial space to critiques of Andrew Dickson White's famous "History of the warfare between science and theology in Christendom"[216] (1896) and of the similar "History of the conflict between religion and science" by John William Draper (1874) and some of the political background of their times.

The flat-earth myth — that the church taught that the earth was flat, and had to recant when Columbus proved otherwise — is delightfully exploded. As shown by J.B.Russell *Inventing the flat earth* (Prager, 1991) this fairy tale can be proved fictitious by documentary evidence. The earth's sphericity was known from Greek antiquity and promulgated throughout the middle ages by the Venerable Bede, Roger Bacon, Thomas Aquinas, and others, who represented the cosmological orthodoxy within Christianity, not the rare enlightened individual. History texts prior to 1870 rarely mention the flat-earth myth, while almost all those after 1880 do. It is not a coincidence then, that the flat-earth myth gains its currency at just about the time of the warfare advocates, and that both White and Draper cite it as a prime example of warfare. Gould points out that the celebrated exchange between Bishop

Wilberforce and T.H.Huxley on the descent of man took place at an 1860 meeting of the British Association whose formal paper was an address by the same Draper on the "intellectual development of Europe considered with reference to the views of Mr. Darwin". In other words, it arose not in the context of a scientific debate, but following an early discussion of "social Darwinism".

Gould cites with approval the physiologist J.S.Haldane, whom he calls a "deeply religious man", in whose *Gifford Lectures* for 1927 a most telling phrase appears "If my reasoning has been correct, there is no real connection between religion and the belief in supernatural events of any sort or kind". This is the religion that Gould has in mind as the candidate for NOMA, because he says "... NOMA does preclude the additional claim that such a God must arrange the facts of nature in a certain set and predetermined way. For example, if you believe that an adequately loving God must show his hand by peppering nature with palpable miracles, ... then a particular, partisan (and minority) view of religion has transgressed in the magisterium of science ..."[217]

The creationism and evolution textbook debate is one in which Gould was directly involved. Two important general points that he makes are that there is probably a majority of clergy (as well as scientists) against imposition of specific theological doctrine on the science curricula of public schools; and that the controversy is a remarkably American phenomenon. "No other Western nation faces such an incubus as a serious political movement". He attributes the latter predominantly to America's "uniquely rich range of sects". I think there may be more cogent reasons[218]. Gould's recounting of the Arkansas Scopes trial of 1925 is interesting in focusing on the difference between the reality and the 1955 cinematic version of *Inherit the Wind*, not to mention the polemic of H.L.Mencken. Both the Dayton creationists and their opponents, the ACLU, were looking forward to a guilty verdict so that the case could move on to higher courts where the real issues of constitutionality were to be fought. The conviction was overturned on the technicality that the judge had no authority to impose the fine of $100 (exceeding his limit of $50) and although this is portrayed by evolutionists as a victory, it was more like a defeat for both sides, since it prevented the real issues from being joined.

Gould also writes passionately about William Jennings Bryan, the famous creationist prosecutor of the Scopes trial, recalling that, far from being by nature a benighted traditionalist, he was, for his whole political career, a liberal and progressive reformer. Gould attributes Bryan's uncharacteristic position to his misunderstanding.

> Bryan's attitude to evolution rested upon a three-fold error. First, he made the common mistake of confusing the fact of evolution with the Darwinian explanation of its mechanism. He then misinterpreted natural selection as a martial theory of survival by battle and destruction of enemies. Finally, he fell into the logical error of arguing that Darwinism implied the moral virtuousness of such deathly struggle.[219]

While acknowledging that Bryan was in part responding to the misuse of Darwinism by scientists and their acolytes, he concludes that "The originator of an idea [Darwin] cannot be held responsible for egregious misuse of his theory"

I take Gould's intentions in advocating what he calls NOMA to be entirely constructive. He undoubtedly has an agenda to defend the independence of science. But there seems no reason to doubt his genuine concern to find a place in intellectual thought for morality and value. He associates these (though not uniquely) with religious underpinnings, rather than with any vain attempts to derive ethics from science or natural history.

Gould's NOMA principle has been much criticized. As we've seen, it does not satisfy the militant atheists, of course, but it also does not satisfy militant, or even tolerably robust, theists. The weakness of Gould's position is primarily that it is scientistic. When he identifies the magisterium of science as "our drive to understand the factual character of nature" he is saying that facts are discovered by science (alone), or in other words that the only real knowledge is scientific. Undoubtedly Gould wishes to set up a contrast between facts (science) and values (religion). The problem with this common opposition is that values are not the natural disjoint of facts. The plain converse of the view that *facts* are the domain of science is that the domain of religion is *feelings*, or worse still *fantasy*. Gould does not mean that converse (I think), and intends to express respect for religion; but he can't avoid the implication. To be fair, he does qualify the "facts" by the phrase "of nature", and were it not for the rest of his exposition, that might leave open the possibility of there being facts "of something else". But he never refers to the domain of religion as being a question of knowledge or fact. The religion that he is making room for is a religion empty of any claims to historical or scientific fact, doctrinal authority, and supernatural experience. Such a religion, whatever may be its attractions to the liberal scientistic mind, could never be Christianity, or for that matter, Judaism or Islam.

For all of his justified critical analysis of Andrew Dickson White's polemic of 100 years earlier, and for all that he aspires to a more balanced interpretation of history, the logic of Gould's position is therefore scarcely different from White's. White was at pains to say that science's warfare was *not* with religion but with "theology". By this, as he clearly stated in his introduction, White meant distinctive religious doctrines that he called sectarian, but which might more descriptively be called confessional or foundational. In White's portrayal, religion's claims to knowledge or authoritative teaching are what science is disputing. For White, and for Gould, there is room for a vague religiosity which serves useful purposes as a civic religion and as an emotional source of moral authority. Both men welcome, and even promote, that religiosity. But neither has left room for anything that looks like orthodox Christianity, based on unique events two thousand years ago: the life, death, and resurrection of Jesus of Nazareth.

9.3 Behind the mythology

Science and Christianity have had a lot of interactions during and since the Scientific Revolution, but none has become so iconic as that of Galileo and the Roman Catholic church.

The popular image of this confrontation is wonderfully captured in the painting by Cristiano Banti, Figure 9.3[220]. Galileo stands in a heroic pose, his head set-off by what almost seems a halo of light behind it. His interrogators have their backs to the wall literally as well as figuratively. The unhappy faces of the passive inquisitors, one of which is partly shrouded by a hood, are

Figure 9.3: Galileo before the Inquisition, Cristiano Banti, oil on canvas.

averted from the brightness of Galileo's face. The central accuser leans forward to confront Galileo, pointing to an open scroll, next to which stands a quill and ink. He is commanding Galileo to sign a confession or a recantation. The plain wall is bright behind them, with only the legs of a crucifix visible. It seems almost as if the brightness has come directly from Galileo's saintly head, metaphorically illuminating the darkness of the nether regions and benighted religious with the breaking light of science.

Of course this portrait deliberately sets out to make a statement and to promote a viewpoint: that Galileo was an early martyr and hero in the long war between science and Christian faith. What is really interesting about it, though, is not so much its portrayal, as its date: 1857. This is the image of Galileo that was promoted in the mid-nineteenth century, more than two hundred years after the events. Almost all the empirical philosophers of the Scientific Revolution in the seventeenth century soon did adopt the heliocentric model of the solar system, in whose defense Galileo had fallen into papal disfavor. But even those who were Galileo's friends and admirers could hardly have seen the events of the confrontation in the way Banti paints them. Galileo's scientific evidence was weak, and some of his theories were plain wrong. He had been allowed remarkable latitude, in those troubled times, to pursue his science, provided he kept out of theology and Bible interpretation. The pope himself had been his friend and encourager. But Galileo had drained all this good-will, enraged his enemies, and alienated most of his powerful friends by publishing through what seemed like subterfuge an arrogant populist imagined dialogue promoting his ideas and portraying their opponent as 'Simplicio', the Simpleton. Both the heliocentric solar system and also Galileo's approach to scriptural interpretation are now commonplace inside and outside the Roman church. And by 1857 one could see that these and other key contributions had been fully vindicated. Yet in his time, Galileo did not heroically stand on principle embodying the light of science before the ignorant Inquisition; the frightened old man would do whatever he had to do to preserve his life and comfort. One should not blame him for that. Besides, he remained a good Catholic, and so far as we can tell had not been seeking to alienate the church, or to undermine its authority, except in so far as it was represented by the schoolmen. So, to summarize, Banti's painting is revealing not of the events or the spirit of the seventeenth century, but of the attitudes towards science, and the scientism, of the mid-nineteenth.

There had not, in the minds of most scientists, been an entrenched warfare or even much of an ongoing intellectual confrontation between science and Christianity in the intervening centuries. But it served the purposes of many academics to persuade themselves that there had been. Andrew Dickson White was just beginning his campaign with Ezra Cornell to found a new model of university. They considered the influence of what they called sectarian religion to be detrimental to learning and to society; so their intention was to spearhead a new movement of essentially secular education, in place of the Christian universities which still dominated academia. Cornell University was to be an institution in which religious doctrine was to have no place[221]. The content of the pamphlets and articles that were his propaganda in support of this campaign eventually became White's famous book *The warfare of science with theology in christendom* (1896). In it he gathered and recounted numerous historical examples of areas in which the growth of what he called science encroached upon traditionally religious intellectual territory. Each development is portrayed as initially meeting with stubborn resistance from the entrenched theological power structures, but eventually from sheer force of evidence and argument overthrowing that resistance and moving forward into greater knowledge and enlightenment. The theme is repeated over and over in this long and eventually tedious book, but it lends itself to stirring melodrama, complete with martyrs, heroes and villains; intrigues and battles; and all the elements that go to make a good story.

White, like many of his contemporaries, used the word science with an enormously wide meaning; so that it encompassed the entirety of liberal scholarship. In addition to astronomy, chemistry, geology and the other natural sciences, his book has chapters on Egyptology and Assyriology, philology, comparative mythology, economics, and biblical criticism, referring to all as science, and implying that the intellectual methodologies of all are similar.

This book, and presumably the pamphlets before it, captured the imaginations of many of the academics of the day and its thesis gradually became accepted even by many Christians as representing a fact of history that science and theology were perpetually at war. For academics, who at that stage almost universally regarded science as the guiding example of all rational thought, it meant so much the worse for religion. For Christians whose faith ruled their lives, it meant, by contrast, so much the worse for science. And thus the warfare metaphor as it was gradually accepted by both sides became a self-fulfilling prophecy.

The relationship of science and Christianity in the three centuries prior to this transition had been complicated, and sometimes tense. But the men who pushed forward the growing knowledge of nature, during that period, were more often pious believers than they were outspoken infidels or scientistic secularists. The universities were of course Christian foundations, Oxford and Cambridge required their ordinary college fellows to be ordained if they remained beyond a limited tenure. But even scientists outside the universities were often either independent gentlemen motivated in part by Christian commitments, or parish clergy who saw no inherent contradiction between their professional religion and their amateur science. The tensions that exist between the 'Experimental Philosophy' and Christianity were a concern for Robert Boyle, one of the founders of the Royal Society. In the terminology of

Figure 9.4: The importance of religion in the founding and life of ancient universities is still evident in the dominance of the chapels among their buildings. This, for example, is the Chapel at King's College Cambridge.

1690 someone who understood and cultivated experimental philosophy was frequently referred to as a 'virtuoso'. In his book *The Christian Virtuoso*[222], Boyle's intention was to show "that, by being addicted to Experimental Philosophy, a man is rather assisted than indisposed to be a good Christian". He addresses himself to the puzzlement apparently expressed that that he should be both "a diligent cultivater of experimental philosophy, [and] a concerned embracer of the Christian religion". So the question of the compatibility of science and Christianity was, even then, a live one. But the danger Boyle addressed was less that of a philosophical atheism than it was of a practical atheism: "... the profane discourses and licentious lives of some virtuosi, that boast much of the principles of the new philosophy. And I deny not, but that, if the knowledge of nature falls into the hands of a resolved atheist, or a sensual libertine, he may misemploy it to oppugn the grounds, or discredit the practice, of religion." While Boyle therefore is familiar with those for whom he considers "their immorality was the original cause of their infidelity", he says his personal observations make him think atheists are rarer among scientists than is popularly imagined. "And though my conversation has been pretty free and general among naturalists, yet I have met with so few true atheists, that I am very apt to think, that men's want of due information, or of their uncharitable zeal, has made them mistake or misrepresent many for deniers of God..."

Protagonists over the whole spectrum of scientific and non-scientific debate, in those days, frequently charged their opponents with religious heterodoxy, when it served their rhetorical purposes. But that was simply a characteristic of an age when religion was the foremost intellectual authority.

Undoubtedly there were many occasions when the presumptions of cosmologies based upon traditional interpretations of the Bible were challenged by the development of science, whether it was the demonstration of the vastness of the universe or its far greater age than imagined by those who interpreted Genesis as literal history. In this sense there was an ongoing process of accommodation and reinterpretation. The scientific revolution had accelerated the pace of discovery, and thereby of this accommodation and reinterpretation. But it had a long prior history. Augustine had, at the end of the fourth century A.D. wrestled with the meaning of the first chapters of Genesis. Lest incorrect interpretation and ignorant Christian speech be the cause of ridicule by a more knowledgeable unbeliever, he warned against jumping to conclusions and said he had "explained in detail and set forth for consideration the meanings of obscure passages, taking care not to affirm rashly some one meaning to the prejudice of another and perhaps better explanation."[223]

It certainly was *not* the case that religion and science were thought non-overlapping magisteria. The Bible was widely taken as a serious guide to life, in respect of morality, yes, but also in respect of history, politics, cosmology, and much else. What the virtuosi recognized was that much of what passed for Christian theology, particularly in areas that overlapped with empirical philosophy, was not Biblical, but Aristotelian. Moreover, they saw that there was a much more fruitful approach to understanding the empirical world than the scholastic logic-chopping that characterized the schoolmen. This new empirical approach was also supported by a fully Christian perspective that Bacon had expressed as "... let no man, upon a weak conceit of sobriety or an ill-applied moderation, think or maintain that a man can search too far or be too well studied in the book of Gods word or in the book of Gods works; divinity or philosophy;"[224]. Both of the *two books*, scripture and nature, according to this widespread viewpoint, told of God's majesty and complemented each other in what they revealed to the scholar. It was of course held that the two books could not contradict one another, but it was not at all the view that their concerns were non-overlapping. When overlapping claims seemed incompatible, it called for reinterpretation either of the science or of the Bible.

The early development of the field of Geology, representative of late eighteenth century concerns, is full of interesting examples of intellectual conflict and confrontation, such as the competition between uniformitarian and catastrophist theories of the earth's past. But as has been amply documented[225], the conflict was predominantly not what has often been portrayed: between hidebound scriptural literalists and open-minded scientists; it was between rival scientific interpretations held by equally religious, and equally scientific, advocates.

By the nineteenth century this process was two-hundred years on. The more directly concordist approach, of which Thomas Burnet's work is an early example, was much less plausible in 1890 than it had been in 1690. Not only had science discredited the details of so many such concordist efforts, but also the hoped-for convergence of the two books into a unified picture of the world did not seem to be happening. Science seemed to be progressing toward a comprehensive description of the universe without any assistance from scriptural revelation. And it increasingly strained credulity to suppose that reading the first two chapters of Genesis as natural history — even a highly stylized natural history — was compatible with what seemed to be established by the natural sciences. The disappointment of the simplistic concordist expectations did not greatly perturb Christians who based their faith on historic revelation, the broad sweep of philosophical arguments, and personal experience. And many scientists took this approach. It did, however, seriously undermine a strand of Christian thought and apologetics that had adopted natural theology, and the argument from design, especially in biology, as its primary rationale. The presumption that science was going to *prove* religion was, in effect, a subverting concession to scientism. It had led many Christian thinkers into a blind alley whose end was approaching. There seemed no prospect that this proof was going to be forthcoming, or even that traditional arguments from natural theology were going to emerge unscathed. What seemed more plausible was that science was going to continue its triumphant progress, sorting out the details of physics and taking over more and more of the rest of intellectual endeavor, until it fully unified and actually monopolized knowledge. This scientistic vision allowed a determined push by the university secularizers to win the day. The century since then has seen the philosophical foundation for this monopoly dissolve away, and the compliance of the academy to the scientistic unifying ambitions also substantially decay. Yet many in academia even today speak as if the secular 'defeat' of religion based upon the scientistic outlook of the nineteenth century still holds.

In fact, however, both the scientistic attempt to found religion upon scientific proofs, and also the wider expectation that science will provide a complete unification of all knowledge — the ambition of scientism as a whole — are now intellectually unsupportable. There remain many people, both theists and atheists, who don't realize it, and who continue to thrash out the old arguments. But they are trapped in a nineteenth-century time-warp.

Probably an even greater influence on the nineteenth-century religious debate than science itself was the rise of 'higher criticism' sometimes called 'historical criticism' of the Bible. The Reformation had transformed the Bible from a mysterious religious artifact written in an ancient language incomprehensible to the populace, into the one book that every literate person read. Catholics still granted to the church hierarchy alone the authority to interpret the Bible. Maintaining that authority, in the face of Protestant arguments and armies, was, by the way, undoubtedly a driving factor in the Papacy's handling of Galileo. But Protestant doctrine gave a much greater role to the individual conscience. The Bible was translated into the language of the common people. The first translators had no doubt about its divine inspiration. Their profound commitment was to represent faithfully its meaning in translation. Their concerns naturally led to a scholarly attempt to establish and understand the accuracy and provenance of the text of the Bible — textual criticism. But as subsequent textual criticism gradually became a critique of the supposed sources and content of scriptures, it became more and more dependent upon both linguistic analysis, seen as 'scientific', and also presumptions imported from outside the Bible, from the wider realms of philosophy and science. These supposed-scientific presumptions were increasingly thought to bring into question the Bible's reliability. Eventually, it began to be analyzed by some scholars as if it were simply another book, to be interpreted by whatever were the prevailing academic standards of the day. And by then the prevailing standards were scientistic and naturalistic. It would take us too far from our theme to pursue any significant discussion of the history of historical criticism of the Bible. Today even theologically orthodox and conservative Christian intellectuals, who believe the Bible to be the word of God, acknowledge there is some value in the analysis of its authorship and dating — topics which constitute a large part the critical focus. In the nineteenth century there were deep divisions in the church and in academia about how to respond to higher criticism's challenges to traditional views of Biblical authorship. Much of the controversy arose not because of questions of scholarship, but because of the heterodox theological views of many of higher criticism's champions. For the church, the question was, justifiably enough, whether or not the critics' teaching was still meaningfully Christian. In many cases it was not. And it hardly seems unjustified in those cases for the church to discontinue its sponsorship: to give the offenders the push.

A major part of the strategy of those committed to what would now be called the *liberal* theological perspective, was to portray their position as scientific[226]. But of course hardly any of the analyses that they offered bore any resemblance to the natural sciences, or depended upon science in any significant way. Their presuppositions were indeed often scientistic. It was commonly held that miracles were impossible; so Biblical descriptions of them were, *ipso facto*, clearly false. Or it was believed that prophecy could never be predictive; so one could reliably date writings that referred (even obliquely) to historical events as being *after* the events. In general, naturalistic and physicalistic analysis became not just an important part of Bible scholarship, but by far the *preferred* type of explanation of the whole of the scriptures. It was a crucial part of the rhetoric to argue that the liberal position was progressive and scientific, while the orthodox position was hidebound and dogmatic. The rebuttal, though it was vociferous, was intellectually confused. Science still held a strong appeal for the orthodox. They resisted the worst excesses of the scientistic presuppositions, but were often ill-equipped to differentiate them from science. The rhetorical battle was often lost to a portrayal that the conservatives were — 'once again', as A D White would have had it — blindly opposing the progress of science by their intellectual fossilization. Scientism was the ultimate victor.

9.4   Mutual support

A serious reading of history enables us to escape the mythological grip of the warfare story. When we do so, it becomes possible to recognize that Christian believers were very active in science during its modern development. We see that, while there was a small fraction of the Scientific Revolution's philosophers who entertained atheistic speculations, the majority were Christians; while there were those who in the Age of Reason adopted the anti-religious cause of the philosophes, they were by no means predominant; and while there were some Victorian scientists who thought that science had disproved Christianity, there were more who accorded an independence to scientific professionalism and research, but still personally practised a Christian commitment. In short, science and the Christian faith were not incompatible.

Scientism was adopted by influential individuals for various reasons of conviction or expedience. It had not, during the seventeenth to the nineteenth centuries, achieved the dominance that was present by the start of the twentieth. If we reject scientism, we find room once again for the intellectual significance of religious claims to knowledge, alongside those of science about nature.

In fact, however, history suggests that an even more constructive relationship exists between science and Christianity than mutual toleration. The thesis, as Stanley Jaki puts it, is that there is a "single intellectual avenue forming both the road of science and the ways to God. Science found its only viable birth within a cultural matrix permeated by a firm conviction about the mind's ability to find in the realm of things and persons a pointer to their creator."[227]

One needs to be cautious, and not claim too much for this interpretation of history. It is, like most historical theses, neither rigorously demonstrable nor universally accepted. No one is denying the influences of the historical and social environment as a whole. Key factors may include: the means of dissemination through printing, other vital technologies that were directly used in experiments, and sufficient social stability to allow time and support for science. It is extremely difficult to assess the importance of these practical influences in comparison to the influences of philosophy itself. But the argument for a strong influence of philosophical preconceptions does have considerable evidence to support it.

There are two complementary sides of this analysis. One side is the negative. It is the observation that modern science did not arise in any of the civilizations except that of Europe. The other is positive. It is the observation that there are, in the world-view of Christianity[228], conceptions that are hospitable to science, which in combination may provide a uniquely fertile mental habitat in which modern science first flourished. A.N. Whitehead, in 1925, put the negative side thus

> There have been great civilizations in which the peculiar balance of mind required for science has only fitfully appeared and has produced the feeblest result. For example, the more we know of Chinese art, of Chinese literature, and of the Chinese philosophy of life, the more we admire the heights to which that civilization attained. For thousands of years, there have been in China acute and learned men patiently devoting their lives to study. Having regard to the span of time, and to the population concerned, China forms the largest volume of civilization which the world has seen. There is no reason to doubt the intrinsic capacity of individual Chinamen for the pursuit of science. And yet Chinese science is practically negligible. There is no reason to believe that China if left to itself would have ever produced any progress in science. The same may be said of India.[229]

The interesting question is why? Why didn't these great civilizations of the past produce a scientific revolution? Whitehead's answer is that these and the other civilizations that predated science, the Persians, the Greeks, the Romans, lacked an implicit faith, "the inexpungable belief that every detailed occurrence can be correlated with its antecedents in a perfectly general manner, exemplifying general principles." His "explanation is that faith in the possibility of science, generated antecedently to the development of modern scientific theory, is an unconscious derivative from medieval theology."[230] According to Whitehead, moreover, it was the anti-rationality of the early modern scientists, tempered by this faith, that was the secret of their success. The scholastic philosophers that they rejected were not irrational, or anti-rational, as many modern commentators imply. On the contrary, the schoolmen were the rationalists of the day. It took the virtuoso's revolutionary — and by contemporary standards irrational — insistence on the primacy of empirical "irreducible stubborn facts", studied for their own sake, combined with the whole of society's inherited faith in the world's rationality, to germinate the new synthesis.

Historian of science, R Hookyaas, in his *Religion and the rise of modern science* (1972), sees it similarly. The weaknesses in Greek science, which "medieval science made no move to eliminate", needed to be corrected by "'de-deification' of nature, a more modest estimation of human reason, and a higher respect for manual labor". And he sets out to "... identify some general trends of thought in the Bible which could exert a healthy influence on the development of science ..."[231] I would summarize some of these trends of thought as follows.

The Bible teaches that the world is the *free contingent creation* of a rational Creator — that God had free choices about how the world was to be. Such a teaching implies that the world can't be understood simply by theoretical philosophy, in the way that the Greeks thought it could and should. We need to do experiments to find out how God chose to create it. Experiments are the foundation of modern science.

The Bible teaches that God *declared the Creation "good"*. This teaching contrasts with a common rejection of the physical as intrinsically evil or degrading. On the contrary, it is worthy of detailed study and investigation on its own merits, again motivating the empirical emphasis.

The Bible teaches that *the world is not itself God*. In contrast with the pantheism of the Greeks and Romans, and the nature worship of the tribal neighbors of the Hebrews, the God of Israel is eternal and transcendent. He brings forth a separate creation by his will, and upholds it by his word of power. "[N]ature is not a deity to be feared and worshipped, but a work of God to be admired, studied and managed."[232] Christians can investigate the physical and biological universe without fear of violating the divine.

The Bible teaches that humans have been given a degree of *authority and responsibility over the Creation*. Therefore they have direct permission and duty to probe its secrets, provided they are truly acting as stewards of it, and respecting God's creatures.

The Bible teaches that human rationality is in the *image of the creator*. This gives us reason to believe that we are capable of understanding the creation, at least in part, despite its radical contingency. It provides a rationale for thinking that the order that we see in nature is not merely an arbitrary construction of the human mind, but is a reflection of a deeper rationality: the mind of God.

The Bible teaches that God is a steadfastly-consistent *law-giver*. This gives us reason to believe that we might discover general laws that govern the course of nature, interpreted as the regular orderly progress of the world in accordance with God's ordinances.

These are philosophical, and in fact *theological* encouragements to the work of empirical science. When contrasted with the relative scientific sterility observed in other cultures, they give reason to believe that far from being an atmosphere stifling to science, the Christian world-view of the West was the fertile cultural and philosophical climate in which science was able to grow and flourish.

Obviously science has now become largely self-sustaining. From a purely philosophical viewpoint, in the west we no longer need to be persuaded of the fruitfulness of the scientific empirical approach. An appreciation of the power of science is practically intrinsic to our cultural subconscious, and all too readily grows into a monopolistic scientism. What I wish to argue, though, is that it would make it easier to appreciate the true status of scientific knowledge if we recognize the underlying philosophical developments that served as its midwife. These extra-scientific beliefs and character traits are, I think, not irrelevant to a comprehensive account of knowledge, nor indeed to the continued health of science.

One current concern that illustrates the dependence of science on extra-scientific traits is the question of scientific fraud. Modern science has an elaborate and long-standing system surrounding the publishing of scientific work. Each scientific journal, when it receives the submission of a new article, sends out the article to be reviewed by one or more experts. Their job is to ensure that it constitutes a significant new contribution to the field of the journal, that it positions itself in relation to prior knowledge by appropriate citations, that it meets professional standards of descriptive and mathematical clarity, and that it appears to be free of egregious error. The peer review process is definitely a human and flawed undertaking. Professional and personal rivalries at times distort the results. Seminal papers are sometimes rejected. Erroneous papers are all too often accepted. But it is a process that has developed over centuries and, for all its weaknesses, provides an important contribution to the filtering and evaluation of scientific communication. Incidentally, the job of the expert referees in peer-review is almost universally carried out voluntarily and anonymously. The only reward a referee usually receives is the opportunity to read the latest paper before it is published, and the verbal thanks of the journal's editorial staff. Reviewing perhaps ten papers a year, as I and many of my colleagues do, is a contribution to the scientific enterprise that involves not insignificant effort, but is part of the normal professional life of a scientist.

Conscientious referees obviously read papers carefully to try to ensure they are free from error. What referees do not do is to read a paper with a view to detecting deliberate deception. The starting presumption of referees and editors is that the descriptions submitted are honest. It is perfectly possible for scientists to deceive themselves inadvertently, especially when their results contain random perturbing influences. The apprenticeship in science that is served through post-graduate and post-doctoral education and experience helps to train scientists to avoid self-deception by systematic application of the best practices of data collection and analysis, and of mathematical rigor. The reviewing process helps to enforce the observation of those practices. What reviewers can't easily do, though, is to detect deliberate fabrication or deceptive selection ('falsification') of data. Actually, *inexpert* fabrication or falsification is often easily discernible; and this helps to protect the journals from cranks and nuisance submissions; but falsification by someone who really knows a field is sometimes very hard to detect in the peer-review process. Because of science's focus on reproducibility, significant falsified results — at least results that are contrary to the actual behavior of nature — are *eventually* usually disproved and discounted. This correctability of science is much hailed and important, but not automatic. But in the mean time, false results can have a major impact on the field, and thereby cause extensive and costly misdirection of effort. In the case of engineering, applied science and medicine, they may lead to injury or death.

Perhaps the most famous scientific falsification of the twentieth century was the 'discovery', in 1912, of Piltdown Man: a skull from Sussex, England, purporting to be the fossilized remains of a missing-link in evolution between apes and humans. Although there were puzzles and skepticism about this find from quite early on, it took over forty years for it to be definitively proven to be a fraud, consisting of a relatively recent human skull combined with a small orangutan jaw that had been stained and filed to assist with the deception[233]. Meanwhile, its misleading influence on research into human ancestors was substantial. There have been several high-profile cases of deliberate falsification of scientific results during the past decade or two, which have drawn the attention of the public and politicians. In a society whose public money supports most science it is fully justified for the government to demand stringent efforts to prevent scientific fraud and misconduct.

What this all illustrates is that science depends for its proper functioning on traits of individuals, and society as a whole, that are not scientific. It depends upon honesty, integrity, truthfulness, openness, and so on, which today's society finds, sometimes to its surprise, are not enforced by science. Indeed these traits are the sorts of traits that have traditionally been viewed as the province of religion. Not that religious people or organizations have any monopoly on the practice of them, but that they are moral *virtues* which in the west historically have been taught by Christianity, and enforced as much by the church and the moral expectations of society as they have by legal sanction. So what is clearer than ever today is that science is itself dependent upon certain virtues of individuals and society. This is an area where science and religion are plainly mutually supportive.

9.5   True contradiction

A very important result of properly rejecting scientism, but not science, is that it accords to both scientific and non-scientific rationality their full scope. And it permits them to interact fruitfully. This is true for all non-scientific thought but it is especially significant for religious thought. It is rarely the case that scientific and non-scientific approaches are completely 'non-overlapping'. As I've shown already, science certainly influences religious thought, and religious thought influences science. There is nothing *improper* about these influences provided that they account for the intrinsic character of the different areas of, and approaches to, knowledge. What's more, these interactions need not just be at the level of encouragements or mutual support. In some cases they are going to be mutual correction, and even contradiction.

The fact that religious knowing is non-scientific does not free religion from paying attention to science's knowledge. And the fact that science can proceed without explicit reference to religion does not free it from paying attention to religious knowledge.

A religious faith that depended upon the belief that humans can routinely levitate runs directly up against the scientific demand for a demonstration. This demand is perfectly reasonable if the claim is for *routine* levitation, because that is in effect a scientific claim. It is a claim to a reproducible effect with sufficient clarity to be addressed by scientific tests. In such a situation science and faith might well contradict one another about the same matter. They are not non-overlapping, and most people, myself included, would regard the scientific conclusions as the cogent ones. However, a religious faith that depended upon a belief that levitation was demonstrated on one particular occasion, or by one particular historic character, does not lend itself to such a scientific test. Science is powerless to bring unique events to the empirical bar. It can of course assert that such an event is inconsistent with the normal course of nature. But such an assertion brings nothing to the discussion that we didn't already know. After all, the whole point was that this was apparently impossible under normal circumstances. Science might sometimes be able to help in the analysis of the evidence surrounding that event. The discovery of powerful electromagnets in the basement of the levitating guru, for example, might, in the light of our scientific knowledge, be highly suggestive that well-understood natural forces had been deployed in the phenomenon under discussion. This scientific interpretation would then definitely give rise to what might be decisive legal evidence in deciding whether fraud played a part in the event, as well as convincing us of what the probable explanation of it is. But the situation that is much more often encountered is that no such legal evidence is forthcoming. Then science has little or nothing useful to say.

In matters of natural history, there is also potential for true contradiction. As we've seen, even though science is rarely definitive for distinct events of the past, scientific investigation of the overall development of the universe, and the earth, is increasingly powerful. Religious believers who feel obliged to maintain, for example, that the earth is young, face justifiable scientific skepticism. The overwhelming evidence, which is woven into the fabric of our description of the world in modern physical sciences, is that the earth and the universe are billions of years old. It is possible to save a literalistic Bible chronology of a 6000 year-old earth only by supposing that God has deliberately made it look as if the earth is much older than it actually is[234]. This theory was most notably espoused by Philip Gosse, in his book *Omphalos*[235] published in 1857, two years before Darwin's *Origin*. Gosse frames his argument around the repetitive circularity of nature, cycling through seasons and lives. Into this circle, instantaneous creation is obliged to break, but Gosse says it must do so by creating the requisite history of prior cycles. Thus Gosse concludes that Adam had a navel, even though he did not need this remnant of the umbilical cord, since he was not *born*. But God could create him with one, nevertheless. (Omphalos is Greek for navel.) While the view that God created the world with the appearance of age is a position that can't be *logically* disproved, it is *theologically* disastrous. It makes God into a deceiver, deliberately misleading us mortals by placing deceptive evidence into nature that leads us to think the earth is old, when 'really' it is young. Even Charles Kingsley, Gosse's friend, called the idea a proposal that God had "written on the rocks one enormous and superfluous lie for all mankind"[236].

It is not so much that the view is obscurantist as that it dismisses the faithfulness of God, which presumably is the main rationale for the young-earth viewpoint. The argument for a young-earth creationist position is that the Bible is the revelation of God, and that since God is faithful, his revelation is free from error; consequently the Biblical account of creation ought to be accepted as true. But if the 'acceptance' advocated leads to the conclusion that God has deceived us by constructing a world that appears to be different from (older than) what it really is, we have undermined our starting premise. Such a deceiver God is not faithful; and thus we have no reason to continue to suppose that what the Bible says is inerrant.

In light of this contradiction, the intellectually consistent position for a Christian who holds a high view of Biblical inspiration, but also recognizes the compelling force of the scientific evidence, is to adopt a different 'acceptance' of the creation account. It is to recognize that the scriptural account was addressed originally to an ancient and unscientific people, and expressed in context and metaphor that reflects the wider culture of that age. This is precisely the position most Christian scientists adopt. The American Scientific Affiliation, is a fellowship of Christians in science, whose members are required to assent to a statement of faith of which the first article is "We accept the divine inspiration, trustworthiness and authority of the Bible in matters of faith and conduct". In other words, these members are theologically conservative Christians who hold a high view of scriptural authority. The ASA polled its membership in 2010 on various questions concerning creation and human origins[237]. Approximately 86% of the respondents affirmed the statement "The universe is approximately 14 billion years old" is "supported by credible scientific evidence". Plainly science has had a very important influence on the opinions of these Christians, many of whom are thought-leaders on the topic of science and faith in their communities. Science does influence, and sometimes contradict, aspects of religion.

The influence of religion on science, beyond the philosophical and cultural encouragement we have already discussed, and the personal motivations of individual believing scientists, comes to a matter of contradiction mostly in topics where religion finds its most potent authority. The ethical and moral acceptability of scientific practices is strongly dictated by religious beliefs and commitments. Every research institution that receives financial support from the US government is required by federal law[238] to have an

Institutional Review Board that evaluates the use of human subjects in research. At a minimum this review board must ensure
that risks to subjects are minimized, consent is obtained, the data
is monitored and privacy observed, and that possibly vulnerable
subjects are protected. There is therefore already in our system
an acknowledgement that science practice must be subject to some
ethical restrictions. The hot-button topic in the past decade in
respect to ethical restrictions on research has been the question of
research using embryonic stem cells. These cells, which are capable
of growing indefinitely in a laboratory environment, and can differentiate into almost any body tissue, are technically very useful for
biological research. It is thought that the research that they enable
has the potential for producing, in the future, powerful medical
treatments for deadly diseases. However, their use generally involves the destruction of a human embryo, which raises questions
of great moral significance for the dignity and value of human life.
Opinion is divided on where the limits ought to be drawn on this
sort of research, but plainly the decisions ought not to be made on
purely technical grounds. The religious component of this discussion is of immense importance, and cannot be excluded. Science,
thoughtfully understood, does not have to exclude it. Scientists,
who may or may not be believers themselves, can take the opinions of religious and moral philosophers seriously. Unfortunately
there has been a more belligerent response from some scientists
and activists, who have argued that religious viewpoints have no
legitimate voice in the discussion; that purely pragmatic considera-
tions overrule any foundational ethics; and that pragmatic, secular,
ethics leads to a much more liberal attitude in the employment of
these cells. One thread of this debate implies that it is somehow
improper for science to be subject to religious criticism. This viewpoint often finds its rationale in a scientistic world-view. After all,
if science is all the real knowledge we have, then it does seem to
follow that there is nothing outside of science that can legitimately
regulate the activities of science. But whether scientistic or not,
an intransigent insistence of the freedom of science-practice from
contradiction or constraint by non-scientific arguments, including
religious ones, seems almost a mirror image of a religious fundamentalist denial of science.

In summary, then, there *is* an intellectual rivalry, involving mutually contradictory claims of priority and authority, that might reasonably be spoken of as warfare. This war is not between science and religion. It is between scientism and a whole lot of other routes to knowledge, including religious faith.

Chapter 10

Integrating knowledge

10.1 The Christian and science

Christianity understands the universe as created and upheld by God; a God who is the foundation of all reality, but nevertheless a personal God who loves and cares for his creation. The immensely persuasive scientific descriptions of the normal course of the world, which sprang from scientific revolution, are deliberately impersonal. The success of those impersonal descriptions made plausible to eighteenth and nineteenth-century skeptics the sub-Christian idea of Deism: that a creator God set the universe in motion but subsequently allows it to proceed without his personal attention or intervention. The atheist of the twentieth or twenty-first century goes further and discards the whole notion of a creator. He finds it more convenient simply to postulate the universe than to postulate the universe's creator, especially if the creator has no relevant participation in the day to day business of the world.

It is more convenient also because doing away with the deity allows freedom to construct moral codes in accordance with the desires of today, rather than being encumbered with the belief that there actually is an external standard represented by the will of God, which is good and guides us to the good and to which humans are held accountable. There are some distinct *in*conveniences with the relativist and pragmatist moral position at which atheism arrives. The lack of any foundation for ethical 'ought' is a notable one that no appeal to common sense or sentiment, evolutionary fitness, or pragmatic self-interest can logically overcome. The consequence is that ethical standards are increasingly becoming an unmoored 'correctness', imposed by the loudest or most fashionable voices. But that is the inescapable price.

Scientific theories and experiments work without appeal to personality. The normal course of the world is, so far as science could possibly tell, uniform and repeatable. It is normal, because the normal course is what science sets out to describe. However, Christians see the uniformity not as ruling God out from his creation but as the outworking of his faithfulness in it. The laws of nature are what they are because God designed them that way, and continuously sustains them by his will. Science is the discovery of the scheme of the universe in so far as it is reproducible and comprehensible. It is the discovery of the workings of God's plan, and of his ongoing action. God has not set the mechanism of the universe in motion independent of his attention and gone on vacation. Nor has he set it in independent motion and allowed himself the liberty of an occasional intervention or adjustment. He continuously sustains it "by his word of power" and science is discovering the coherent character and law-like stability of that sustainment.

Such a comprehensive view of God's sovereignty raises an important challenge to understanding his fairness. Is God then responsible also for all the suffering and evil in the world? If so, how can we maintain that God is good? The Christian message takes this challenge with deadly seriousness, and asserts that God has addressed it in the most remarkable and comprehensive way through the Incarnation. Whether one believes that message is, as a practical matter, the deciding factor in one's stance with respect to Christianity. And it is also in Christian theology the touchstone of one's relationship with God. But in any case, this is not the place to enter into a detailed exposition of *theodicy*, the theological justification of God's goodness. We must content ourselves with the observation that the Christians who helped make science what it is generally recognized both the constraints that the faithfulness of God places on his actions, and also the possibility that he can act in unusual ways, which reveal his personal love and character. In other words, they believed both in God's laws, including natural laws, and in the possibility of miracles.

10.2   Levels and perspectives

Without scientism's artificial constraints, we are at liberty to understand human knowledge as it really is. It has many facets. We have many different types of descriptions, each of which may contribute additional insights. Sometimes it is helpful to regard these as different *levels* of description, in a hierarchy. This hierarchical view is commonplace within science itself.

Physics has identified four forces of nature: gravity, electromagnetism, the weak force, and the strong force. And it has identified a scheme of 16 particles — quarks, leptons, neutrinos, and bosons — that are apparently *elementary*. The interaction of these particles through the fundamental forces can be considered the foundational level of our current description of the physical universe. Elementary particle theorists are working hard on descriptions of the world that might be *more* fundamental than this. String theory, supersymmetry, and the "landscape", refer to mathematical ideas that are interesting possibilities but so far have no experimental evidence to support them — and also have many theoretical difficulties. They are trying to find what might be called an even lower level of description than the standard model of 4 forces and 16 particles. But even within physics there are higher levels of description than our current elementary particle picture. For example, solid state physics is the study of the ways that nuclei and electrons interact so as to determine the properties of solids. The orderly arrangements of atoms in crystal structure and the quantum-mechanical behavior of electrons moving under their influence give rise to a rich variety of electrical and optical phenomena which are the basis for all of modern integrated electronics, imaging detectors, solid-state lasers, and so on, as well as providing a fundamental understanding of how materials respond to stress, corrosion, heat, and age. In solid state physics, quarks are essentially never mentioned. The interactions of interest are atomic, and electromagnetic, rather than nuclear. Solids are made up of quarks and leptons, but no sensible scientist tries to analyze them at the level of quarks. Instead she understands them at a different level: the level of atomic and electromagnetic interactions, appropriate to the phenomena under consideration.

My own field, plasma physics, the study of the collective behavior of the ionized gaseous state, has similar hierarchical relationships to other fields of physics. It also has within itself different levels of description. The ions and electrons that together make up the plasma move freely and randomly within the plasma at speeds that reflect the high temperatures involved, anywhere from ten thousand to a hundred million degrees Celsius or more. Sometimes we need to calculate the trajectory of individual particles. But more often, since we are dealing with the collective interaction of trillions of particles, we must focus on statistical descriptions. Sometimes the description treats the plasma as an assembly of particles, but often the description can be in terms of a conducting fluid, acted on by electromagnetic forces. This treatment is analogous to the calculation of the dynamics of water, for example how droplets form in a water stream, based on the representation of the fluid as a continuous medium, even though we know that 'really' it is made up of individual atoms. The whole hierarchy of descriptions of a plasma is useful for different purposes, and each level provides useful insights that help us to understand the behavior. A significant part of the skill of an experienced plasma physicist is to decide judiciously when to appeal to the different levels of description.

What is more, physics has shown that different descriptions at the *same* level, not separated by a natural hierarchy, sometimes must simultaneously be considered. Quantum mechanics has taught us that complementary descriptions are completely inescapable. Particles behave to some extent like waves, and waves behave to some extent like particles simultaneously, even though we have no way to visualize how that could possibly be true.

When we consider the other sciences, different hierarchical levels become predominant. Chemistry is focused on the interaction of atoms through bound electrons, which form the chemical bonds that determine the structure and reactions of molecules. In a sense, chemistry is reducible to physics, but that sense is only formal. It does not account properly for the different approaches to understanding that are commonplace within chemistry. Chemists are not just physicists struggling with complicated problems. Similarly, biology springs out of chemistry, and we now know a great deal about how biotic information is encoded in molecules and how the folding and unfolding of molecules underlies many biological mechanisms. But despite the scientific value of studying the ways in which different levels of description are related to one another, and the spectacular progress in recent decades in molecular biology, the descriptions of biology are not *just* chemistry. They are qualitatively different, even at the level of the cell, because they identify and analyze biological function and the coordinated behavior of the whole, not just the individual molecules.

We could move further up the scientific levels of description and discuss botany, zoology, physiology, and so on. But I think the point has been made. Science itself recognizes the importance of descriptions at different levels — from different perspectives. The fact that we believe there is a continuity between the different levels of description, that phenomena at higher levels are founded upon the behavior at lower levels, in ways that we can sometimes trace, does not disqualify the higher level descriptions. Biology is not explained away by chemistry, or chemistry by physics. We might believe in reductionism to the extent that biological phenomena obey the laws of fundamental physics, but that does not reduce biology to physics. Biological phenomena are at the very least 'emergent'. That is, truly new types of description are required for them, even if the behavior emerges from physical laws at a lower hierarchical level.

What the descriptions of natural science, at all levels, share is their dependence upon reproducibility and Clarity. But there are other types and levels of description in which those characteristics cannot be expected or attained. In that case it is even more obvious that even if the laws of physics remain fully in force, non-scientific knowledge is not explained away by physics, nor is it disqualified from being knowledge just because it does not conform to the requirements of natural science.

So yes, I am an assembly of electrons and quarks interacting through quantum chromodynamics and the electroweak forces; yes, I am a heterogeneous mixture of chemical elements predominantly hydrogen, oxygen, and carbon and their compounds; yes, I am a wonderful system of biochemical processes guided by genetic codes; yes, I am a vast and astoundingly complex organization of cooperating cells; yes, I am an mammal, with hair and warm blood; yes I am a person, husband, lover, father; yes, I am a sinner saved by grace. I am all of these things and not one of them is less true than any other. In no case is it correct to say I am *nothing but* one of these descriptions. Not one of these descriptions necessarily rules out the others, once we set scientism aside. The kind of evidence one might seek to establish each of these assertions will be appropriate to the character of the assertion. For the scientific assertions it will be scientific. For the others it will not.

Sometimes it is helpful to regard the different descriptions of the world as different *perspectives*. This is illustrated by C.A.Coulson (Professor of Applied Mathematics at Oxford) in his *Science and Christian Belief*[239]. He was responsible for the building of an underground laboratory, and recounts:

> While the laboratory was in course of construction, we had frequent occasion to consult the architect, and look through the large sheaf of drawings that he had in his office. Some of these were plans, showing us what the floor space would look like to an imaginary observer overhead: others were elevations, from one side or one end: or they were sections, in different directions and at different levels. Many of the diagrams looked utterly unlike the others: some showed features not present in the rest. ...
>
> Now despite all these differences, we know perfectly well that there is only one building. These are representations of it, in the form appropriate to a piece of paper which is only two dimensional. We need to have several of these drawings before we can say that we know what the building is really like. From one point of view, not a single one among all these drawings is ultimately redundant; and every drawing will have something particular to tell us about the building. ...
>
> This is the analogy. ... the building stands for the reality God, who is being described in the separate disciplines (or diagrams).

Incidentally, the analogy might equally well be applied in the same spirit to a secular world-picture, provided the world-view allows for knowledge beyond that of science. So, while Coulson wants to emphasize — as I do — his belief that God is the underlying reality, nevertheless, the crediting of different perspectives of reality, each contributing to the overall understanding, is not unique to a religious viewpoint. It is just good sense.

It is good sense that liberates rationality as a whole from the suffocating artificial constraints of scientism. It does not endorse irrationality, or undermine rigor of thought. It does not imply that anything or everything is to be believed. Instead it understands that cognition is complex and multifaceted, and that no single approach to knowledge can rightfully monopolize our assent. If scientific knowledge is woven of individual strands of theory and experiment that together combine to create a mutually supporting, strong and coherent fabric, then our overall knowledge is like a garment. Its different fabrics are stitched together in a coordinated patchwork to create a practical covering, fitted to our cognitive stature and to the needs of our environment, in which no single fabric can claim overall priority, but all are necessary. The formal disciplines like literature, history, economics, theology, and the no-less-vital underlying practical skills on which they depend, such as the ability to communicate, the comprehension of everyday language and of mathematics, the sympathetic understanding of other persons and creatures, and the ability to plan and organize — all these are equally important aspects of human knowledge.

10.3 The place of faith

According to the skeptic, faith is belief without warrant. In the popular caricatures it is believing in the teeth of the evidence. "Believing what you know ain't so" is how Mark Twain says the schoolboy puts it. The militant atheists want us to see the contrast as between a tentative — yet supremely sure and self-correcting — science that believes nothing unless demonstrated, and a credulous faith that stubbornly believes its religious authorities regardless of demonstration or counter-evidence.

Actually of course, science itself requires a kind of faith. It requires the belief that the world has stable coherent characteristics that can be uncovered by a pursuit of reproducibility and Clarity. This is a belief that science has validated only *a posteriori*. It finds its confirmation not from prior logical proof, but from the fact that it seems to work rather well. Scientism goes further. It elevates the limited faith that under-girds science into a philosophy whose ambition is nothing less than to encompass all knowledge. What we've been exploring in this book are the arguments and evidence showing that this escalated scientistic faith is itself actually a belief in what "ain't so"; and that it does not take too much thoughtful reflection to realize that we "know" scientism "ain't so". Scientism's fault does not lie in the mere fact that it is based upon prior unproven commitments. Science and most other areas of endeavor are similarly based. It lies in the pretense that it has no prior commitments, and in the consequent arrogance that it can and will replace all the other subjective disciplines with an objective science.

There are doubtless benefits and merits to a tentative approach to knowledge and action. If we can, without cost, put off deciding an uncertain question till a later time when we expect to have better information, we are generally well advised to do so. But more often than not, the luxury of awaiting decisive evidence is too costly. We usually have to decide on action with insufficient evidence. Humans make decisions on minimal evidence beyond personal preference and impulse every moment of their waking lives. It is what it means to be sentient. Many of these decisions are of little significance; but others are life-changing. And if history is any judge, it is those who act boldly with determination and commitment, even in the face of risk and in the absence of complete information, who are successful in this world. Such people, men and women of *action*, illustrate one of the primary qualities of faith. They act in accordance with a view of the world that is plausible but unproven. That is faith. And religious faith is quite simply the same principle applied to matters of God and the spirit.

Moreover, the man of action is not inclined to retreat or give up at the first sign of opposition or disadvantage. He shows commitment. If the going gets tough, he is persistent. This is a facet of faith. And religious faith calls for the same sort of commitment and persistence. What's more, as we've seen, scientists themselves show similar sorts of commitment to the theories and ideas they have. Contrary evidence rarely immediately causes a scientific theory that has prior successes to be dropped. Science is more robust than that. It is correctable, but not in a way that supports the simplistic identification of science as falsifiable knowledge in contrast with religion as unfalsifiable superstition. The best science comes out of a deep commitment to ideas, evaluated by unspecifiable criteria, and rigorously pursued to their logical consequences. Many of the most celebrated scientists have spoken of that commitment in religious terms. For some it was in directly Christian terms. For others, their faith might not be identifiable with any organized religion. But it is faith nevertheless. What ever might be the eventual epistemological status of scientific knowledge, there is no doubt that faith plays a crucial part in the processes of discovery and the lives of scientists.

The other facet of faith lies in relationships. It is not too much of an exaggeration to regard the dominant intellectual presumption of the West today as being that there is no reality beyond what is discovered by natural science and no authority or good higher than the freedom of the individual. Both science and individual freedom are good, but Christians have a different ultimate view. We believe that both the deepest reality and the highest moral meaning and authority are found in *loving relationship*. We believe that the universe exists because a God whose nature is love, expressed in relationship, has willed it and loves it. We believe that individuals are loved by God, and find their true fulfillment by entering willingly into loving relationship with Him, and into loving relationship with one another.

A relationship cannot be reduced down to a description in terms of physics or biology. It is something that is both intrinsically a holistic, higher-level, phenomenon, and also inherently lacking in the Clarity that science demands for its kind of descriptions. Indeed, a relationship cannot fully be encompassed by purely rational arguments. My love for my wife, for example, is not something that I can rationally explain. Nor is it something I feel obliged to provide a scientific demonstration of. There may be reasons for it. There may be evidence of it. I hope there is. But the relationship does not consist of satisfaction of a set of scientific criteria. It depends much more upon sympathetic understanding, which is an intrinsically subjective form of knowledge, not capable of being objectively codified. A loving relationship like marriage has to be lived out in a faithful and trusting partnership. And this sort of faith, Christians say, is what is called for in our relationship with God. It is not a tentative, uncommitted, distant, rationalistic, or scientistic evaluation. It is a committed, intimate, passionate, and personal involvement. That is what is meant by faith. And in the Bible it is also referred to as the *knowledge* of God. This knowledge does not contradict what we know from natural science about the regular course of the world. It does go beyond what science is competent to describe. But then, scientists themselves are committed, intimate, passionate, and personally involved in their science, and the scientific community. Relationships are as important to most scientists as they are to any professionals. Scientists may be focusing on describing the world in terms of impersonal inter- actions and reproducible laws; and they may hold fiercely to the standards of scientific demonstration which under-gird that scien- tific knowledge; but their approach to the scientific enterprise and other scientists is just as human as any other profession, and just as dependent on relationships.

Faith, then, though they don't study it and may not be aware of it, is not something alien to scientists. It is a background and foundation for what they do.

Knowledge is not one-dimensional. It is not arrived at by one strategy or method. The methods of natural science, while uniquely powerful in their chosen domain, are not applicable to much of the knowledge we know. Attempting to extend the boundaries of natu- ral science to encompass all of knowledge, as has been the program of scientism for centuries, is doomed to failure. To presume that anything which remains outside of science's scope fails to qualify as knowledge is not justified by science or any other argument, and is, in fact, self-contradictory. Adopting the scientistic presumption has a suffocating effect on all non-scientific thought, including religion, and is unhealthy for science itself. What is required of knowledge is not that it all become science, but that the different perspectives be given appropriate scope and credit; that the mutual dependen- cies and boundaries between different approaches to knowledge be understood, and the relative authorities be respected.

In short, my argument is that, rather than *monopolizing* knowl- edge, as scientism tries to do, true rationality should insist upon *integrating* knowledge.

Bibliography

Jeremy C. Ahouse and Robert C. Berwick. Darwin on the mind. evolutionary psychology is in fashion-but is any of it true? *Boston Review*, 1998. April/May edition.

Denis Alexander. *Rebuilding the Matrix. Science and faith in the 21st century*. Zondervan, Grand Rapids, Michigan, 2001.

Elizabeth Allen, Barbara Beckwith, Jon Beckwith, Steven Chorover, David Culver, Margaret Duncan, Steven Gould, Ruth Hubbard, Hiroshi Inouye, Anthony Leeds, Richard Lewontin, Chuck Madansky, Larry Miller, Reed Pyeritz, Peter Bent, Miriam Rosenthal, and Herb Schreier. Against "sociobiology". *New York Review of Books*, 22(18), 13 November 1975.

Claude Alvares. Science, colonialism and violence. In Ashis Nandy, editor, *Science, Hegemony and Violence*. Oxford University Press, Delhi, 1988.

Saint Augustine of Hippo and Roland J Teske. *De Genesi ad litteram*. Catholic University of America Press, Washington D.C., 1991.

Francis Bacon. *The Advancement of Learning*, volume 1. Henrie Tomes, 1605. Available at
http://www.gutenberg.org/etext/5500.

Mara Beller. The Sokal Hoax: at whom are we laughing. *Physics Today*, September:29–24, 1998.

Mario Biagioli. *Galileo, Courtier*. University of Chicago Press, 1996.

Thomas Birch, editor. *Robert Boyle,, The Works*. Georg Olms Verlangsuchhandlung, Hildsheim, 1966.

Michael Bulmer. *Francis Galton Pioneer of Heredity and Biometry*. Johns Hopkins University Press, Baltimore, 2003.

William T Cavanaugh. *The Myth of Religious Violence*. Oxford University Press, Oxford, 2009.

Alan Chalmers. *What is this thing called science?* University of Queensland Press, St Lucia, Queensland, 3rd edition, 1999.

Edward P. Cheyney. Presidential address delivered before the american historical association. *American Historical Review*, 29(2):231–48, 1924. http://www.historians.org/info/AHA_History/epcheyney.htm.

R G Collingwood. *An Essay on Metaphysics*. Oxford University Press, Oxford, 1940.

C A Coulson. *Science and Christian Belief*. Fontana, London, 1958.

Erasmus Darwin. *Zoonomia; or the Laws of Organic Life*, volume 1. Guttenberg Books, 1794.

Richard Dawkins. *The Blind Watchmaker*. New York. Norton, 1996 edition, 1986.

Richard Dawkins. *The God Delusion*. Houghton Mifflin, Boston, 2006.

Daniel C. Dennett. *Breaking the Spell. Religion as a Natural Phenomenon*. Viking Penguin, New York, 2006.

René Descartes. *Discourse on the Method of Rightly Conducting the Reasons and Seeking the Truth in the Sciences*. Maire, Leiden, 1637.

Denis Diderot and Jean le Rond d'Alembert, editors. *Encyclopédie, ou dictionnaire raisonné des sciences, des arts et des métiers*. André Le Breton, Michel-Antoine David, Laurent Durand, and Antoine-Claude Briasson, Paris, 1751-77.

Dinesh d'Souza. *What's so great about Christianity*. Regenery, Washington, D.C., 2007.

Pierre Duhem. *The Aim and Structure of Physical Theory*. Princeton University Press, 1954. Originally published as *La Théorie Physique: Son Objet et sa Structure*, Marcel Riviera & Cie., Paris (1914).

A S Eddington. *The Philosophy of Physical Science*. MacMillan, Cambridge, 1939. (Tarner Lectures).

Jacques Ellul. *The technological society*. Knopf, New York, 1964.

Paul Feyerabend. *Against Method*. NLB, London, 1975.

Francis Galton. Hereditary talent and character. *Macmillan's Magazine*, 12:157–166,385–327, 1865.

Martin Gardner. Games. *Scientific American*, 223:120–123, 1970.

Karl Giberson. *Saving Darwin*. Harper One, New York, 2008.

Philip Henry Gosse. *Omphalos: an attempt to untie the geological knot.* John van Voorst, London, 1857.

S J Gould and R C Lewontin. The spandrels of san marco and the panglossian paradigm: A critique of the adaptationist programme. *Proc Roy Soc, B.,* 205:581–98, 1979.

Stephen J Gould. *Rocks of Ages.* Ballantine, New York, 1999.

Paul R Gross and Levitt Norman. *Higher Superstition: The academic left and its quarrels with science.* John Hopkins University Press, Baltimore, MD, 1994.

Susan Haack. *Defending science – within reason. Between scientism and cynicism.* Prometheus Books, New York, 2003.

Jürgen Habermas. *Knowledge and human interests.* Beacon Press, Boston, 1971. Translated by Jeremy J Shapiro.

Sandra Harding. *Whose Science? Whose Knowledge?* Cornell University Press, Ithaca, NY, 1991.

Mike Hawkins. *Social Darwinism in European and American Thought.* Cambridge University Press, Cambridge, 1997.

F A Hayek. *The counter revolution of science studies on the abuse of reason.* Free press of Glencoe (Macmillan), New York, 1955.

Jane Heal. Pragmatism and choosing to believe. In Alan R Malachowski, editor, *Reading Rorty: Critical Responses to Philosophy and the Mirror of Nature (and Beyond),* pages 101–4. Basil Blackwell, Oxford, 1990.

C. G. Hempel. Studies in logic and confirmation. *Mind,* 54:1–26, 97–121, 1945.

David J Hess. *Science Studies.* New York University Press, New York, 1997.

Richard Hofstadter. *Social Darwinism in American Thought 1860-1915.* University of Pennsylvania Press, Philadelphia, 1944.

R Hooykaas. *Religion and the rise of modern science.* Scottish Academic Press, Edinburgh, 1972. Regent College Publishing reprint, 2000.

Stanley L Jaki. *The Road of Science and the Ways to God.* University of Chicago Press, Chicago, 1978.

Phillip Johnson. *Darwin on Trial*. Regenery Gateway, Washington, D.C., 1991.

Phillip Johnson. Is scientific naturalism scientific? In Scott B Luley, Copan Paul, and Stan W Wallace, editors, *Science: Christian Perspectives for the New Millenium*, volume II, pages 79–106. Christian Leadership Ministries and Ravi Zacharias Ministries, Addison, Texas, and Norcross, Georgia, 2003a.

Phillip Johnson. What is darwinism? In Scott B Luley, Copan Paul, and Stan W Wallace, editors, *Science: Christian Perspectives for the New Millenium*, volume II, pages 19–36. Christian Leadership Ministries and Ravi Zacharias Ministries, Addison, Texas, and Norcross, Georgia, 2003b.

Samuel Johnson. *A Dictionary of the English Language*. Richard Bentley, London, 1755.

W A Jurgens. *The Faith of the Early Fathers*, volume 3. Order of St Benedict, Inc, Collegeville Minnesota, 1979.

D J Kelves. *In the Name of Eugenics*. Harvard University Press, Cambridge, Massachusetts, 1995.

Alfred Kinsey. *Sexual behavior in the Human Male*. Indiana University Press, Bloomington, Indiana, 1948.

Philip Kitcher. *Abusing Science*. MIT Press, Cambridge Massachusetts, 1983.

Philip Kitcher. *Vaulting Ambition: Sociobiology and the Quest for Human Nature*. MIT Press, Cambridge, MA, 1985.

S Kühl. *The Nazi Connection: Eugenics, American Racism, and German Socialism*. Oxford University Press, Oxford, 1994.

Thomas Kuhn. *The Structure of Scientific Revolutions*. University of Chicago Press, Chicago, 1962.

Jay A Labinger and Harry Collins, editors. *The One Culture? A conversation about science*. University of Chicago Press, Chicago, 2001.

J B Lamarck. *Philosophie zoologique, ou exposition dex considérations relative à l'histoire naturelle des animaux*. Dentu, Paris, 1809. Translated by Hugh Elliot, Macmillan, 1914.

L E Lisiecki and M E Raymo. A pliocene-pleistocene stack of 57 globally distributed benthic $\delta^{18}o$ records. *Paleoceanography*, 20:PA1003, 2005.

Jack Lynch, editor. *Samuel Johnson's Dictionary: Selections from the 1755 Work that Defined the English Language*. Walker, New York, 2003.

Jean-François Lyotard. *The Postmodern Condition: A Report on Knowledge*. University of Minnesota Press, Minneapolis, 1984. Translation from the French by Geoff Bennington and Brian Massumi.

Thomas Babbington (Lord) Macaulay. *The History of England from the accession of James the second*. G. P. Putnam, New York, 1898.

Thomas Babington (Lord) Macaulay. *Critical and Historical Essays*, volume 2. Longman, Brown, Green and Longmans, 5th Ed., London, 1848. Lord Bacon, July 1837, available at http://oll.libertyfund.org.

Donald M. MacKay. *The clockwork image*. Intervarsity Press, London, 1974.

George M Marsden. *The soul of the american university*. Oxford University Press, New York, 1994.

Georges May. Observations on an allegory: The frontispiece of the "encyclopédie". *Diderot Studies*, 16:159–174, 1973.

J Richard Middleton and Brian J Walsh. *Truth is stranger than it used to be. Biblical faith in a postmodern age*. Intervarsity Press, Downers Grove, Illinios, 1995.

Kenneth Miller. *Finding Darwin's God*. Harper Perennial, New York, 2002.

Simon Mitton. *The Crab Nebula*. Charles Scribner's & Sons, New York, 1978.

Jacques Monod. *Chance and Necessity. An essay on the natural philosophy of modern biology*. Vintage, New York, 1972. Translated by Austryn Wainhouse from the French "Le Hasard et la Necessité", 1970.

J. P. Moreland. *Christianity and the nature of Science*. Baker, Grand Rapids, MI, 1989.

Ernest Nagel. *The Structure of Science*. Harcourt and Brace, New York, 1961.

Isaac Newton. Answer to the foregoing letter. *Philosophical Transactions of the Royal Society*, 85:5014–5018, 1672.

Isaac Newton. A letter of Mr. Isaac Newton, Professor of the Mathematicks in the University of Cambridge; containing his New Theory about Light and Colors. *Philosophical Transactions of the Royal Society*, 80:3075–3087, 1672a.

Isaac Newton. *Philosophiæ Naturalis Principia Mathematica*. Joseph Streater for the Royal Society, London, 1687. English translation 1729 at http://books.google.com/books?id=Tm0FAAAAQAAJ.

Richard G. Olson. *Science and Scientism in Nineteenth-Century Europe*. University of Illinois Press, Urbana and Chicago, 2008.

Working Group on Teaching Evolution. *Teaching about Evolution and the Nature of Science*. National Academy of Sciences, Washington, D.C., 1998.

H. Allen Orr. Darwinian storytelling. *New York Review of Books*, 50(3), 2003.

David Papineau. The rise of physicalism. In M W F Stone and Jonathan Wolf, editors, *The Proper Ambition of Science*. Routledge, London and New York, 2000.

Blaize Pascal. *Pensées*. Dutton, New York, 1958. Available at http://www.gutenberg.org/files/18269/18269-h/18269-h.htm.

J R Petit, J Jouzel, D Raynaud, N I Barkov, J M Barnola, I Basile, M Bender, J Chappellaz, J Davis, G Delaygue, M Delmotte, V M Kotlyakov, M Legrand, V Lipenkov, C Lorius, L Nipin, C Ritz, E Saltzman, and M Stievenard. Climate and atmospheric history of the past 420,000 years from the vostok ice core, antarctica. *Nature*, 399:429–436, 1999.

Steven Pinker. *How the mind works*. W.W.Norton, New York, 1999.

Michael Polanyi. *Person Knowledge: Towards a Post-Critical Philosophy*. Chicago University Press, 1958.

Karl Popper. *The Logic of Scientific Discovery*. Routledge, New York, 2002.

Neil Postman. *Technopoly The Surrender of Culture to Technology*. Random House, Vintage, New York, 1993.

W Provine. Evolution and the foundation of ethics. *MBL Science*, 3:25–29, 1988.

W. V. Quine. Two dogmas of empiricism. *The Philosophical Review*, 60(1): 20–43, 1951.

Richard Rorty. *Philosophy and the Mirror of Nature*. Princeton University Press, Princeton, NJ, 1979.

Lionell Rubinoff. The Autonomy of History: Collingwood's critique of F.H.Bradley's Copernican Revolution in Historical Knowledge. In Leslie Armour and James Bradley, editors, *Philosophy after F. H. Bradley*, pages 127–146. Thoemmes Press, Bristol, 1996.

Michael Ruse. *Can a Darwinian be a Christian*. Cambridge University Press, Cambridge, 2000.

Steven Shapin. *The Scientific Revolution*. University of Chicago Press, Chicago, 1996.

Vanda Shiva. Reductionist science as epistemological violence. In Ashis Nandy, editor, *Science, Hegemony and Violence*. Oxford University Press, Delhi, 1988.

Alan Sokal and Jean Bricmont. *Fasionable Nonsense: Postmodern Intellectual's Abuse of Science*. Picador USA, New York, 1998. First published as *Impostures Intellectuelles* by Editions Odile Jacob, 1997.

Tom Sorell. *Scientism Philosophy and the infatuation with science*. Routledge, London and New York, 1991.

Herbert Spencer. A theory of population, deduced from the general law of animal fertility. *The Westminster Review*, 57([New Series, Vol I, No. II]):468–501, 1852.

Herbert Spencer. *The Study of Sociology*. Henry S King, London, 1873.

Todd M Squires. Optimizing the vertebrate vestibular semicircular canal: Could we balance any better? *Physical Review Letters*, 93:198106, 2004.

Rodney Stark. *For the Glory of God: how monotheism led to reformations, science, witch-hunts, and the end of slavery*. Princeton University Press, Princeton, N.J., 2003.

Robert Stauffer. Speculation and Experiment in the Background of Oersted's Discovery of Electromagnetism. *Isis*, 48:35, 1957.

F Richard Stephenson and David A Green. A millennium of shattered stars - our galaxy's historical supernovae. *Sky and Telescope*, 105(5): 40–48, 2003.

F J Sulloway. Birth order and evolutionary psychology. *Psychological Inquiry*, 6:75–80, 1995.

Paul Thagard. *The brain and the meaning of life*. Princeton University Press, 2010.

Ann Thwaite. *Glimpses of the Wonderful: The Life of Philip Henry Gosse, 1810-1888*. Faber, London, 2002.

Richard S Westfall. *The life of Isaac Newton*. Cambridge University Press, Cambridge, 1993.

Andrew Dickson White. *A history of the warfare of science with theology in christendom*. Appleton, New York, 1896.

Alfred North Whitehead. *Science and the Modern World*. Mentor Book Edition, New York, 1948.

Edward O Wilson. *Human Nature*. Harvard University Press, Cambridge, Massachusetts, 1978.

John Ziman. *Reliable Knowledge*. Cambridge University Press, Cambridge, 1978.

Notes

[1]See, for example, Marsden [1994].

[2]Figure 1.1 shows the allegorical frontispiece of the Encyclopédie, which was described by the artist in the following way "We see the Sciences in the act of discovering Truth. Reason and Metaphysics try to remove her veil. Theology waits for her light from a ray originating in the Sky: next to her Memory and History, ancient and modern. Next and below are the Sciences. On the other side Imagination approaches with a garland, to adorn Truth. Beneath her are the various Poetries and Arts. At the bottom are several Skills deriving from the Sciences and the Arts." A detailed commentary is given by May [1973], available at http://www.jstor.org/stable/40372425.

[3]Diderot and d'Alembert [1751-77]

[4]Johnson [1755]

[5]or in later abstracted editions *A dictionary of the English language: in which the words are deduced from their originals, explained in their different meanings, and authorized by the names of the writers in whose works they are found*

[6]Cited in Lynch [2003], p5

[7]Figure 1.2 is from
http://www.gutenberg.org/files/19222/19222-h/images/imagep006.jpg.

[8]Macaulay [1898], v1, p54

[9]Macaulay [1898], v1, p324

[10]Macaulay [1898], v1, p335

[11]Macaulay [1898], v1, p350

[12]Macaulay [1898], v2, p89

[13]Macaulay [1898], v1, pXV

[14]Between the writing of Macaulay and Cheyney stands F. H. Bradley's *The Pre-suppositions of Critical History*, first published in 1874. This work was regarded as a foundation of the "scientific" approach to history. The *scientistic* aspects of Bradley's approach were criticized by R. G. Collingwood, as has been described by Rubinoff [1996] p137-8 as follows: "In keeping with the tradition of Hume and J.S.Mill, Bradley conceived the 'scientific method' along the lines of the methods of the natural sciences. He was, to this extent, a positivist for whom the natural sciences provided the paradigm of rationality against which all other modes of rationality are to be measured. The historical method thus becomes a mere species of the universal method of science whose generic essence is determined by what is in fact only one of its species, namely the species known as natural science now elevated to the rank of a universal. Without recognizing the category mistake involved in this equation Bradley held this view of the scientific method together with the belief, as we have already noted, that there was an essential difference between the historical processes and those of nature. *A Parte Objecti*, nature is the permanent amid change; history, the changes of the permanent; natural events are mere illustrations, while historical events are embodiments. It was left for Collingwood to expose the inconsistency of these positions concerning the methodology and ontology of history, and to

articulate a conception of method more in keeping with the ontological distinction between nature and history to which both Collingwood and Bradley were committed."

[15]Cheyney [1924]

[16]Collingwood [1940]

[17]My philosopher friends point out to me that the word metaphysics is used more technically these days by many of them in ways that are complementary to science. I am not here doubting that metaphysics and science may have much to say to one another and may be mutually supportive. What I am addressing is that in popular perception, at least, metaphysics is in part defined by a *distinction* from natural science

[18]Shapin [1996]

[19]I am indebted to Hooykaas [1972] for his compact summary of scientific history, on which I depend heavily in this section.

[20]Dawkins [1986].

[21]Newton [1687]

[22]Newton [1672] cited by Westfall [1993] p 89.

[23]Birch [1966] volume 5, p167-9.

[24]Michael Faraday, engraved by J. Cochran, from National Portrait Gallery, volume V, published c.1835, after the painting by Henry William Pickersgill.

[25]Stauffer [1957] retrieved from
http://www.clas.ufl.edu/users/fgregory/oersted.htm

[26]Macaulay [1848]

[27]Bacon [1605] Book 1, section v, paragraph 11

[28]Reproduced from the first edition in MIT's Archives and Special Collections by kind permission. With particular thanks to Stephen Skuce, Rare Books Program Coordinator.

[29]Newton [1672a] available at
http://www.newtonproject.sussex.ac.uk/catalogue/record/NATP00006

[30]See for example Mitton [1978]. Or a more recent discussion is found in Stephenson and Green [2003]

[31] Figure 2.4 credit NASA/ESA, , J. Hester and A. Loll (Arizona State University), 2005.
http://www.nasaimages.org/luna/servlet/detail/NVA2 8 8 14234 114775:A-Giant-Hubble-Mosaic-of-the-Crab-N

[32]See http://www.astronomy.com/asy/default.aspx?c=a&id=5638

[33]Figure 2.5 obtained from
http://en.wikipedia.org/wiki/Image:Vostok-ice-core-petit.png, based on the data of Petit et al. [1999]

[34]Lisiecki and Raymo [2005]

[35]Hess [1997] p 16.

[36]Hess [1997] p 28.

[37]Macaulay [1898] Vol 3 p 71.

[38]Descartes [1637] available on line at http://www.gutenberg.org/ebooks/59

[39]Descartes [1637] Part IV.

[40]There is some technical philosophical debate as to whether "one plus one equals two" is a good example of an analytic statement, but for present purposes I am glossing over some nuances

[41] Figure 3.1 from
http://en.wikipedia.org/wiki/File:Denmark%E2%80%99s_K48_Kilogram.jpg

[42] The reliance on an artifact is considered somewhat unsatisfactory. For one thing it now seems to disagree with its replicas to a measurable extent. There are proposals afoot to change the definition. So far, though, the replacement techniques are substantially less precise than using the standard artifacts. See the article by Robert P Crease in "Physics World", Volume 24, No 3, March 2011, p39.

[43] Ziman [1978].

[44] Ruse [2000] p78.

[45] One of the more extreme versions of this position is "eliminative materialism". The common-sense interpretation of the behavior in terms of agents is termed "folk psychology". And eliminative materialism eagerly anticipates the displacement of folk psychology by neurophysiology. Eliminativism holds that the mental concepts such as beliefs, desires, and subjective experiences do not actually exist. Its champions include G.Rey, B.F.Skinner, P.M. and P.S.Churchland, and (with a technically different twist) Daniel Dennett.

[46] Dawkins [1986] p 12ff.

[47] MacKay [1974] p 43.

[48] Monod [1972] p 21.

[49] At least, not e.g. according to logical positivist philosopher of science, Ernest Nagel, "It is a mistaken assumption that teleological explanations are intelligible only if the things and activities so explained are conscious agents or the products of such agents." Nagel [1961] p 24.

[50] in 2010

[51] Hayek [1955], p 13.

[52] An important recent historical study of nineteeth-century scientism is Olson [2008], which reviews and expands on much the same topics.

[53] Hayek [1955] p 120.

[54] Hayek [1955] p 170.

[55] From *The New World of Henri Saint-Simon* Frank Manuel, Harvard University Press (1956) cited by Olson [2008] p 52.

[56] Hayek [1955] p 153

[57] See Olson [2008] pp 185-7.

[58] Profound developments in the foundations of mathematics were later to correct the over-confidence that a complete axiomatic understanding of mathematics was in hand.

[59] Haack [2003] chapter 2.

[60] *The Old and New Logic*, Rudolph Carnap, in *Logical Positivism* A. J. Ayer (ed), Free Press of Glencoe (1959) p 145. Cited by Haack [2003] p 32.

[61] Popper [2002]

[62] Hempel [1945]

[63] Duhem [1954] p 187, available at
http://plato.stanford.edu/entries/scientific-underdetermination/

[64] Quine [1951]

[65] Kuhn [1962]

[66] Feyerabend [1975]

[67] See for example Kitcher [1983].

[68]See Giberson [2008] p 94.

[69]The ID movement's primary claim is that design in nature can be detected *scientifically*. It denies far less of scientific cosmology than the earlier Creation Science movement.

[70]For example Moreland [1989].

[71]Chalmers [1999], p250.

[72]I am here using the expression natural law as an abbreviation for laws of nature, not as a reference to a basis for civil laws rooted in nature.

[73]Gardner [1970].

[74]Squires [2004].

[75]Dawkins [1986] p 39.

[76]Dawkins [1986] p 287.

[77]Philosophers answer this question by saying that there is a qualitative difference in the type of thing that is being referred to. God as Final Cause is not subject to infinite regress because reference to Final Cause is not the same type of explanation as reference to law of nature or to history. To treat them as the same sort of thing is a Category Mistake.

[78]Accessible at http://humanorigins.si.edu/

[79]Available at http://www.nsf.gov/statistics/seind08/c7/c7s2.htm

[80]Miller [2002] p 166.

[81]Miller [2002] p 167.

[82]on Teaching Evolution [1998] p 58, at
http://www.nap.edu/openbook.php?record_id=5787&page=58

[83]Provine [1988] cited by Miller [2002] p 171.

[84]Johnson [2003a] p 93

[85]Johnson [2003b] p 25.

[86]The first meaning, {1}scientific naturalism, is an extension of *naturalism*, which "assumes the entire realm of nature to be a closed system of material causes and effects, which cannot be influenced by anything from 'outside'," to *scientific naturalism*, which "makes the same point by starting with the assumption that science, which studies only the natural, is our only reliable path to knowledge".'[Johnson [1991] p114,115] I've already pointed out the problematical character of the use of "nature" or "natural" as if we intuitively know what they mean. In my terminology, what Johnson means by scientific naturalism is a combination of physicalism and scientism. (This combining of attributes is one cause of confusion.) I take it here that Johnson's {2}science refers to the scientific epistemological enterprise, the attempt to understand the world as far as it can be understood through the methods of natural science. He leaves it unclear whether the {1}physicalism actually is a limitation of {2}science, or whether it is just said to be. However Johnson's view is that adopting physicalism places (by implication improperly) the limitations of {2}science upon reality. This far the argument sounds pretty close to the view I've been advocating. Indeed, I'd say it is about right. But then the terminological fog descends. He says this limitation of reality is "in the interest of maximizing the explanatory power of {3}science". What can this mean? I don't see how it can really mean a maximization of the correct explanations of reality by the scientific epistemological enterprise. Limiting reality doesn't increase the explanatory extent of {2}science. Instead, I think it can only rationally mean that applying {2}science's

limitations improperly to all of reality provides improper cultural power to the practitioners and communities that go to make up {3}science. But then when he advocates that we can study organisms on the premise that all were created by God, {4}scientifically — if it means anything different from what we already do in science — this must be yet a different meaning of science. It must mean in accordance with a different epistemological enterprise, not subject to these improper limitations of physicalism. This final broader enterprise: {4}science, we are to understand is (or would be) a Good Thing, but what is it? Perhaps one should regard {4}science as being simply systematic knowledge, or in other words, the historical definition of science of the Encyclopédie or of Collingwood, even though that definition does not readily lend itself to transformation into an adjective or adverb. But to revert suddenly to that archaic usage in the middle of a discourse that has plainly been using the word in the modern sense is very peculiar.

[87] Johnson [2003b] p 31.

[88] Darwin [1794] available at
http://www.gutenberg.org/files/15707/15707-h/15707-h.htm

[89] Lamarck [1809] translations cited at
http://www.ucl.ac.uk/taxome/jim/Mim/lamarck6.html

[90] Hawkins [1997] p 42.

[91] A Desmond *The Politics of Evolution* 1989, cited by Hawkins [1997] p 43.

[92] Hawkins [1997] p 34.

[93] Spencer [1852] available at
http://www.victorianweb.org/science/science_texts/spencer2.html

[94] Autobiography I 502, cited by Hawkins [1997] p 84.

[95] Spencer [1873] p 86. Available at
http://files.libertyfund.org/files/1335/0623_Bk.pdf

[96] Hofstadter [1944] p 31.

[97] Hofstadter [1944] p 35.

[98] Bulmer [2003] p 79, citing Galton's *Inquiries into Human Faculty*.

[99] Galton [1865] p 164, cited by Bulmer [2003].

[100] Galton [1865] p 165.

[101] Galton *Hereditary Genius* 1869, p3 62, cited by Bulmer [2003] p82.

[102] Kelves [1995] p 94, cited by Bulmer [2003] p 83.

[103] From *Eugenics. Its definition and scope* 1904, cited by Bulmer [2003] p 83.

[104] Bulmer [2003] p 89, citing Kühl [1994].

[105] Hayek [1955] p 107.

[106] Kinsey [1948].

[107] Wilson [1978] p 6.

[108] Wilson [1978] p 7.

[109] Wilson [1978] p 32.

[110] Wilson [1978] p 33.

[111] Allen et al. [1975] available at http://www.nybooks.com/articles/9017

[112] Wilson [1978] p 196.

[113] Wilson [1978] p 198.

[114] Wilson [1978] p 201.

[115] I prefer the designation 'physicalist' to the perhaps more widespread 'materialist' because materialism logically implies a more specific basis in *matter*, which

is contradicted by modern theories of physics. But I don't mean to draw philosophically significant distinction between physicalism and a loose meaning of
materialism: that everything in the world is made from entities that obey the
laws of physics.

[116]Sorell [1991] p4.

[117]Papineau [2000]

[118]Papineau [2000] p 178.

[119]In Eddington's famous analogy, Eddington [1939].

[120]Thagard [2010] p8.

[121]Thagard [2010] p41.

[122]Thagard [2010] p15.

[123]Eugenie Scott of the National Center for Science Education has frequently made
the assertion that ID is a "science stopper." See, for example, "Evolution and Intelligent Design," September 28, 2001, Religion and Ethics Newsweekly, Episode
no. 504, at

http://www.pbs.org/wnet/religionandethics/week504/feature.html

[124]It might be argued that sociology of scientific knowledge, and the strong program in science studies, don't have all that much in common with postmodern
literary theory, with narrative, and with hermeneutics. But I am avoiding fine
distinctions with this admittedly broad-brush depiction. And in the broad sense,
the sociological critiques do repudiate the 'modern' (i.e. Enlightenment) view
of science.

[125]Lyotard [1984] p xxiv.

[126]Lyotard [1984] p xxiii.

[127]Lyotard [1984] p 7.

[128]Lyotard [1984] p 18.

[129]Lyotard [1984] p 27.

[130]Lyotard [1984] pp 55ff.

[131]Gross and Norman [1994] pp 86-8.

[132]Sokal and Bricmont [1998].

[133]Beller [1998]

[134]In an exchange in the New York Review of Books, 3 October 1996

[135]It may be accessed at http://www.nybooks.com/articles/1409

[136]The opinions arising from a 'peace' workshop have been published in
Labinger and Collins [2001].

[137]Trevor Pinch in Labinger and Collins [2001], p19

[138]A very balanced, succinct outline has been given elsewhere by Heal [1990].

[139]Rorty [1979] p12.

[140]Rorty [1979] p317.

[141]Rorty [1979] p142.

[142]Rorty [1979] p146.

[143]Rorty [1979] p170.

[144]Rorty [1979] p317.

[145]Rorty [1979] p320.

[146]Rorty [1979] p332.

[147]Rorty [1979] p352.

[148]It should not escape our notice that Kuhn's scientific "revolutions", analogous
in Rorty's mind to the non-science state, are the heroic moments in the history

of science. So by this reading, non-sciences are the most exciting, heroic, phase of knowledge.

[149]Middleton and Walsh [1995] p 71.

[150]Habermas [1971] p 306.

[151]Habermas [1971] p 315.

[152]Harding [1991] p 15.

[153]Harding [1991] p 5.

[154]Harding [1991] p 10.

[155]Harding [1991] p 40.

[156]Alvares [1988] p 89.

[157]Alvares [1988] p 91

[158]Shiva [1988] p 232.

[159]Ellul [1964] p (x).

[160]Ellul [1964] p 59.

[161]Ellul [1964] p 84.

[162]Ellul [1964] p 92.

[163]Ellul [1964] p 96.

[164]Ellul [1964] p 128.

[165]Ellul [1964] p 134.

[166]Ellul [1964] p 430.

[167]Postman [1993] p 48.

[168]Postman [1993] p 161.

[169]Postman [1993] p 184.

[170]Postman [1993] p 198.

[171]I use the adjective militant in its standard dictionary definition and usage to mean vigorously active and aggressive, especially in support of a cause. Though its derivation is of course associated with warfare, it does not necessarily imply literal violence. Moreover, while I criticize the recent atheist militancy as misinformed and misleading especially in their scientism, I intend the word militant as a factual description not as an insult

[172]Dawkins [2006] p 48.

[173]Dawkins [2006] p 50.

[174]Dawkins [2006] p 58.

[175]Dawkins [2006] p 57.

[176]Dawkins [2006] p 58.

[177]Pinker [1999] p X.

[178]Pinker [1999] p 156.

[179]Pinker [1999] p 166.

[180]Pinker [1999] p 451-2.

[181]Sulloway [1995].

[182]Pinker [1999] p 555.

[183]Dennett [2006] p 9.

[184]Dennett [2006] p 14.

[185]Dennett [2006] p 17.

[186]Dennett [2006] p 18.

[187]Dennett [2006] p 30.

[188]Dennett [2006] p 33.

[189]I don't see how this is really a worry, because religious believers presumably don't think that killing all the specimens of religion is possible, and atheists don't worry about it, they want it.

[190]Dennett [2006] p 43.

[191]Dennett [2006] p 68.

[192]Dennett [2006] p 70.

[193]Fig 9.1 is the first figure from Gould and Lewontin [1979], reproduced by permission.

[194]Dennett [2006] p 114.

[195]Ahouse and Berwick [1998], Kitcher [1985], Orr [2003].

[196]http://www.bostonreview.net/BR23.3/pinker.html Originally published in the Summer 1998 issue of Boston Review.

[197]Allen et al. [1975].

[198]http://www.bostonreview.net/BR23.3/berwick_ahouse.html Originally published in the Summer 1998 issue of Boston Review.

[199]Dennett [2006] p 70.

[200]I don't mean to say that the atheists claim to have disproved religion *logically*. Scientific demonstration is, after all, not formally deductive. Their predominant claim is that the "God Hypothesis" is shown by science to be highly unlikely. Lest it be thought that I am overstating the atheists' claims, I cite the title to Victor J Stenger's 2008 opus, fulsomely endorsed by Christopher Hitchens: *The God Hypothesis—How Science Shows That God Does Not Exist.*

[201]Polanyi [1958] p286.

[202]Polanyi [1958] p284.

[203]Polanyi [1958] p 279,280.

[204]Dawkins [2006] p 181.

[205]Dawkins [2006] p 184.

[206]Dawkins [2006] p 187.

[207]Pascal [1958] Pensée 894, originally published posthumously in 1670.

[208]See for example Stark [2003] or d'Souza [2007], for a discussion of the estimates of deaths under the Inquisition relative to Stalinism and Nazism.

[209]Dawkins [2006] p 271. Any thoughtful observer who has paid any attention to what Martin Luther King actually said and wrote must acknowledge that his Christian faith is absolutely central to his motivation and to his arguments.

[210]Dawkins [2006] p 278.

[211]A recent scholarly study of the question of religious violence, Cavanaugh [2009], shows how (and why) most commentators fail to maintain a stable meaning for the term. It also shows that the religious nature of the so-called "Wars of Religion" is largely a myth.

[212]Gould [1999] p 5.

[213]James Clerk Maxwell famously responded in very similar terms to the Bishop of Glouster and Wells concerning the significance of the "aether".

[214]Gould [1999] p 42.

[215]Biagioli [1996]

[216]White [1896].

[217]Gould [1999] p 94.

[218]I believe the misinterpretation of the first amendment to exclude religion from schools is the dominant factor.

[219]Gould [1999] p 154.

[220]Image obtained from http://commons.wikimedia.org/wiki
/File:Galileo_facing_the_Roman_Inquisition.jpg

[221]White was careful to draw a distinction between *sectarian theology*, meaning broadly doctrinal or confessional Christian faith which his book condemned, and his own vaguer liberal religiosity, which he regarded as enlightened, but which excluded any requirement of Christian orthodoxy

[222]Birch [1966] volume 5, p 508ff.

[223]Augustine of Hippo and Teske [1991] 1, 20 available on line as passage number 1685 in Jurgens [1979]. http://books.google.com/books?id=rkvLsueY_DwC

[224]Bacon [1605], cited by Darwin in the front page of the *Origin of Species*.

[225]See for example Alexander [2001] chapter 6, for a summary of the content of the early geological rivalries.

[226]A D White's tendentious chapter on Higher Criticism is rife with expressions of this sort, even to the point of invoking approvingly Auguste Comte's positivism. Perhaps this is appropriate since the positivist George Eliot was the first to translate the works of the German critics Strauss and Feuerbach into English.

[227]Jaki [1978].

[228]And, by derivation, Judaism, but I can't represent modern Judaism knowledgeably.

[229]Whitehead [1948] p 13.

[230]Whitehead [1948] p 19.

[231]Hooykaas [1972] p xiii.

[232]Hooykaas [1972] p9.

[233]See for example the 50 year anniversary talk by Chris Stringer, 2003. On-line at http://www.talkorigins.org/faqs/homs/piltdown2003.html

[234]It might be argued that the Enemy, Satan, is responsible for this deception, but such a view is not consistent with Christian understanding of God's sovereignty.

[235]Gosse [1857].

[236]Cited in Thwaite [2002]

[237]http://www.asa3online.org/asa/survey/OriginsResults.pdf

[238]Title 46 part 46. Available at http://www.hhs.gov/ohrp/humansubjects/guidance/45cfr46.htm

[239]Coulson [1958] p86.

Index